IMAGES
of America

EUREKA AND SEQUOIA PARK

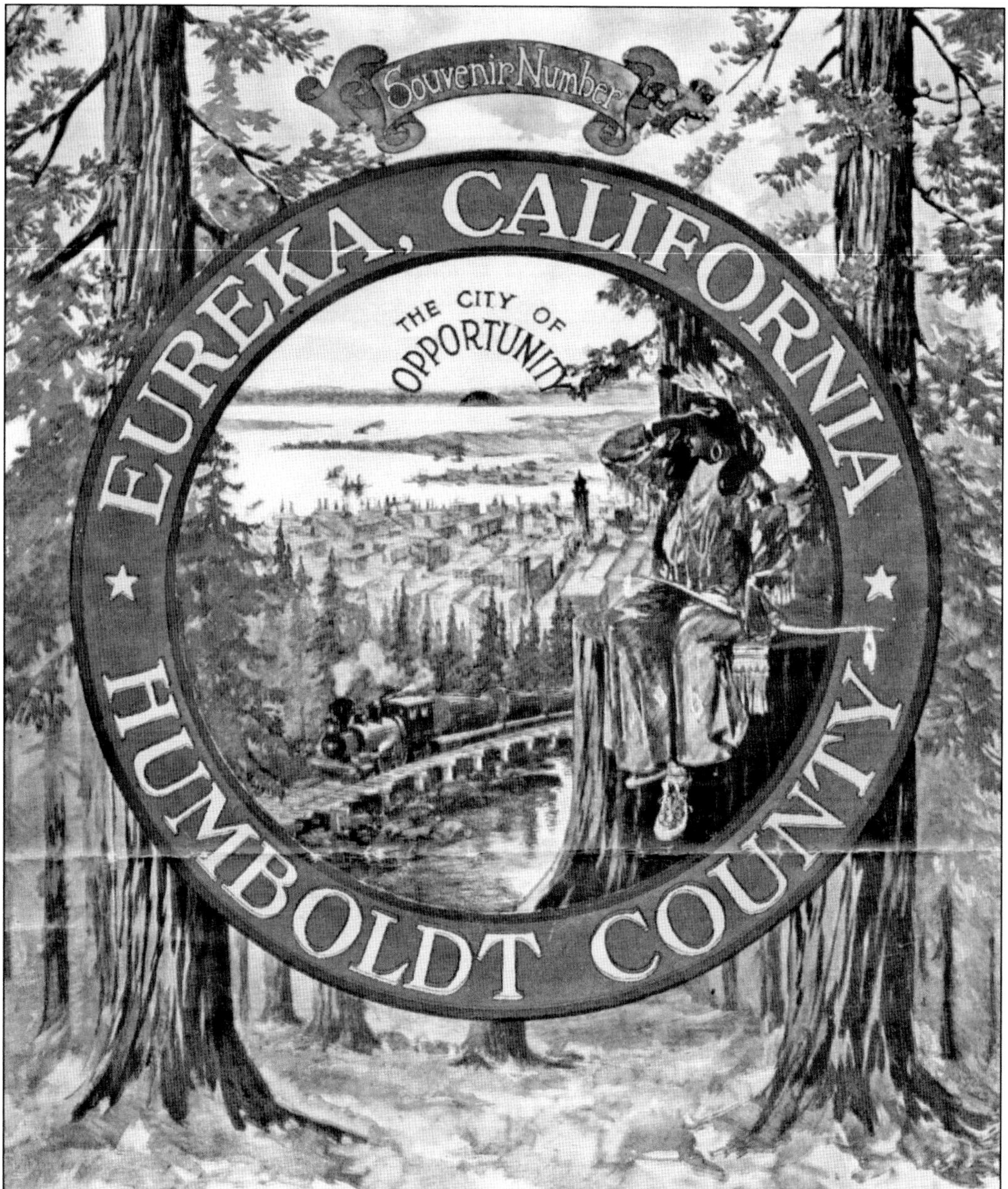

This image from the cover of *The Californian* in 1911 shows Eureka, "City of Opportunity," in microcosm: the Humboldt Bay in the background with tall ships sailing, the city pushing its way from shore side into the vast forest lands, and a Native American sitting on a large redwood stump. Thousands came to Eureka in search of a better life, which had a considerable negative impact on the native peoples already resident and the forests that vanished at an alarming pace. Notice the steam locomotive pulling a train loaded with virgin timber. (Courtesy of the Humboldt County Historical Society.)

ON THE COVER: This image of Sequoia Park around 1907 shows many of the park's longtime landmarks, including Mirror Lake, the twin trunks of Redwood Island, and the three-tiered Victorian fountain in the background. (Courtesy of the Clarke Historical Museum.)

IMAGES
of America

EUREKA AND SEQUOIA PARK

Dione F. Armand

ARCADIA
PUBLISHING

ISBN 978-0-7385-5573-7

Published by Arcadia Publishing
Charleston, South Carolina

Printed in the United States of America

Library of Congress Catalog Card Number: 2007930843

For all general information contact Arcadia Publishing at:
Telephone 843-853-2070
Fax 843-853-0044
E-mail sales@arcadiapublishing.com
For customer service and orders:
Toll-Free 1-888-313-2665

Visit us on the Internet at www.arcadiapublishing.com

For the redwoods, which have sustained our community in so many ways since the very beginning.

Contents

ACKNOWLEDGMENTS

A work of local history is inherently collaborative, involving countless discussions, reminiscences, fact-finding expeditions, and telephone calls within the community. I would like to express my deep gratitude to the local archives and their talented staffs that contributed their images and their considerable knowledge to this volume: Pam Service (curator), Lynn Wellman (registrar), and Art Barab (registrar) at the Clarke Historical Museum; Joan Berman (special collections librarian) and Edie Butler (special collections assistant) at Humboldt State University; Deborah Meador (research and collections manager), Suzanne Forsyth (*Humboldt Historian* editor), Linda DeLong (research center assistant), Durry Jones (executive director), and the board of directors at the Humboldt County Historical Society.

The City of Eureka Parks and Recreation Department was also generous in allowing me to examine their files. Local historians Mary Jane Phegley, Arlene Hartin, Ray Hillman, and Jerry Rohde offered clues that were helpful. A crucial resource to me was the always wonderful *Humboldt Historian* by which the Humboldt County Historical Society gives to us all, preserving our stories. Local newspapers were also a vital source of information.

Special thanks go to photographer extraordinaire Chris Pennington for providing contemporary images. To Shaun Case, who provided research assistance and cheerleading when it counted most: a heartfelt thank you! For those interested in working to promote biodiversity and native plant survival in Sequoia Park, please join the efforts of the No Ivy League.

For information on planting trees to beautify Eureka, please join the efforts of Keep Eureka Beautiful. See you all in Sequoia Park!

INTRODUCTION

Eureka's Sequoia Park is unique because it is much more than a park. A park can be placed anywhere. Rectangular expanses of asphalt-covered ground can be beautified by planting sod and trees, adding a swing set and a few benches—all the makings of a park. In fact, one of the most well-known parks in California—San Francisco's Golden Gate Park—was built on sand dunes in an act of creation that made a woodland park where once there had been only sand and scrubland. By contrast, Sequoia Park is a saved remnant of one of the mightiest forests in the world. Its 77 acres are filled with native Californian plants and trees from the complex ecosystem of the coast redwood forest. It is also filled with the civic pride and memories of more than century of management by the City of Eureka.

That any of Eureka's once vast forest stands today is a testament to the foresight of a few courageous individuals. Bartlin and Henrietta Glatt made an exchange of land within the city limits in 1894 in order to set aside an area for a city park. Initially called Forest Park, it comprised 20 acres of virgin timberland. Within 10 years, additional transfers of land from the Glatts more than doubled the park's acreage. Forest Park was formed in 1904 by a city ordinance, and its name was changed to Sequoia Park in 1907. Park Street was renamed Harris Street in honor of Valentine Francis Harris, the park's first superintendent, who was responsible for transforming the land from undeveloped forest into a woodland park.

Development in this context is, however, a problematic concept. What has always made Sequoia Park unique is its astounding natural beauty. The mature redwood forest is a veritable feast for the senses with many layers of plant and animal communities. First there are the trees: coast redwood, Douglas fir, Sitka spruce, and grand fir. Flowering shrubs, such as rhododendrons, fill the middle layer. Then there is the forest floor, which is covered in ferns, redwood sorrel, and a variety of berry-producing shrubs such as salmonberry and huckleberry. Even "dead" wood is not dead in a redwood forest, as standing snags are critical to nesting birds and downed trees provide important habitat to amphibians, small mammals, reptiles, and many invertebrate species.

Harris accentuated these natural features by designing well-placed paths through the forest and providing ample rustic bench seating. The few buildings that were placed in the park were designed to be small and in keeping with their natural surroundings. By placing a dam on a naturally occurring spring in the park, Harris created Mirror Lake, the diminutive version of what is known today as the duck pond. He gave thought to the kinds of activities that would draw people together to enjoy their park. Facilities for cooking, for music to be performed, and niceties such as electric lighting added to the festive atmosphere in early Sequoia Park. What Harris did in sum is what any manager of a city park must do: maintain a wild resource in the face of many financial and development pressures.

This brings us back to the question of what makes Sequoia Park different from any other city park in the nation. The answer lies in the forest itself and in the choices the community makes to sustain that forest. In order that Sequoia Park continue to thrive, it is critical that the forest itself be seen for the rare treasure that it is. The Sequoia Park forest, as with any natural system, seeks its own dynamic equilibrium, a process that requires every part of the forest ecosystem—from the largest to the smallest. From the mycorrhizae in the soil, to the redwood duff that carpets the forest floor and from the living trees and those that have fallen or remain as standing snags, every part of the forest is important to the whole. To serve this goal, not only is there a need for a moratorium on the removal of redwoods in the park, but there is also a need for a renewed commitment to the replanting of trees lost to storms. Community restoration days, where local community members and organizations gather to remove invasive plants or trash, will continue to make an important contribution to Eureka and Sequoia Park.

The story that will unfold in the pages of this book is in its own way a unique story. Eureka and Humboldt County have been isolated from the rest of California by the same forests, mountains, and rivers that served to sustain their communities. Unlike most areas of the country, rail service did not come to the county until 1914. Until that time, the only way in or out was by ocean vessel or by the overland stage route used by the U.S. mail service. Treacherous fog and other adverse weather conditions made both routes a risk not to be underestimated. Access to transport became a significant factor in land speculation, as parcels adjacent to rivers or local railroads could make or break a timber operation.

Inside the city limits, a trolley system provided convenient transport around the city. Sequoia Park was the terminus of one of the southbound trolley lines. Early Sequoia Park attracted picnickers and community organizations, as well as traveling performers and politicians. The Sequoia Park Zoo, started in 1907 as a small menagerie but now an American Zoological Association–accredited zoo, has delighted and inspired visitors for a century. In the meantime, the fight to protect our heritage forestlands continues. Revisiting Walt Whitman's "Song of the Redwood Tree," excerpted from his 1902 volume *Leaves of Grass*, is an apt way to start our journey into the story of Eureka and Sequoia Park:

> The choppers heard not—the camp shanties echoed not;
> The quick-ear'd teamsters, and chain and jack-screw men, heard not,
> As the wood-spirits came from their haunts of a thousand years, to join the refrain;
> But in my soul I plainly heard.
>
> Murmuring out of its myriad leaves,
> Down from its lofty top, rising two hundred feet high,
> Out of its stalwart trunk and limbs—out of its foot-thick bark,
> That chant of the seasons and time—chant, not of the past only, but the future.

One

Forest Conservation and Civic Pride

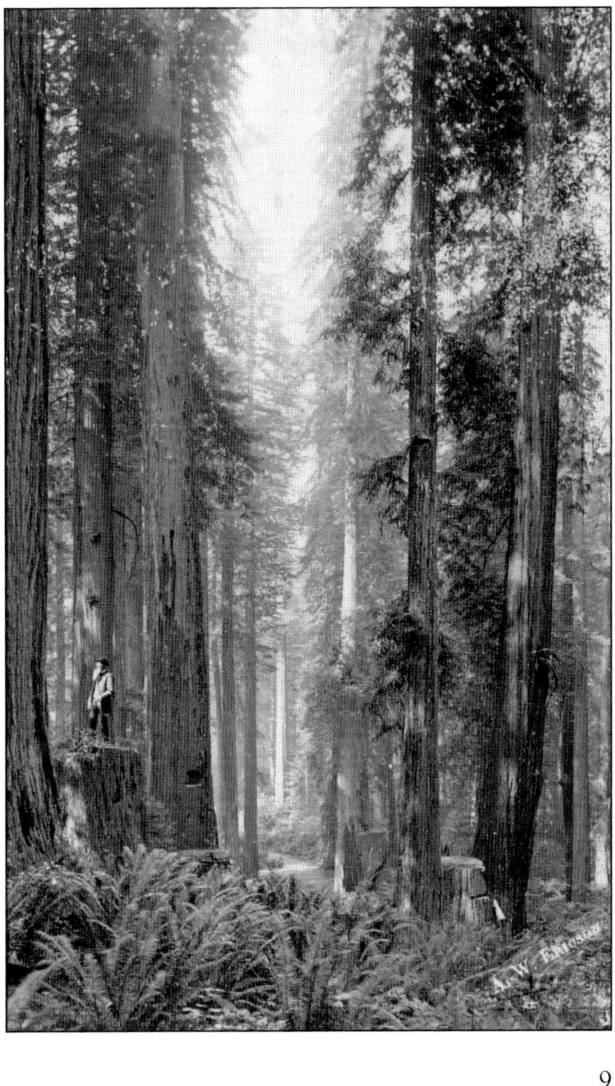

The tension between an abiding appreciation of the unique coast redwood forest and the economic centrality of the timber trade has long been present in Eureka and Humboldt County. Starting in the 1850s, logging became more than a trade; it became a way of life. By 1881, Eureka supported 22 sawmills fueled by the U.S. Homestead Act, which allowed the purchase of 160-acre tracts of prime virgin timberland by any man, many of whom were paid $50 a piece to turn over their newly acquired deeds to timber speculators. Between 1889 and 1893, the years just before Bartlin and Henrietta Glatt donated the original 20 acres of park land to the City of Eureka in 1894, nearly 670 million board feet of redwood lumber left Humboldt County for locales in California as far south as San Diego and internationally to every continent except Antarctica. The alchemy of turning the ancient trees into gold was the growth engine for the entire region. However, the late 19th and early 20th centuries were also a time of increasing public participation in civic activities, including forest conservation and park building. (Courtesy of the Clarke Historical Museum.)

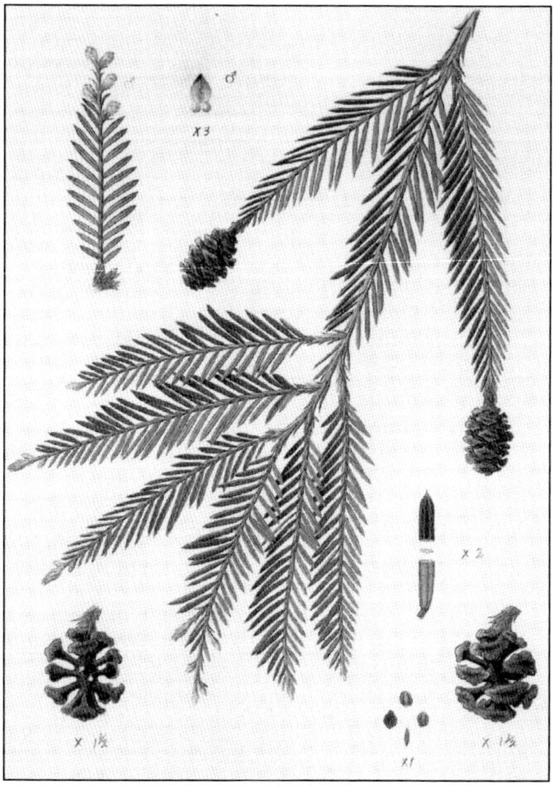

The coast redwood is the Earth's tallest tree and can grow to heights well in excess of 350 feet. Its Latin name—*Sequoia sempervirens*—means "forever green." Fossil records show that redwoods were contemporaries of the dinosaurs. This botanic print by E. O. Murman shows the branchlets and seed-bearing cones of the giant conifer. The cones are only about the size of an olive. (Courtesy of the Murman family.)

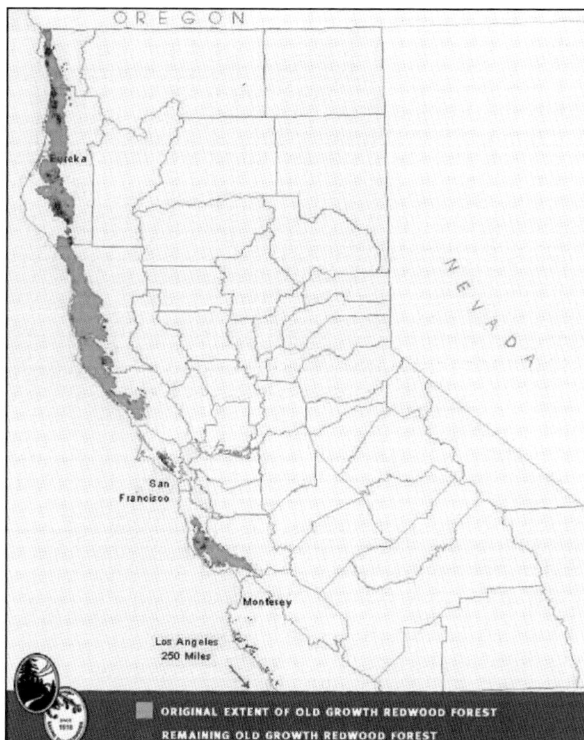

Though they once covered most of the northern hemisphere, coast redwoods now grow in a thin coastal strip from south of Brookings, Oregon, to just south of Monterey, California. Throughout northern California, many place names reflect the former presence of these forests. Today only four percent of the original old growth coast redwood forest remains. (Courtesy of the Save-the-Redwoods League.)

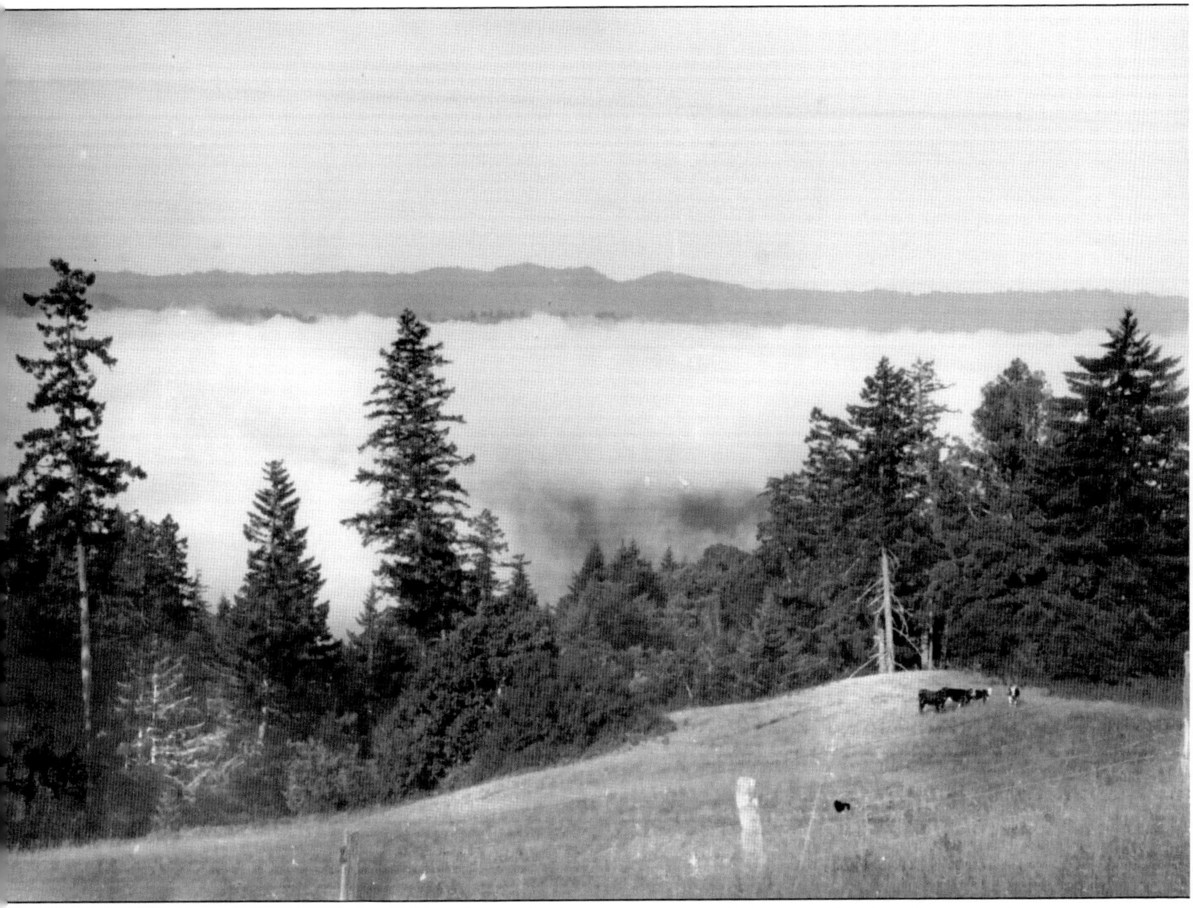

Redwood forests, like this one in Briceland, California, create their own fog in a hydrologic loop that helps the forest to retain water even in summer. Dense redwood needles are such efficient water collectors that in one foggy night, a single redwood can deliver the equivalent of a drenching rainstorm. The redwoods' ability to draw water from fog maintains the wet climate in which they and many other species thrive. (Courtesy of Humboldt State University.)

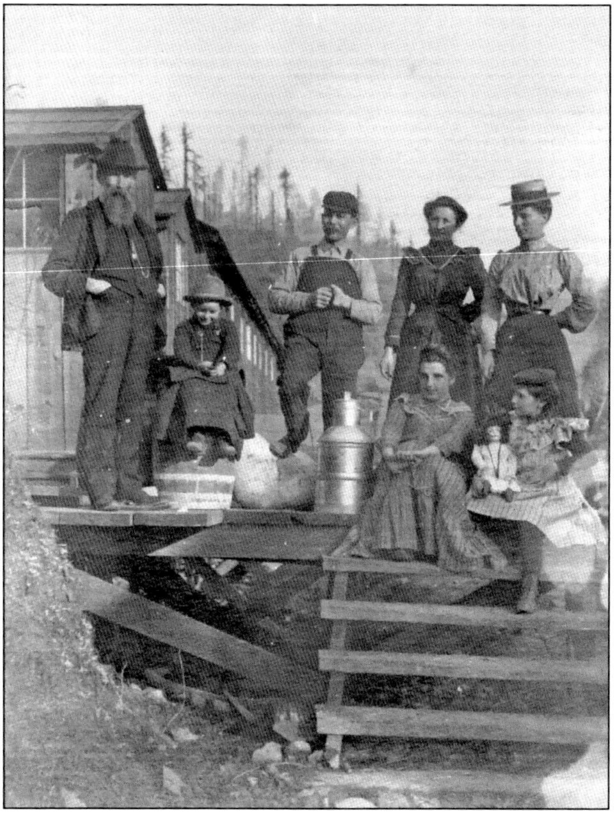

This photograph of the Humboldt pioneer family of Jackson Sawyer shows a typical family and, in the background, the forests they depended upon. Logging camps often had rows of small cottages, one per family, as well as bunkhouses for single men, and were made entirely out of redwood lumber. (Courtesy of the Clarke Historical Museum.)

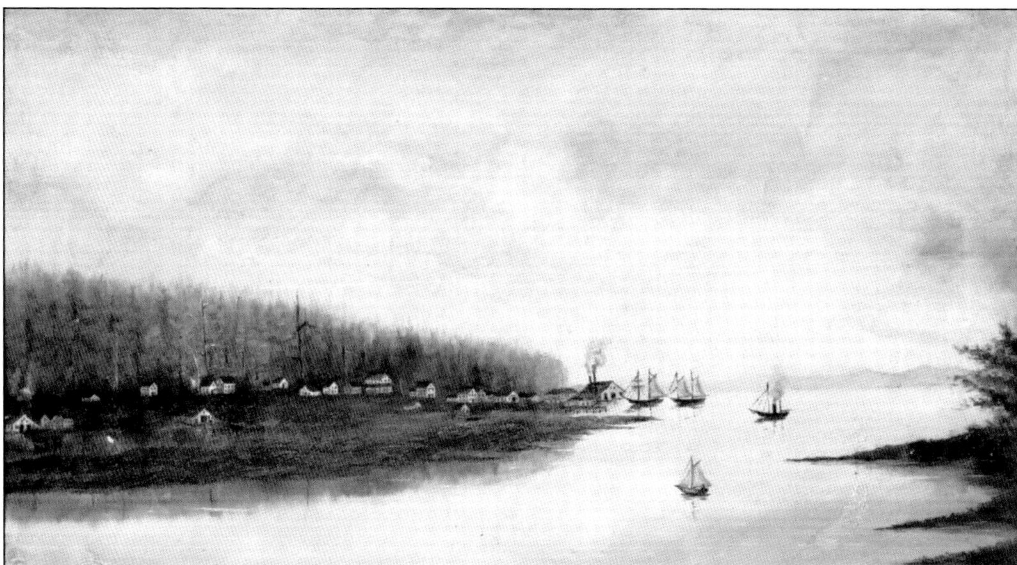

This anonymous oil painting, *Eureka in 1854 as Painted by a Soldier from Fort Humboldt*, is one of the few images of pioneer-era Eureka. It depicts the first lumber mills on the Humboldt Bay and shows that the original redwood and spruce forest extended all the way to the water's edge. The original painting, which measures 29-by-16 inches, belongs to the Clarke Historical Museum in Eureka. (Courtesy of the Clarke Historical Museum.)

In the mid-1850s, Humboldt County pioneers Joseph Russ and his wife, Zipporah, began to buy ranch land, ultimately owning some 50,000 acres. Nearly all the ranches are still owned and operated by their descendants. Their land in Eureka and environs (the Russ Claim) included the land that Bartlin Glatt was eventually to own—and donate—to the City of Eureka for Sequoia Park. (Courtesy of Humboldt State University.)

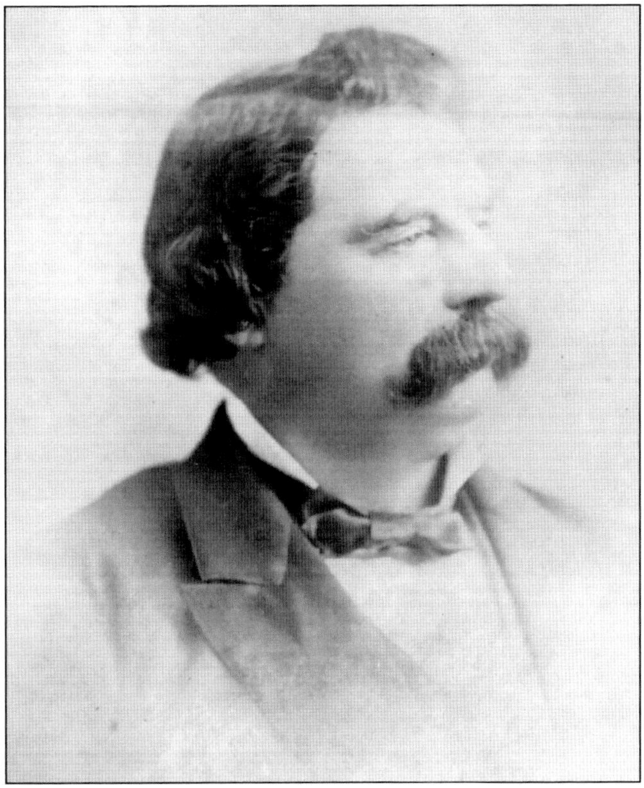

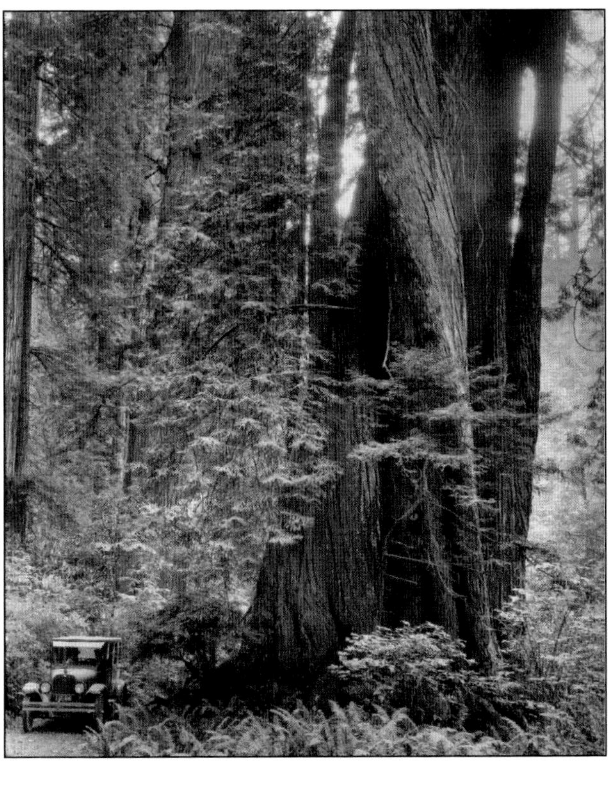

In 1923, Zipporah Russ (neé Patrick), wife of the late Joseph Russ, donated to the State of California 166 acres of redwood forest for inclusion in the Prairie Creek Redwoods State Park. The dedication ceremony on September 2, 1923, included many prominent Eurekans, including Eureka mayor Richard Sweasey. Dr. William Fredric Bade gave the dedication address entitled "An Ennobling Gift." (Courtesy of Humboldt State University.)

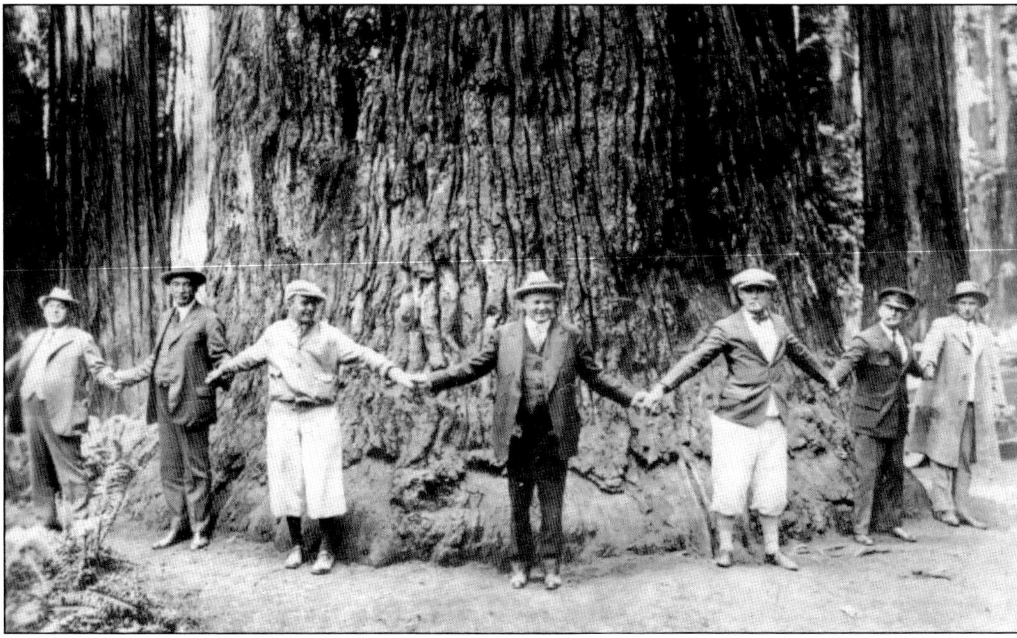

It was on Bull Creek Flat in what is today Humboldt Redwoods State Park that Pres. Herbert Hoover (center) and his party camped in 1928, at which time he expressed the hope that the redwoods would ultimately be preserved for posterity. This photograph was taken in front of the Stout Tree in the first grove donated for Jedediah Smith Redwoods State Park. Gifford Pinchot, first chief of what later became the U.S. Forest Service, is also shown (second from left). (Courtesy of Humboldt State University.)

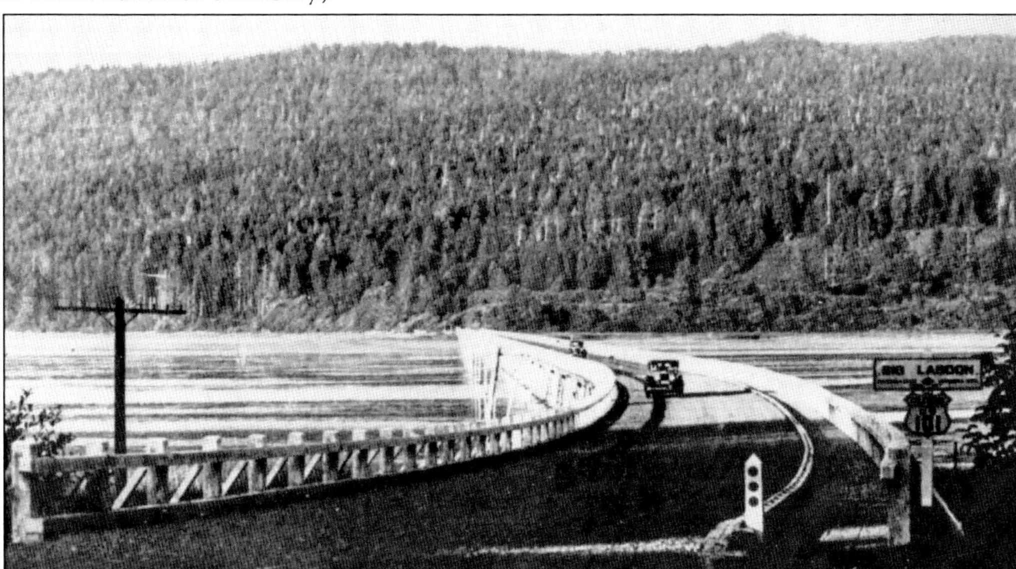

Big Lagoon Bridge is shown here in 1930. Tourists were informed that this span was built almost entirely of local redwood timber. Bridges were one of many items made out of redwood in early California history: sidewalks, shingles, houses, barns, railroad ties, water tanks, wine casks, pickle barrels, and even cigar boxes were made out of the once abundant wood. (Courtesy of the Clarke Historical Museum.)

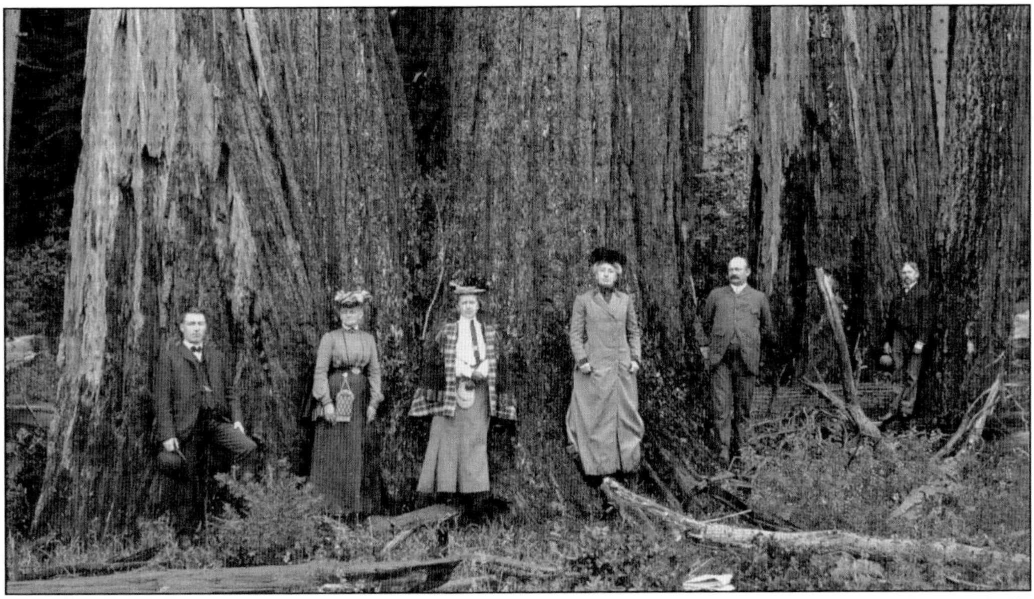

The following was noted on the back of this photograph, "M. A. Burns, Gourley, and Campbell: wealthy Easterners who invested largely in Humboldt timber." By the early 1880s, East Coast investing in West Coast timber had become widespread. Many local booster publications encouraged this investment by providing detailed charts showing the mild climate and abundant natural resources of the county, including acres of timberland, pastureland, and arable land suitable for farming and fruit orchards. With prices on government-owned land set at $2.50 acre through the U.S. Homestead Act, many investors jumped at the chance to cash in. (Courtesy of the Clarke Historical Museum.)

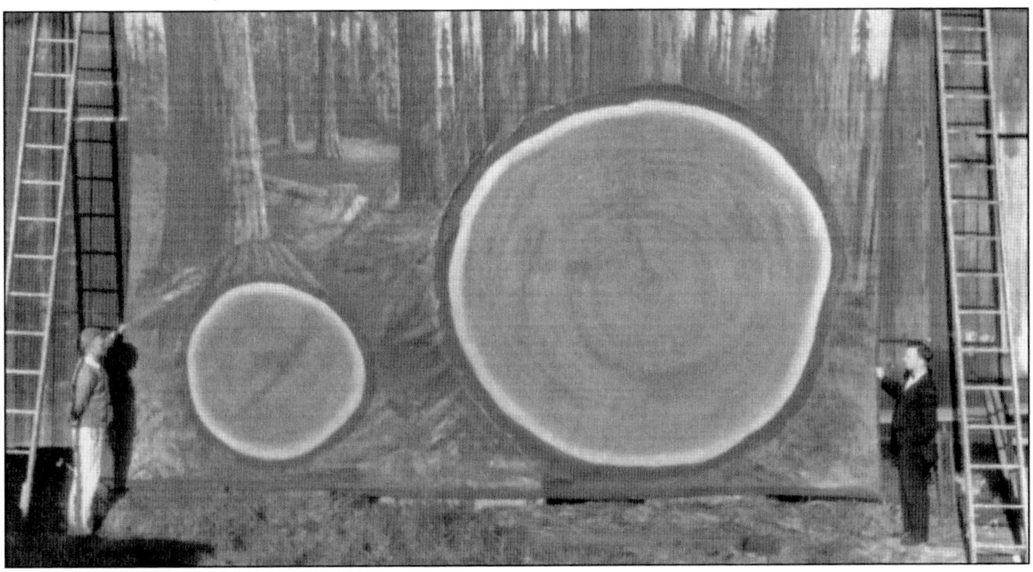

This photograph, most likely taken at a logging convention, shows a presentation of the enormous size and clear grain of virgin redwood timber. Many of the earliest trees to be harvested were even larger, up to 30 feet or more. Logging conventions, which to this day offer annual displays of logging equipment and logger contests, contribute to Humboldt County's community life. (Courtesy of the Clarke Historical Museum.)

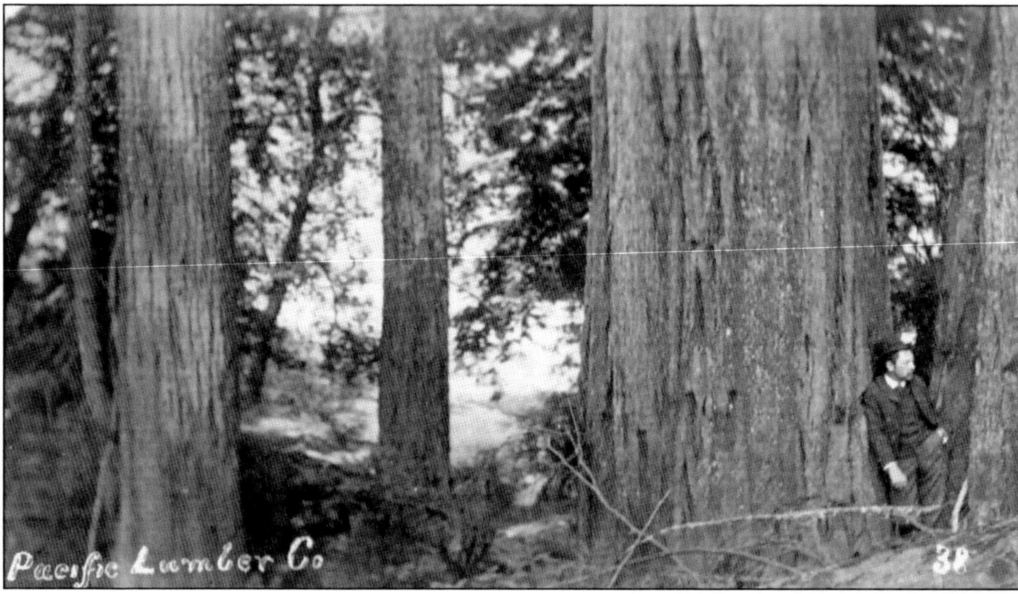

This early advertisement for the Pacific Lumber Company shows an unidentified man leaning up against a large redwood. Pacific Lumber Company was one of the earliest major logging companies on California's north coast. In recent years, the company has been embroiled in a number of controversies surrounding its forestry practices. (Courtesy of the Clarke Historical Museum.)

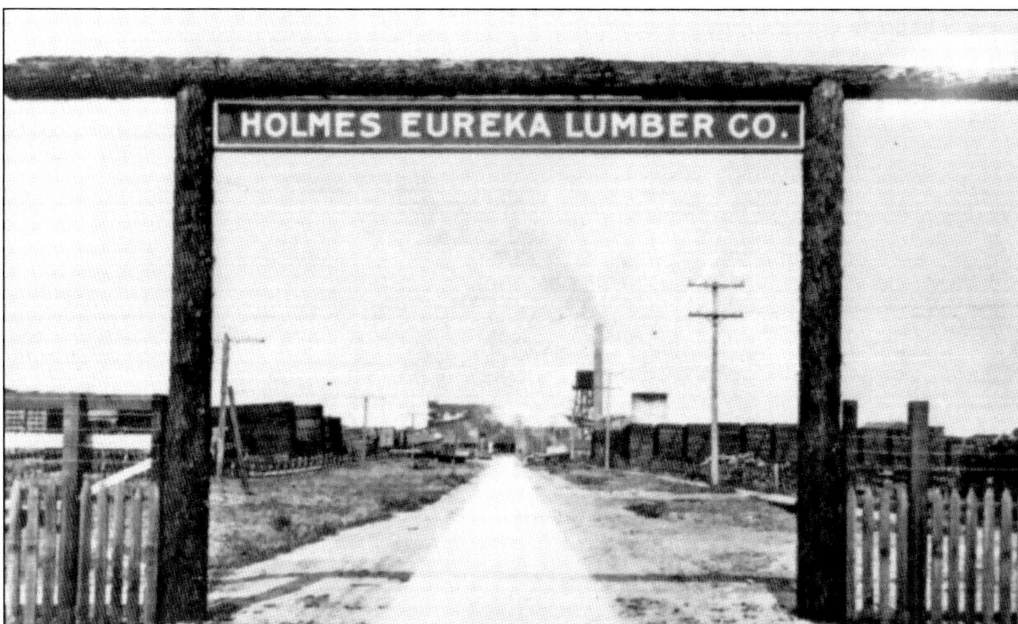

Holmes Eureka Lumber Company, purchased by the Pacific Lumber Company in 1959, was one of Eureka's major timber concerns. Shown in the photograph is the early gate to the facility, which was the scene of a strike and a riot in 1935 in a failed action to unionize the mill. The site is now occupied by the Bayshore Mall. A modern gate structure was installed by the company in 1938 and now stands at the east entrance of Sequoia Park. (Courtesy Humboldt County Historical Society, Phegley Collection.)

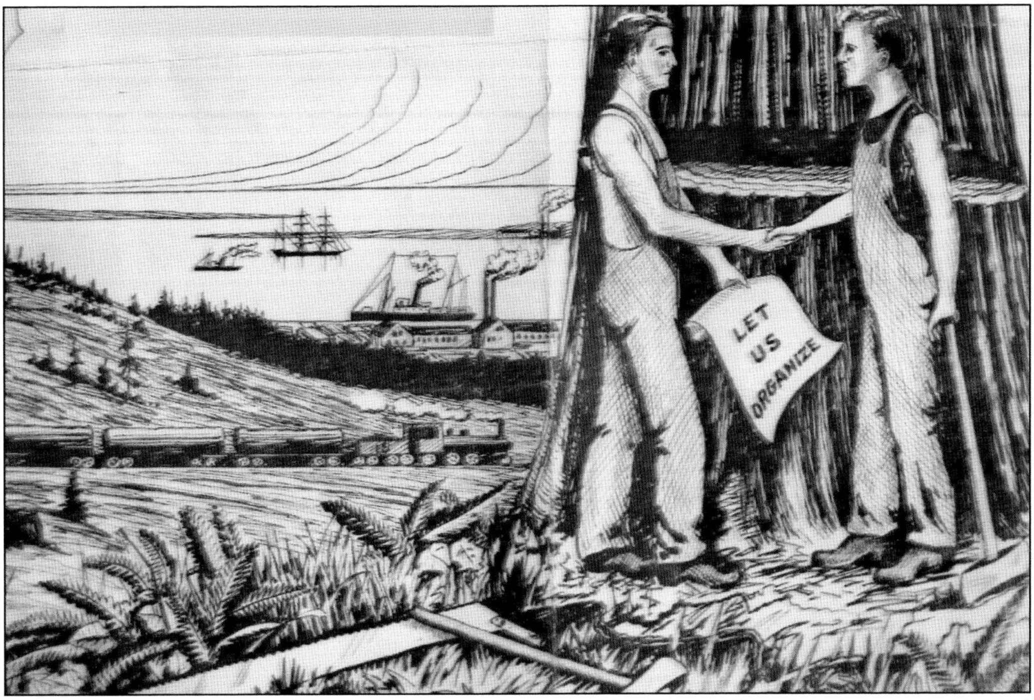

This 1914 cartoon by Torkelsen dramatizes the plight of forests and loggers. Conservation and labor organizations were often at odds, but the fact remained that many lumber companies folded as soon as the timber was cut and sold, causing a loss of local forests and local employment. (Courtesy of the Clarke Historical Museum.)

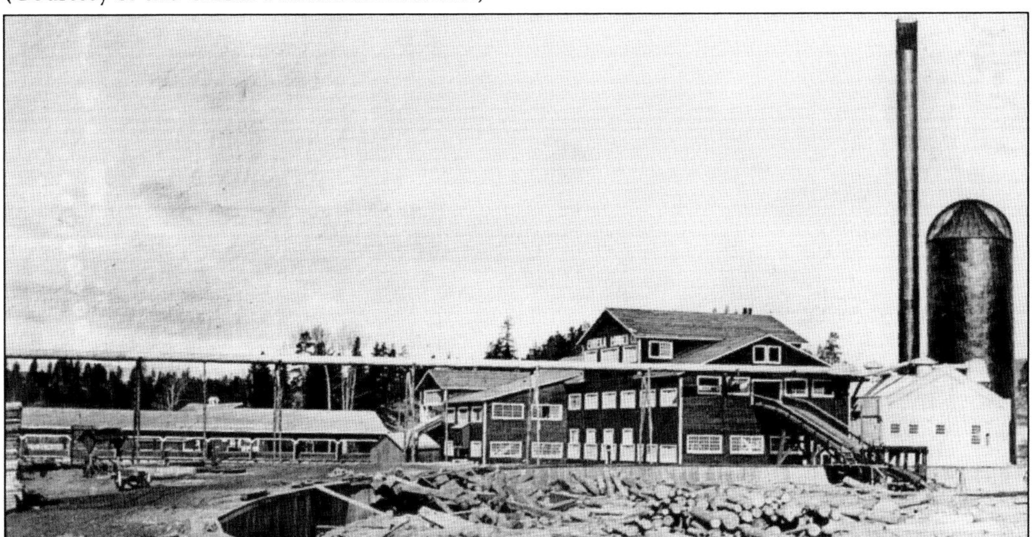

Eureka Lumber Company was one of dozens of lumber mills that operated in the 19th and 20th centuries. This newspaper description of a local mill appeared in September 1902: "Orton Gulch on the Elk River has become a busy place. The mill is solidly built with ample room for three machines. Nine men are employed in the mill, 28 in the woods. The company includes some of Humboldt's best known mill and lumbermen, including Sinclair, A. Connick, and T. W. Hine." (Courtesy of Humboldt State University.)

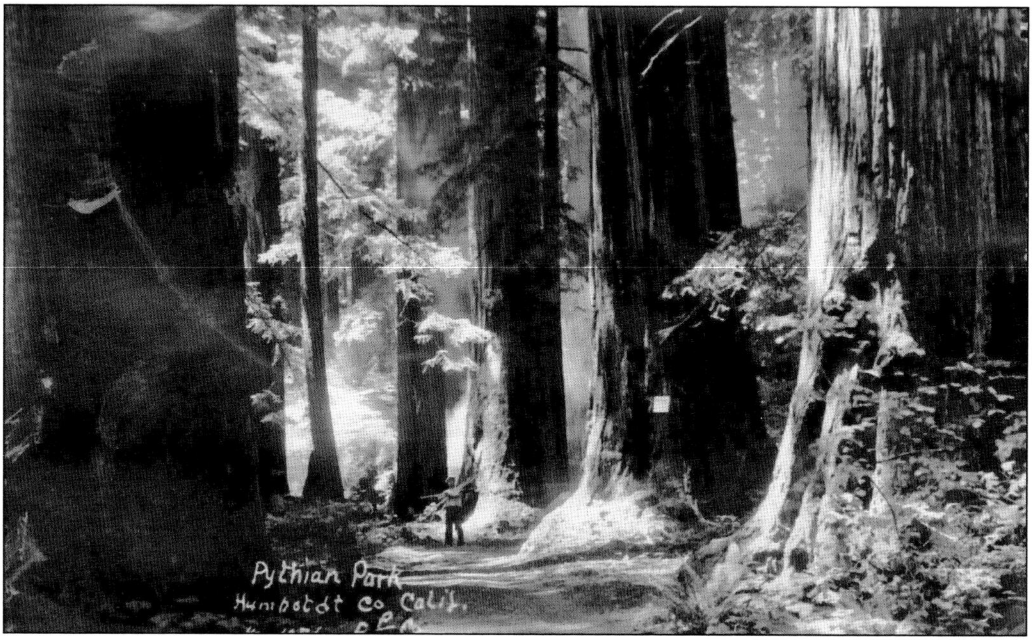

Park building was locally and nationally widespread in the late 1800s and early 1900s. The park pictured here, Pythian Park, was once owned by the Knights of Pythias and is now owned by Humboldt County. The Swimmers Delight swimming hole in the Van Duzen River is still a park favorite. (Courtesy of the Clarke Historical Museum.)

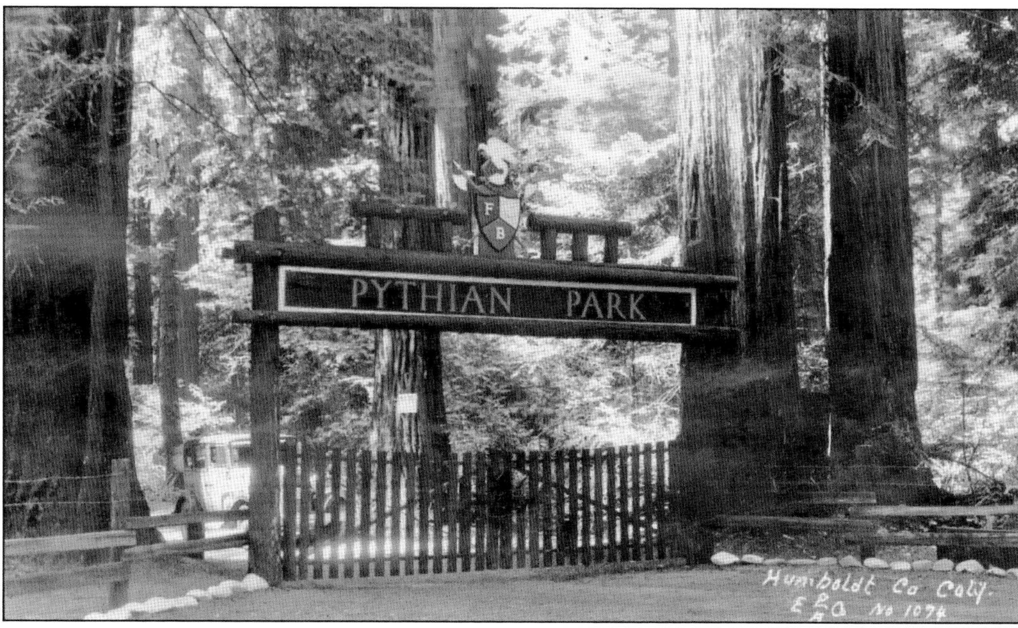

The Pythian Park gate shown in this photograph is comparable to the gate that stood at the Holmes Eureka Lumber Company until it was later donated for use at Sequoia Park, where it now stands. (Courtesy of the Clarke Historical Museum.)

This 1946 photograph captures the drama of felling a 13-foot diameter redwood tree that was considered to be a safety hazard by personnel at the Landing Aids Experiment Station (LAES). The LAES was a joint military project that experimented with low-visibility landings. The government closed the experimental station in 1950 and deeded the property to Humboldt County for use as the Arcata Eureka Municipal Airport. (Courtesy of the Clarke Historical Museum.)

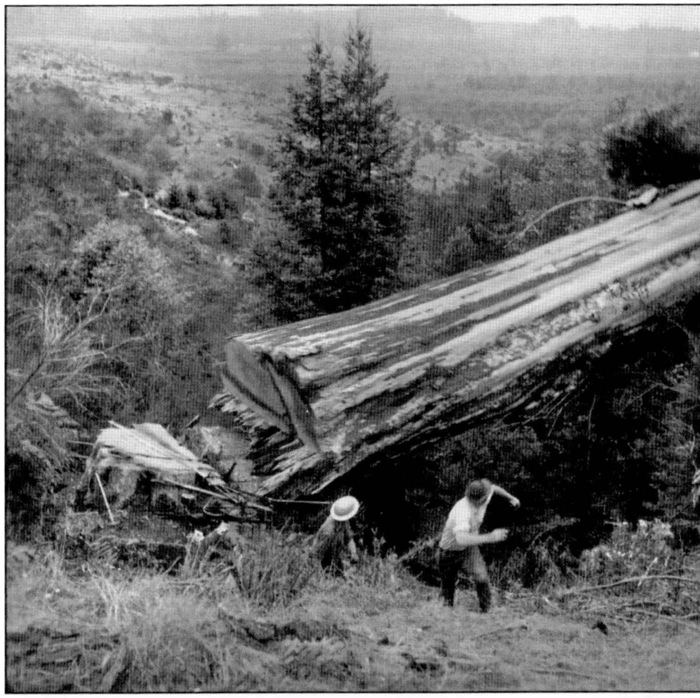

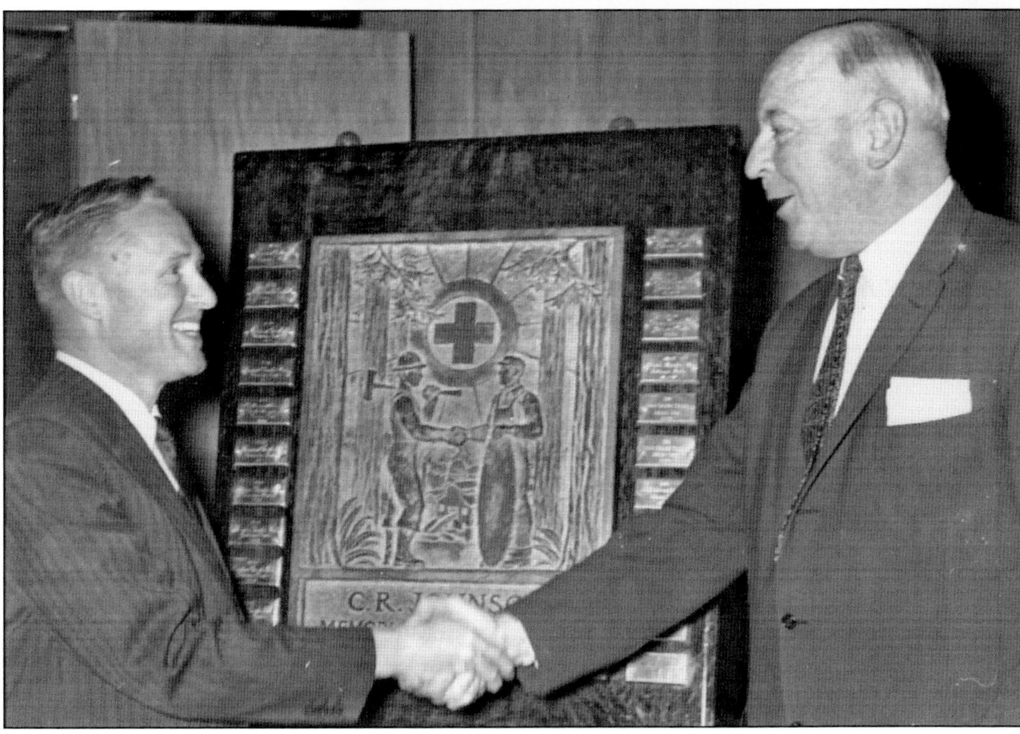

This photograph of two unidentified men shows the acceptance of a safety award called the C. R. Johnson Memorial trophy. The award is given by the California Lumbermen's Accident Prevention Association (CLAPA) for having the best safety record among companies where employees worked more than 100,000 hours. (Courtesy of the Clarke Historical Museum.)

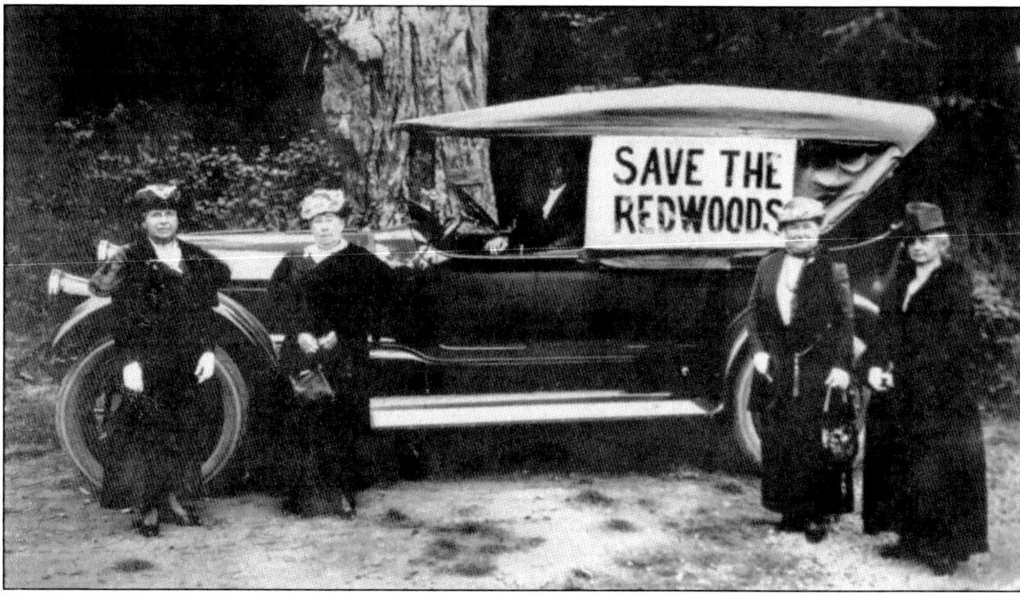

Women's club leaders mobilized conservation efforts both in Humboldt County and in the nation's cities, which broadened women's public influence and greatly expanded both the reach and the impact of the early conservation movement. The four women pictured were prominent in Eureka and Humboldt County in the early fight to save the redwoods. From left to right are Mrs. A. J. Monroe, Mrs. K. Warksc, Mrs. Atkinson, and Mrs. F. Georgeson. (Courtesy of the Humboldt County Historical Society.)

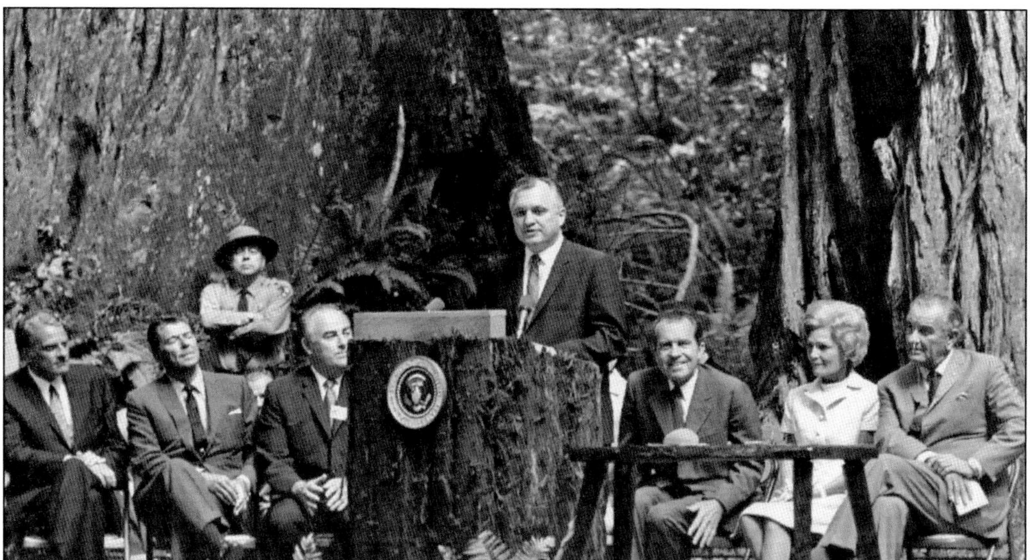

After years of negotiation among local, state, and federal officials, timber interests, and environmentalists, the Redwood National Park finally became a reality. On August 27, 1969, Lady Bird Johnson dedicated the new park in a stand of old growth redwoods named in her honor. Seen at the ceremony (from left to right) are the Rev. Billy Graham, Gov. Ronald Reagan, Congressman Don Clausen, Interior Secretary Walter Hickle, Pres. Richard M. Nixon, First Lady Pat Nixon, and former president Lyndon B. Johnson. (Courtesy of the Clarke Historical Museum.)

Two

EARLY SEQUOIA PARK

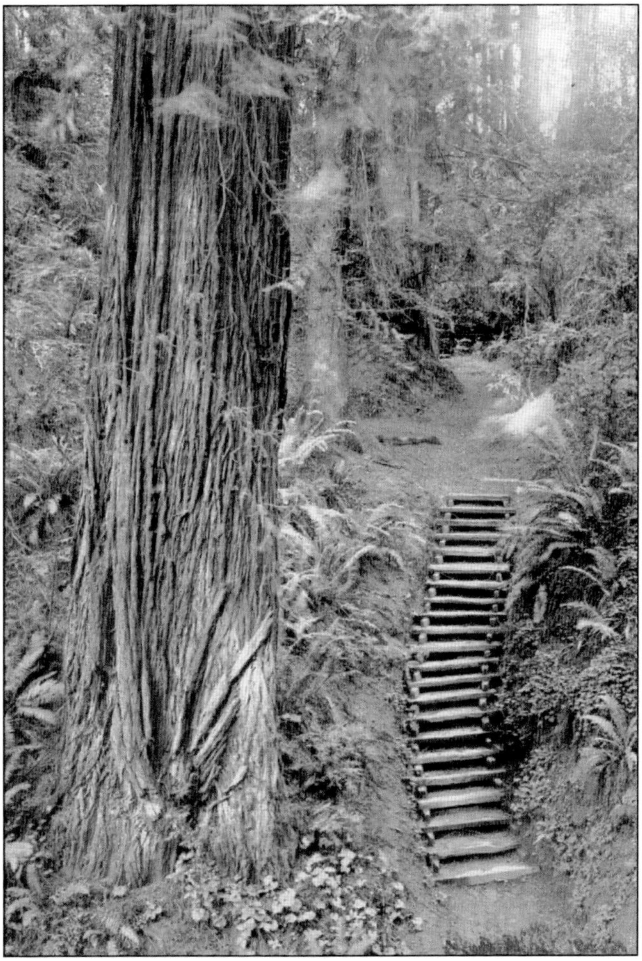

From a 1911 Eureka souvenir brochure comes this delightful description: "Sequoia Park is situated in the center of what was originally an immense redwood forest. On every side of it the timber has been cut away and manufactured into lumber, and there remains within easy reach of the town just this one small spot of timbered land. While the redwood trees of the park are not large ones, the largest one having a diameter of something like twelve feet, yet they are redwoods and some of them are very beautiful trees. They lend a grace and dignity to the park that is not found in man-made playgrounds." (Courtesy of the Clarke Historical Museum.)

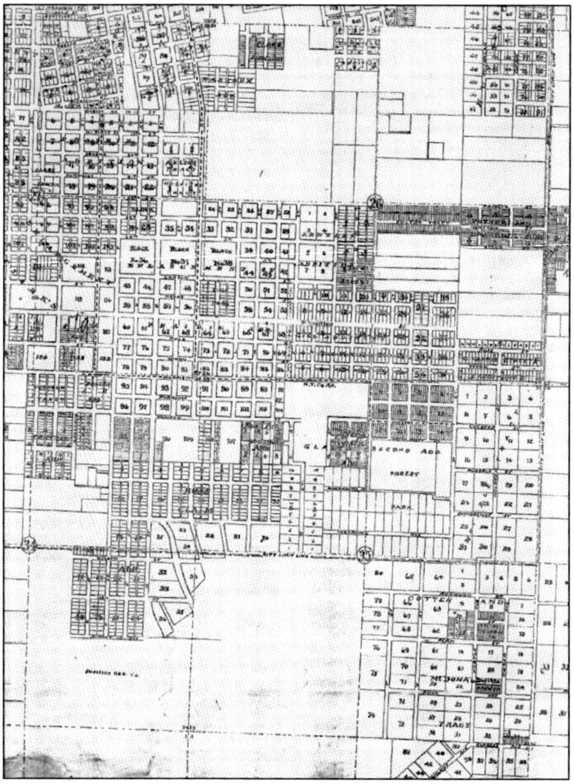

This 1906 map shows the historic Glatt's Second Addition, named after pioneer Bartlin Glatt. Originally, the land set aside for a city park was called Forest Park. To better reflect the unique character of the forest, the name was changed in 1907 by a city ordinance to Sequoia Park. Dotted lines on the map indicate streetcar routes. Other historic timberland parcels later developed into housing tracts include the historic Russ Claim and the Cutten McDonald Tract. (Courtesy of the Humboldt County Historical Society.)

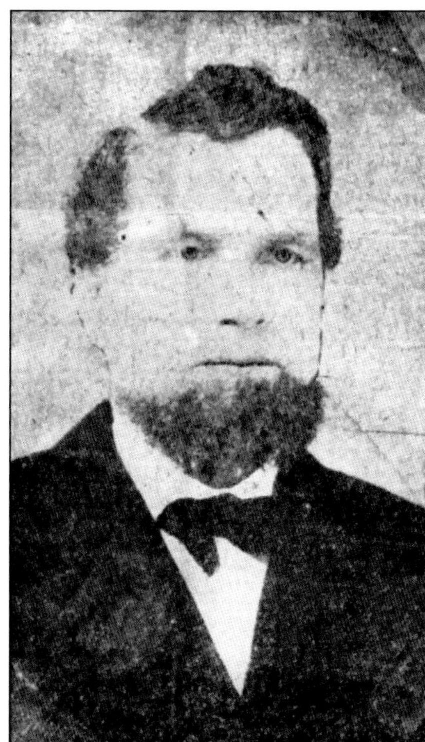

George McFarlan sold the land that became Sequoia Park to Bartlin Glatt in 1874 during a slump in real estate prices. He was one of the earliest pioneers, arriving in Humboldt County during the winter of 1850 in the company of fellow Canadians, including William Carson. After a successful career logging huge tracts of land in south Eureka, McFarlan met his end mysteriously on Christmas Eve 1875 when he was found drowned in the Humboldt Bay. (Courtesy of Humboldt State University.)

Henrietta Glatt (neé Hotzen) was born in 1843 in Germany, immigrated to Illinois in 1847, and moved west with her new husband, Bartlin Glatt, in 1863. After three years of gold mining in Panama, the Glatts arrived in Humboldt County and began investing in timberland in Elk River and in south Eureka. Envisioning the city's first park, Bartlin urged the mayor to exchange some of the city's municipal property for 20 acres of his virgin timberland. Bartlin accepted one city block in exchange and sold additional acreage to the City of Eureka in 1894 and 1896. The park, originally Forest Park, was created by a city ordinance in 1904. The Glatts had eight children. (Courtesy of the Humboldt County Historical Society.)

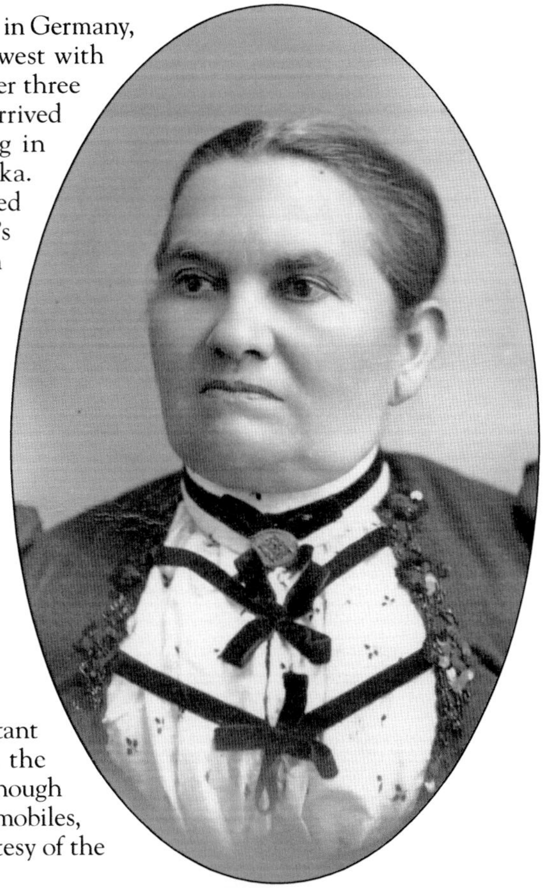

Taken around 1904, this is one of the earliest extant photographs of Forest Park. The road from the upper portion of the park is already present, though still unpaved and generally untraveled by automobiles, which were rare in Eureka at the time. (Courtesy of the Clarke Historical Museum.)

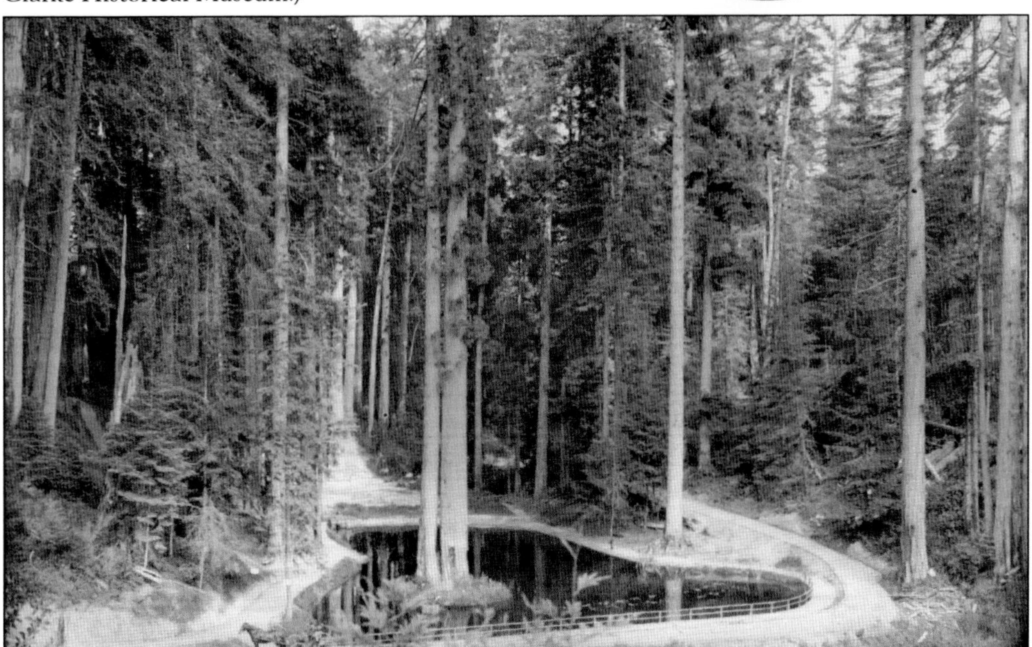

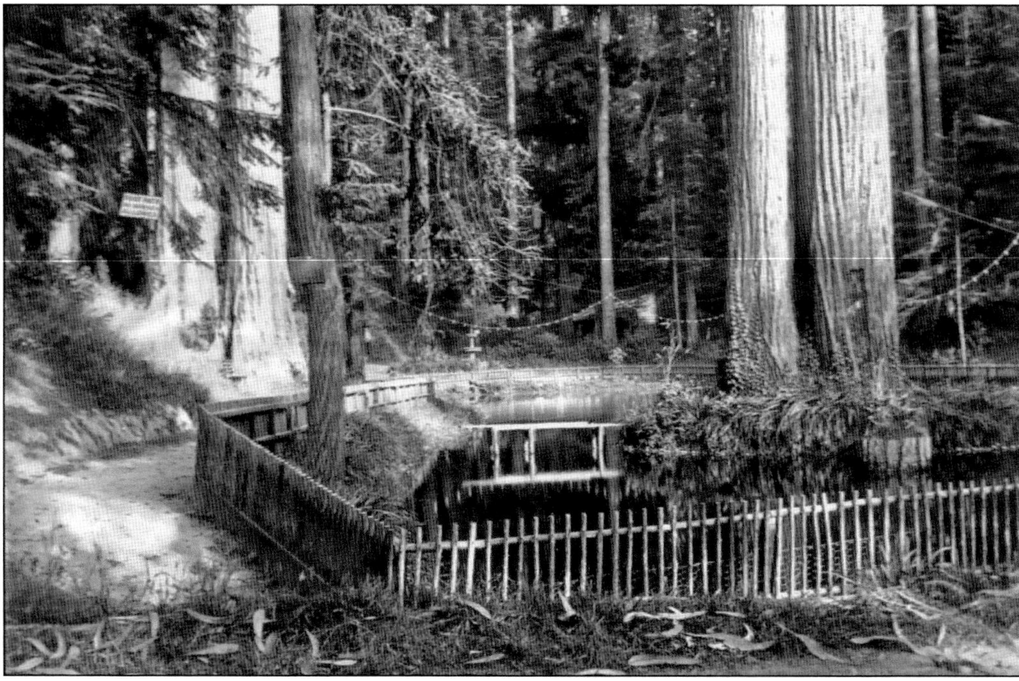

As the sign indicates, horses were not allowed on the footpath. There was a road to be used by horses and the occasional automobile, as well as various footpaths for pedestrians. Interfering with or cutting any of the foliage was also forbidden. (Courtesy of the Clarke Historical Museum.)

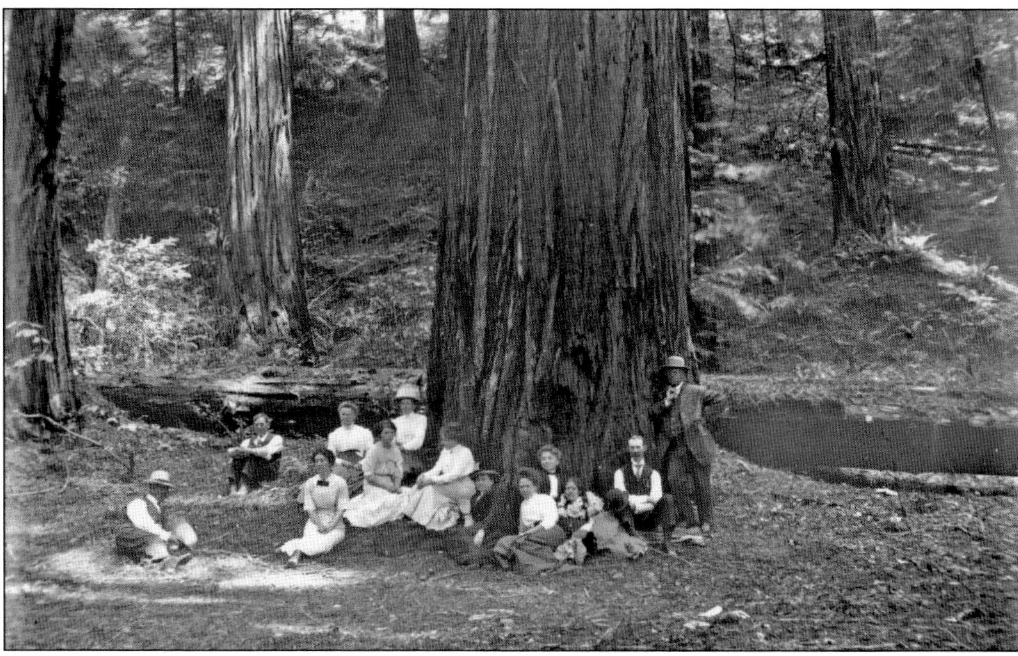

This unidentified party enjoying an afternoon at the base of a giant redwood shows an eight-across span of sitting, standing, and reclining figures. Posing human subjects in front of the great trees was and is a popular way to show the scale of the redwoods. The downed redwood behind the group also provides spatial perspective. (Courtesy of Humboldt State University.)

The forest that became Sequoia Park had abundant water resources. Natural springs flowed from the top of the ravines and into the valley below. One local resident recalled fishing for trout in the park. In Eureka, fishing was widespread at various fishing holes throughout what used to be called Ryan's Slough and Martin's Slough. In fact, one of these springs in present-day Old Town Eureka used to draw people from miles around for its "curative waters." (Courtesy of the Clarke Historical Museum.)

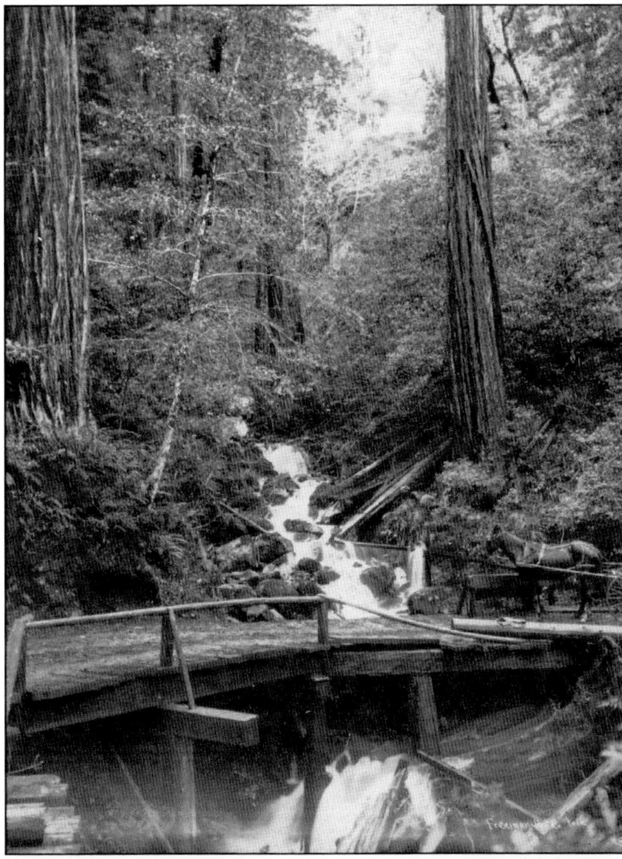

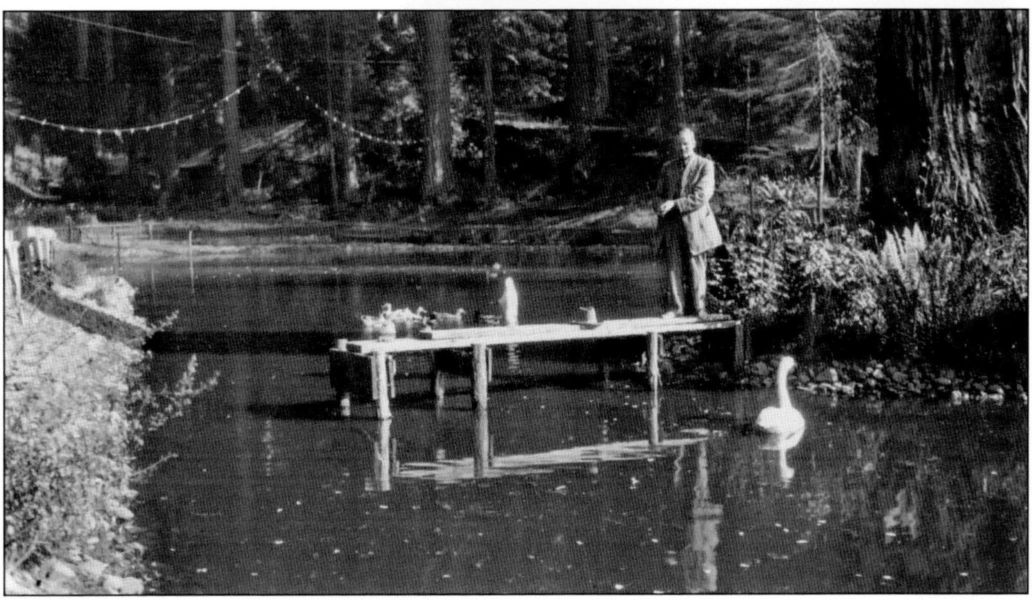

The pictured rudimentary fishing platform was accessed from Redwood Island. Although the island is still there, the platform is not. The swans that were in the park have been replaced by a small flock of ducks. (Courtesy of Humboldt State University.)

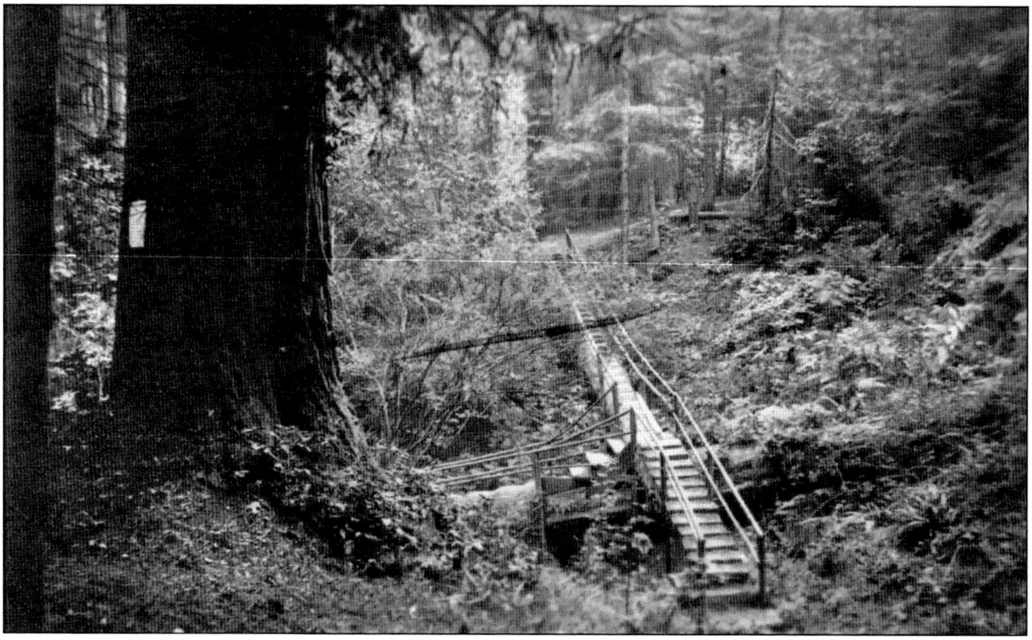

The tiered stairways and other structures in early Sequoia Park were built by the park's first superintendent, Valentine Francis Harris. Harris was born in 1849 in Auckland, New Zealand, and immigrated to San Francisco with his family in 1852. He arrived in Humboldt County in 1871 and was appointed superintendent to Forest Park in 1904. (Courtesy of the Humboldt County Historical Society.)

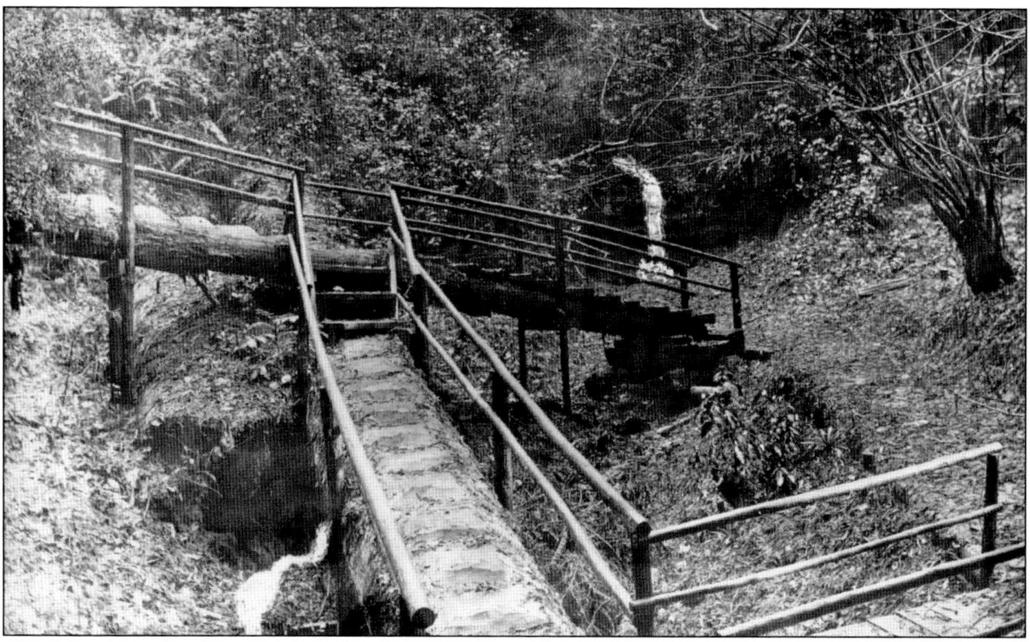

This photograph of a natural timber bridge and stairway in Eureka's Forest Park is another example of park superintendent Valentine Harris's handiwork. An early biography of his work recounts: "Mammoth Sequoias that have fallen he has converted into bridges and others are made into stairways, giving a splendid rustic effect." (Courtesy of the Clarke Historical Museum.)

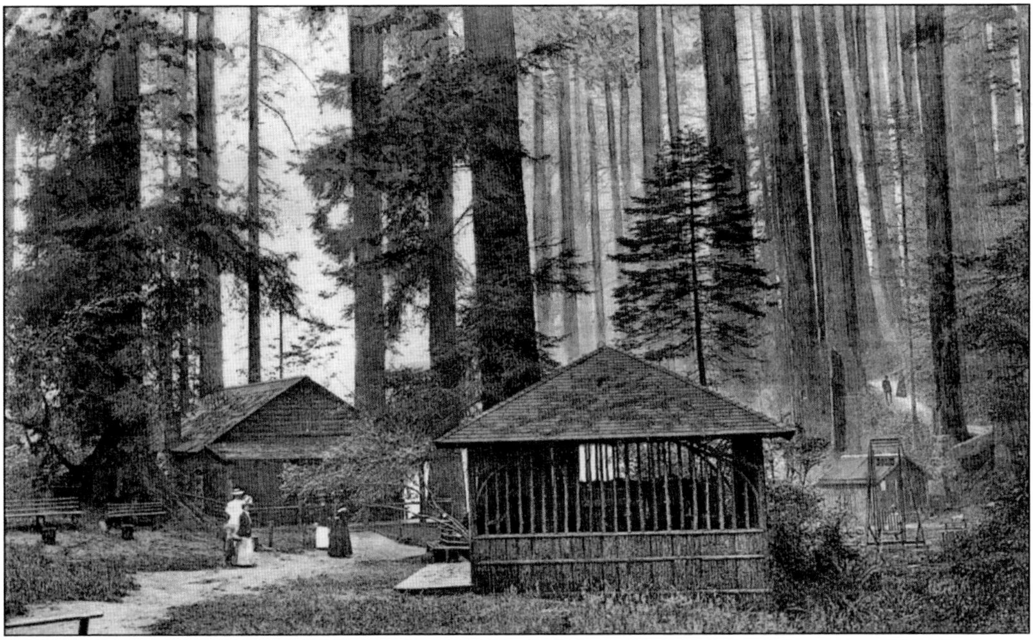

Forest Park was the official name of Sequoia Park from 1904 until July 5, 1907, when the name was changed. This photograph dates from the Forest Park period and shows a family strolling amidst the forest. Many rustic buildings were located in the valley just east of the lake. (Courtesy of the Clarke Historical Museum.)

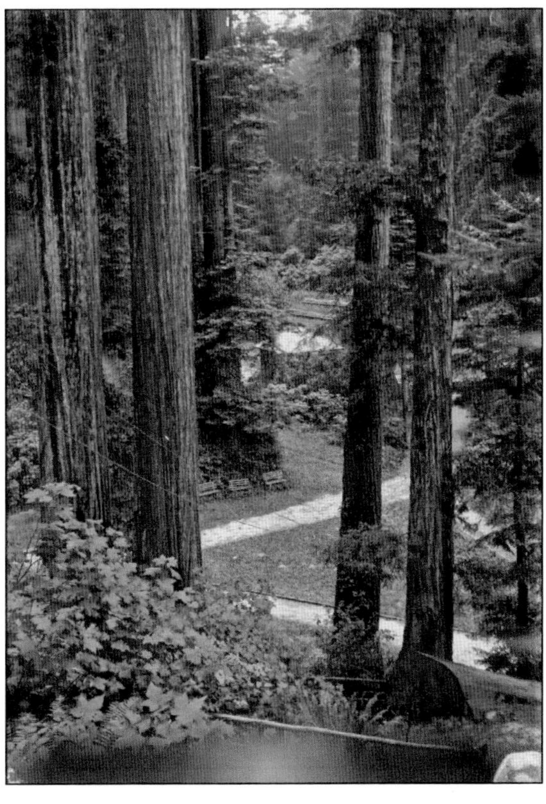

Winding up the hillside behind and above the valley below were a series of footpaths. Although the exact route of these paths has changed over time, footpaths like these remain in today's Sequoia Park. (Courtesy of Humboldt State University.)

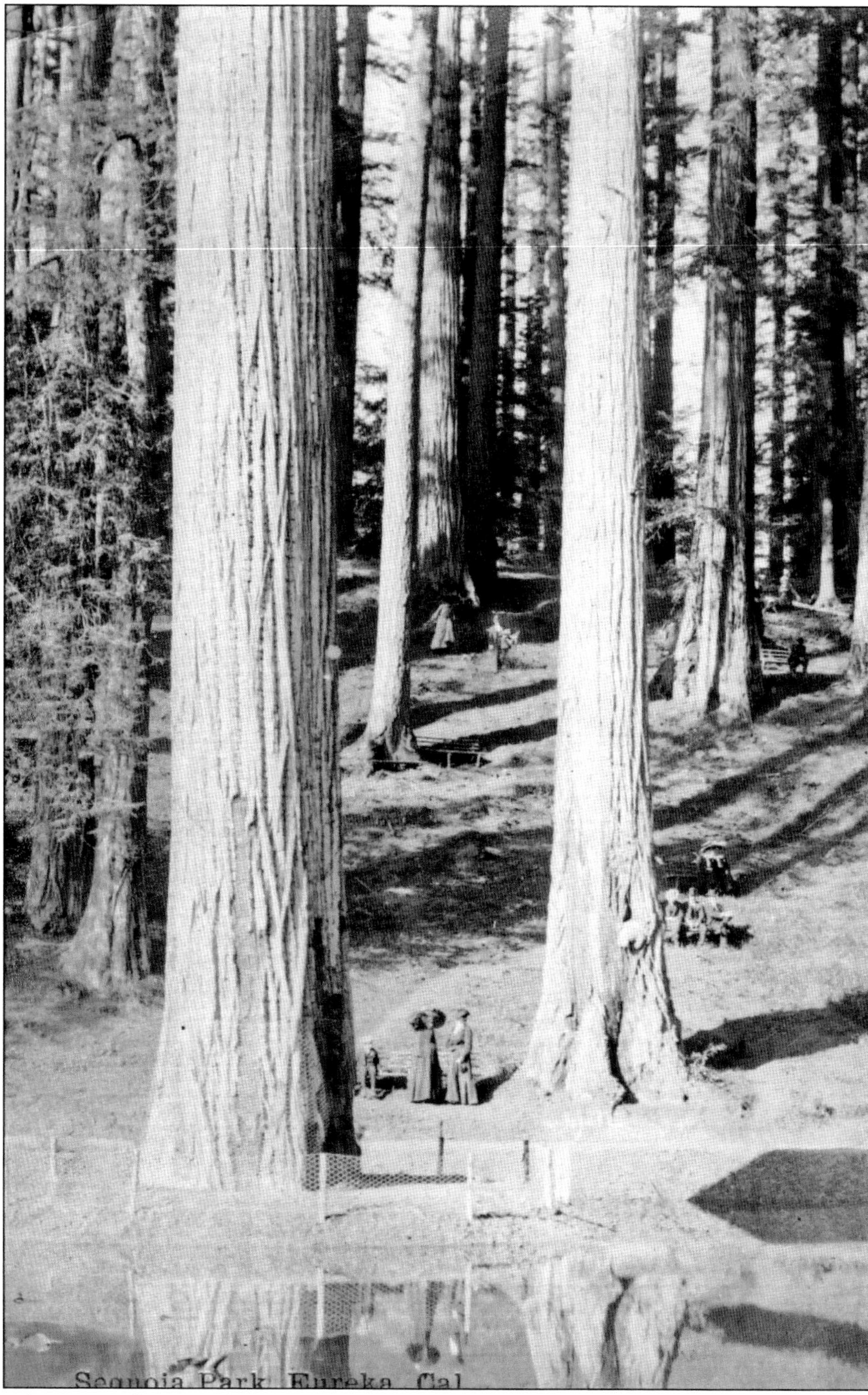

This early postcard image shows the popularity of Sequoia Park in its first years, as well as the scale of the giant redwoods. The photograph was taken prior to the building of the park's rustic fences. A variety of figures are shown peopling the hillside. The Eureka postmark date is January 1910. (Courtesy of the Clarke Historical Museum.)

The photographer, with a sense of humor, took this photograph of three early-20th-century women beneath one of Forest Park's many prohibitionary signs. Although the lower portion of the sign is obscured by the fashionable hat of the berry-picking woman, the message is clear. The posted sign reads: "Warning: All visitors to Forest Park are hereby warned under penalty of arrest not to remove, destroy, or deface any shrubbery or trees." (Courtesy of the Humboldt County Historical Society.)

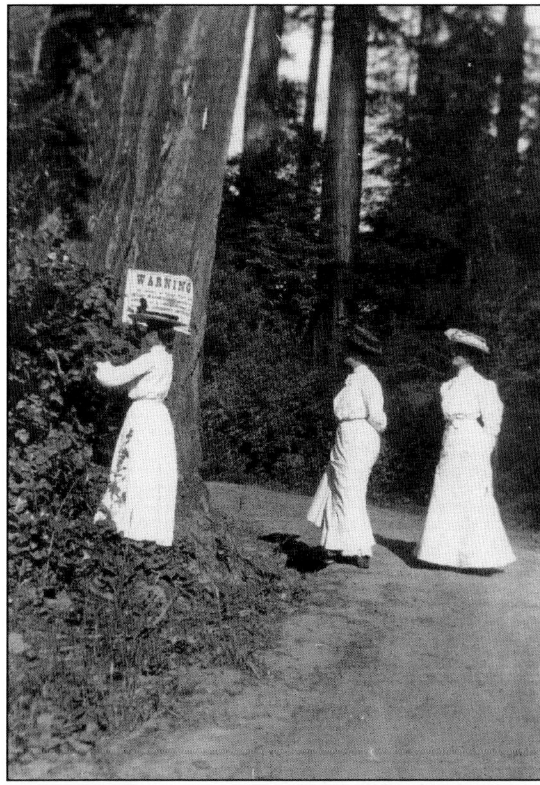

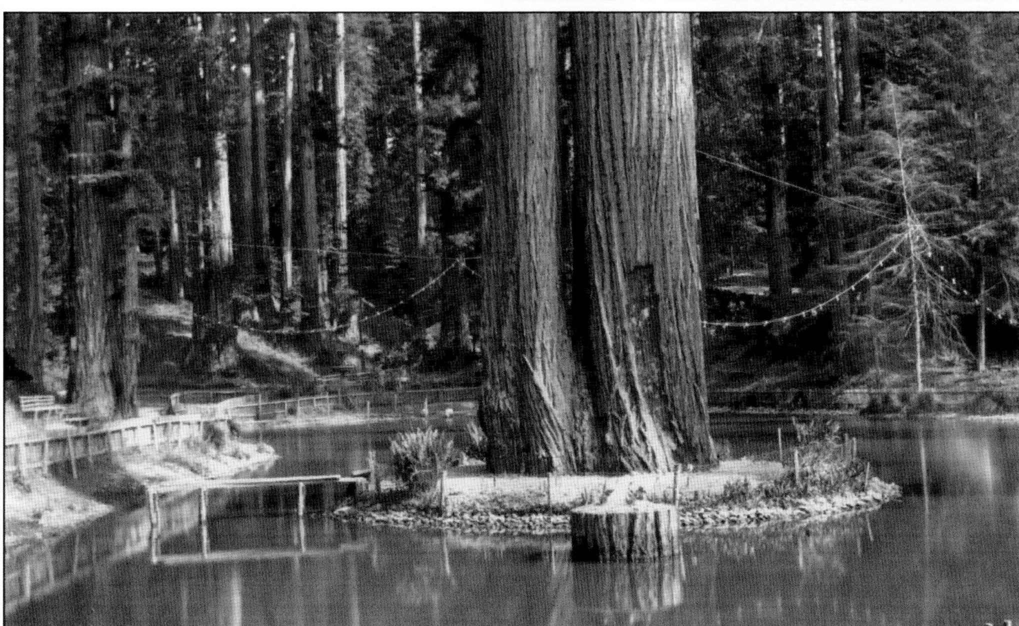

Mirror Lake, as the duck pond was once called, provided a central hub to Sequoia Park visitors. Created simply by damming a natural spring, it was once larger and deeper than it is now. The lake provided a home to swans, ducks, turtles, and fish. Lights strung around the lake provided evening light for strollers. (Courtesy of Humboldt State University.)

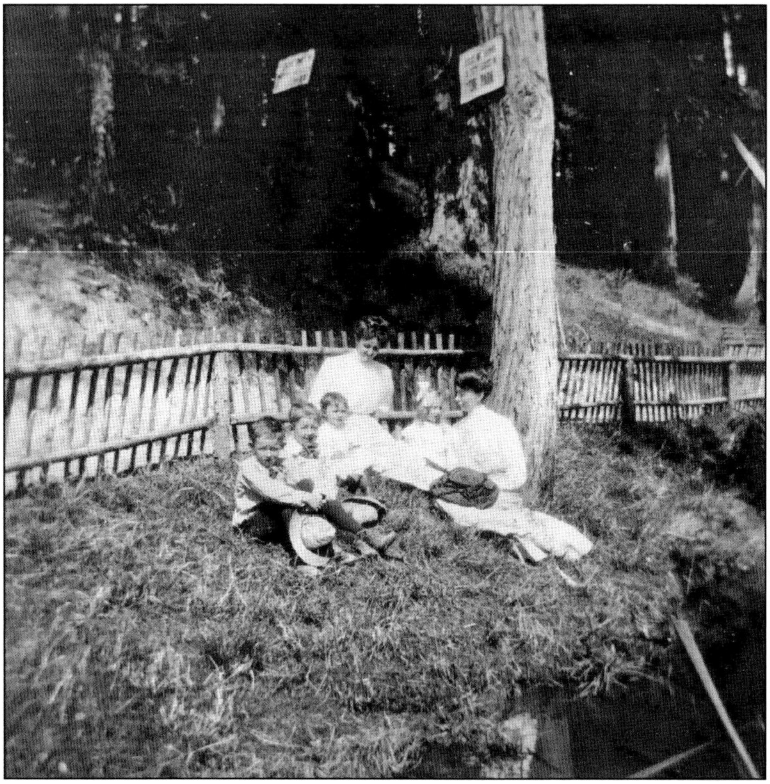

This early-20th-century family poses for a picture while sitting on the banks of Mirror Lake, a practice not possible today due to higher fences and built-up concrete berms at the lake sides. Signs abound: these two admonish park visitors to avoid picking the flowers and to keep all dogs leashed. (Courtesy of the Humboldt County Historical Society.)

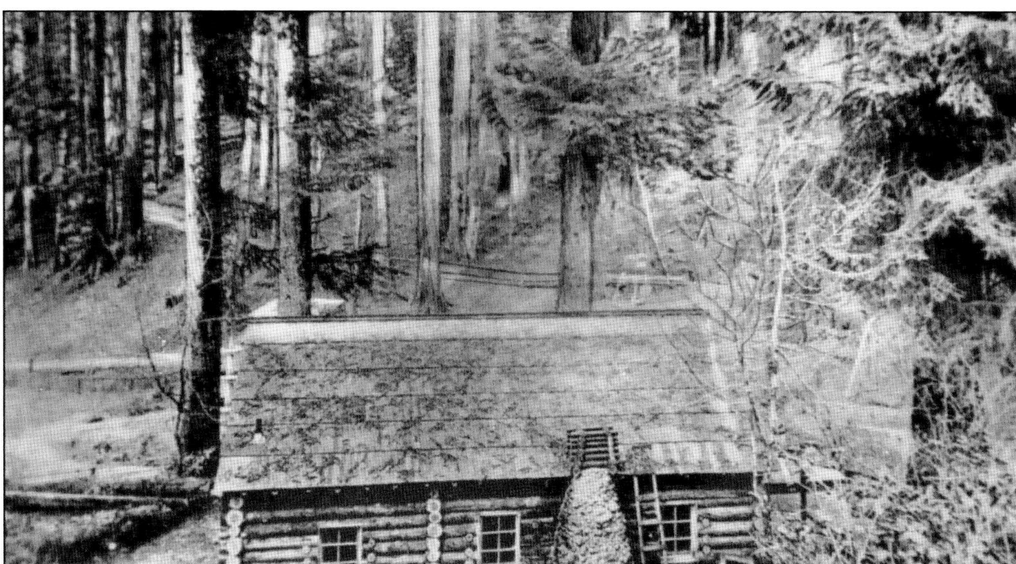

The frontier-style log cabin was built in Forest Park and remained for many years. This rear view of the cabin shows the river rock chimney and the wide planks of the redwood lumber–built roof. The top tier of the fountain at the east end of Mirror Lake is just visible to the cabin's left. (Courtesy of the Humboldt County Historical Society.)

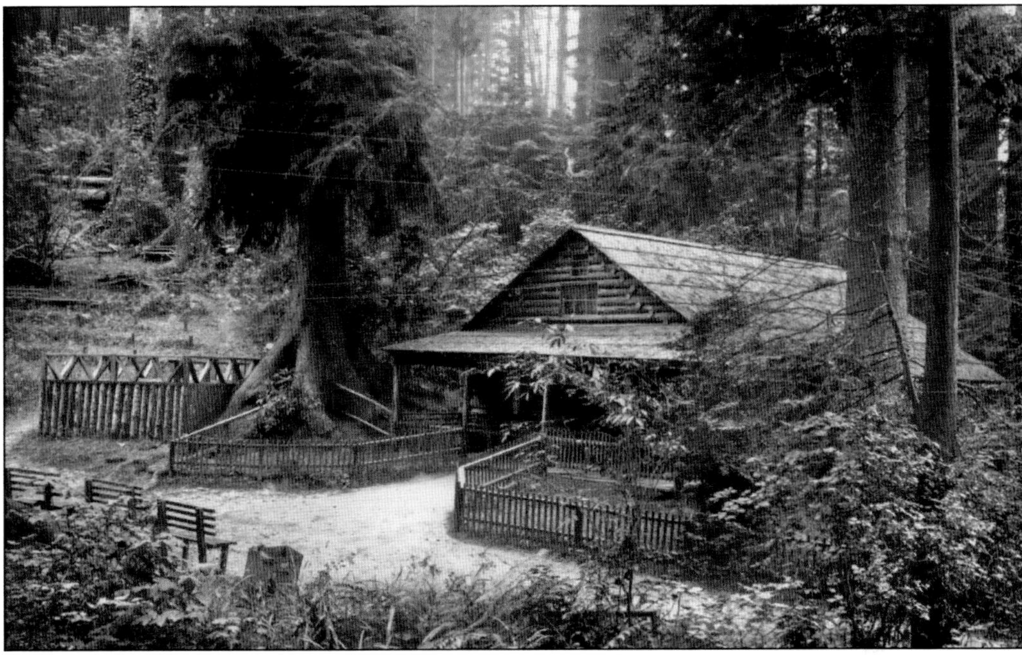

This frontal view of the log cabin shows its rustic beauty and the care with which it was integrated into the park. By 1911, the cabin was described as having a large main room and a ladies dressing room lighted with electric lights. It was also connected to the city telephone system. (Courtesy of Humboldt State University.)

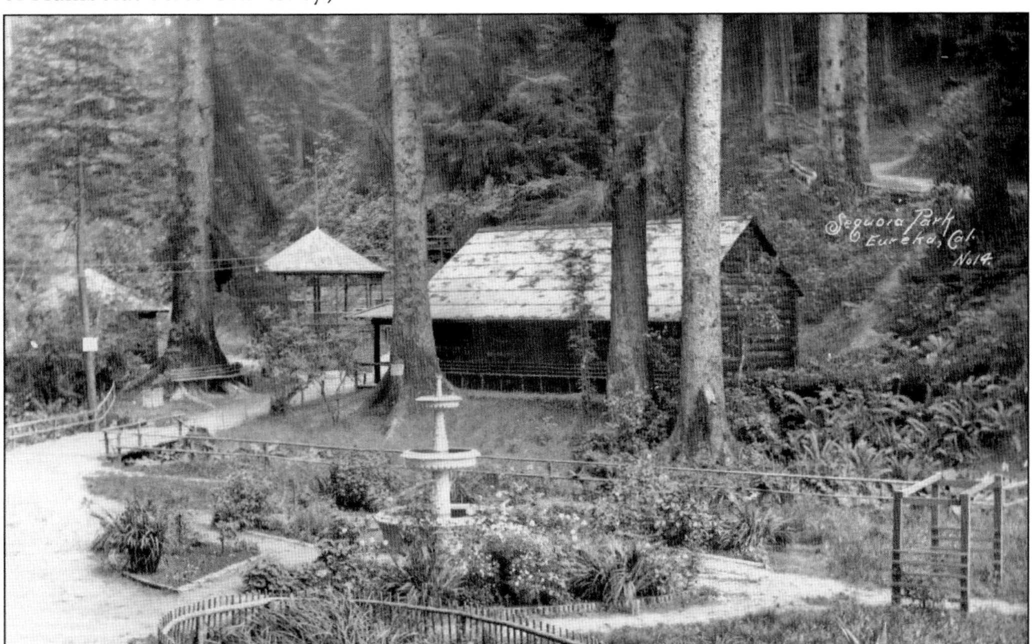

The three-tiered Victorian fountain is a well-known Sequoia Park landmark. It, along with the log cabin, gazebos, and smaller wood structures throughout the park, provided gathering places. Gardens and fences added to the manicured appearance of the Mirror Lake area of the park, currently bounded by Rhododendron Glen. (Courtesy of Humboldt State University.)

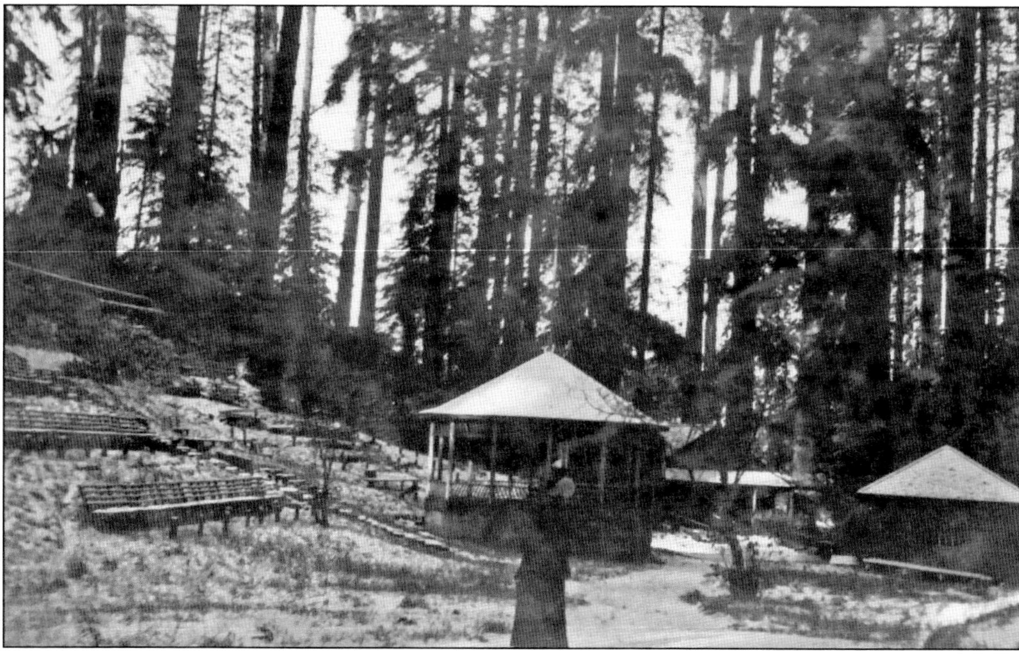

This c. 1907 photograph from an unidentified album page shows Sequoia Park's rustic buildings and amphitheatre-like hillsides after a rare snowfall. In the center of one of the main ravines (not shown), stood a bandstand. The sloping hillsides with benches similar to those shown provided a natural Greek theatre for park concertgoers. (Courtesy of Humboldt State University.)

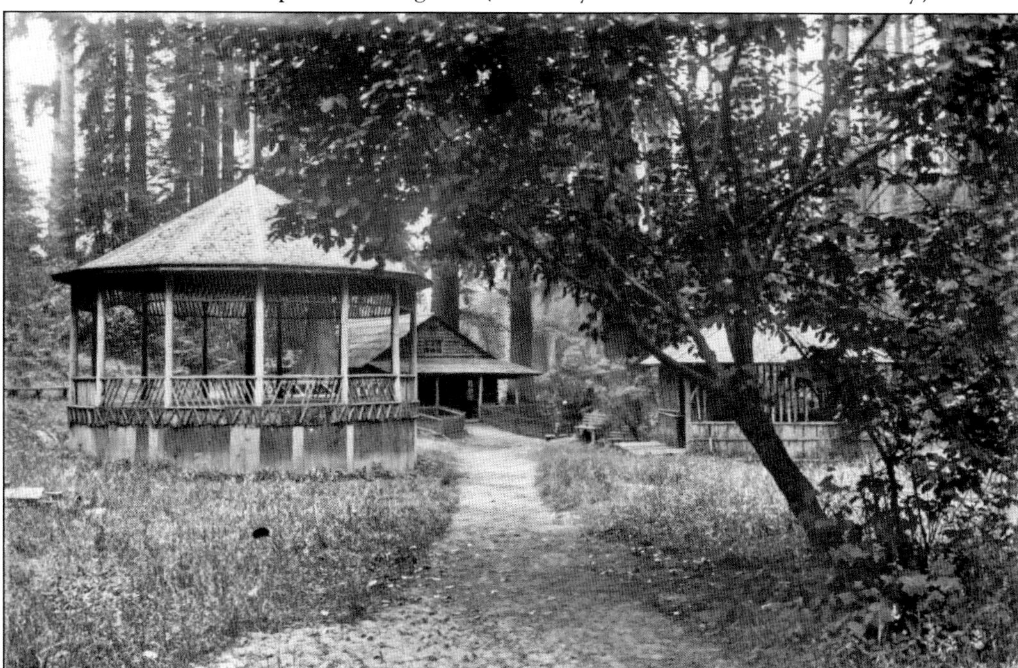

The many pathways through the old pavilion provided visitors with places to relax and to gather, especially on weekends. Nearly every Sunday there were published events in Sequoia Park such as concerts. (Courtesy of Humboldt State University.)

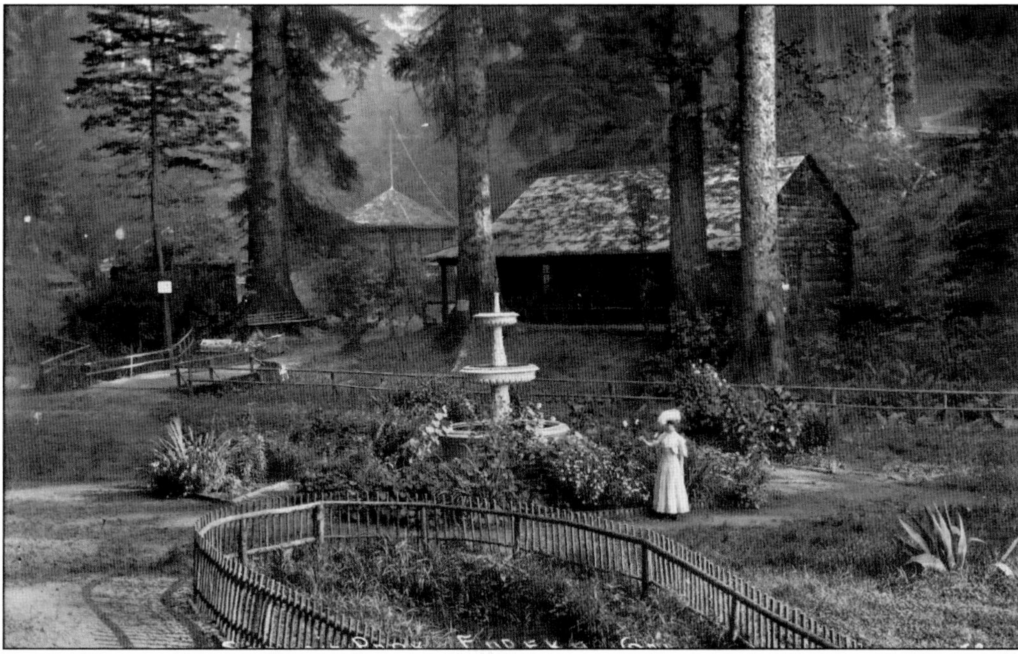

This photograph of an early-20th-century woman shows her admiring the gardens near the three-tiered fountain. Although the photograph is undated, her Edwardian-period dress and hat indicate a date prior to 1910. During this time, the hat, worn atop piled up hair and cantilevered over the face, was an essential element. (Courtesy of Humboldt State University.)

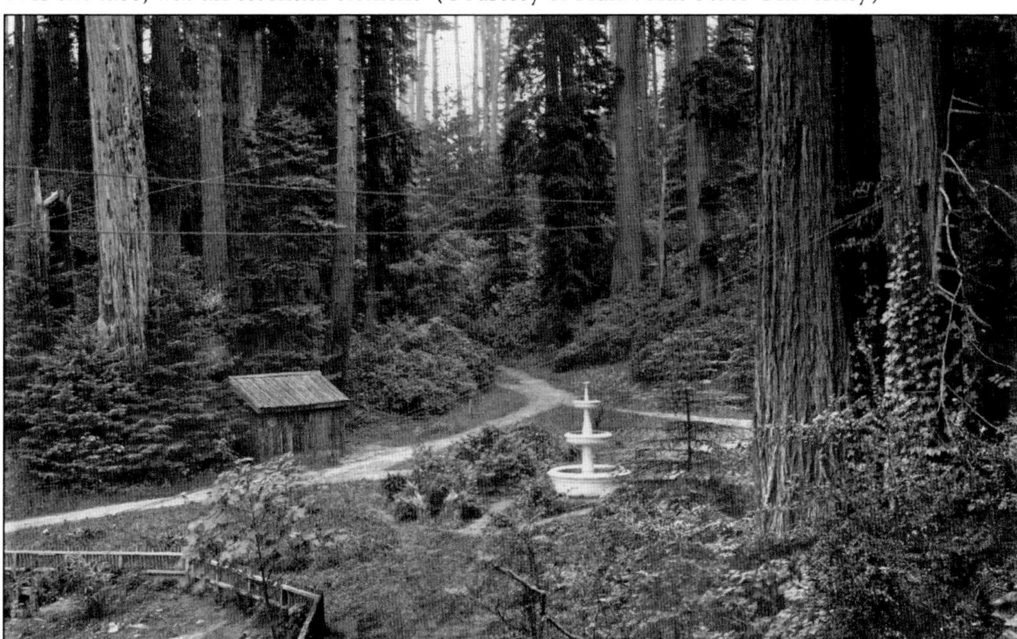

Footpaths through early Sequoia Park were extensive and well maintained. As shown here, there were additional tiered fountains and wooden structures placed throughout the park. This photograph also shows utility lines strung through the trees, most likely to provide electricity for park lighting. (Courtesy of Humboldt State University.)

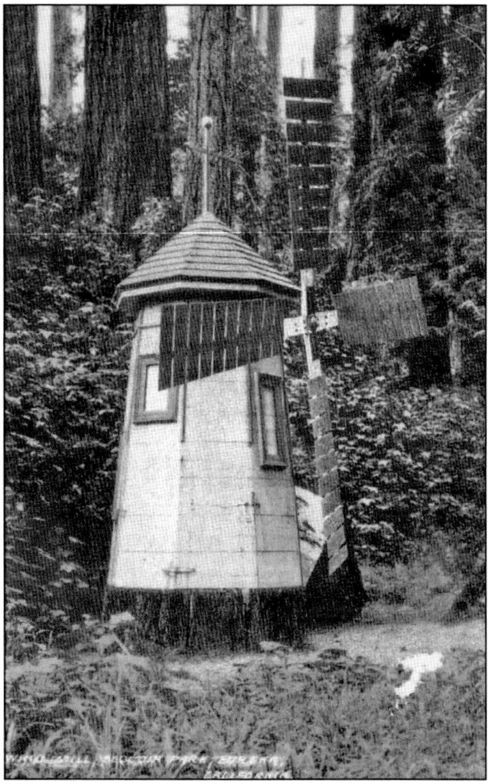

A full-scale Dutch windmill was installed in Sequoia Park amidst the walking paths and giant trees. It is not clear whether the windmill was a working windmill (such as the 1902 windmill still standing today in San Francisco's Golden Gate Park) or whether it was intended only to be decorative. (Courtesy of the Humboldt County Historical Society.)

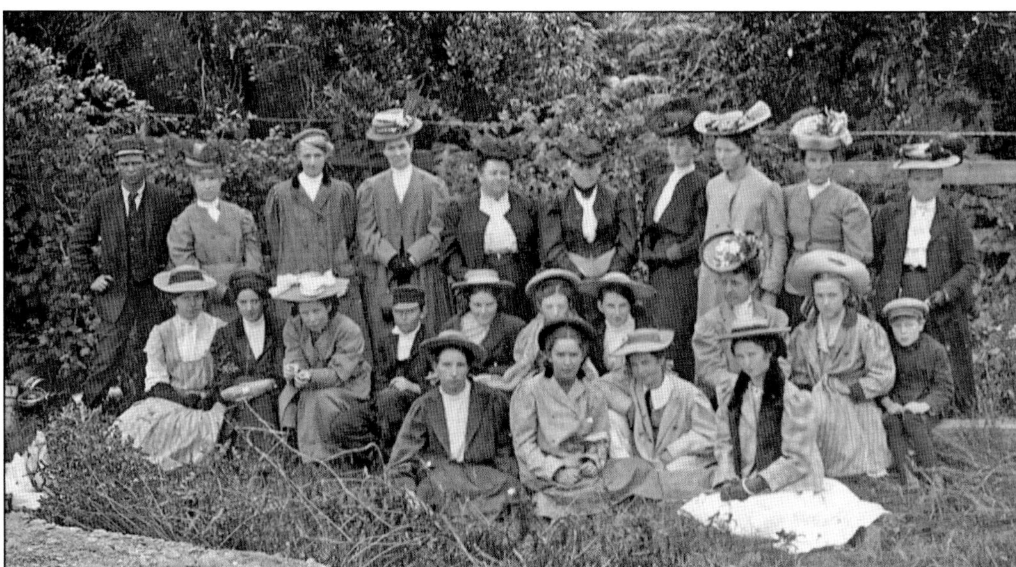

This group photograph identifies two members of Eureka's Hilfiker family: Christine Hilfiker (back row, third from right) and her mother, Christine Davies Hilfiker. The Hilfiker family has a long history of contributing to Sequoia Park and to the Sequoia Park Zoo. A plaque on one of the park's giant redwoods memorializes H. O. Hilfiker. Nancy Hilfiker's memory is honored by the 5,000-square-foot aviary in the Sequoia Park Zoo. (Courtesy of the Humboldt County Historical Society.)

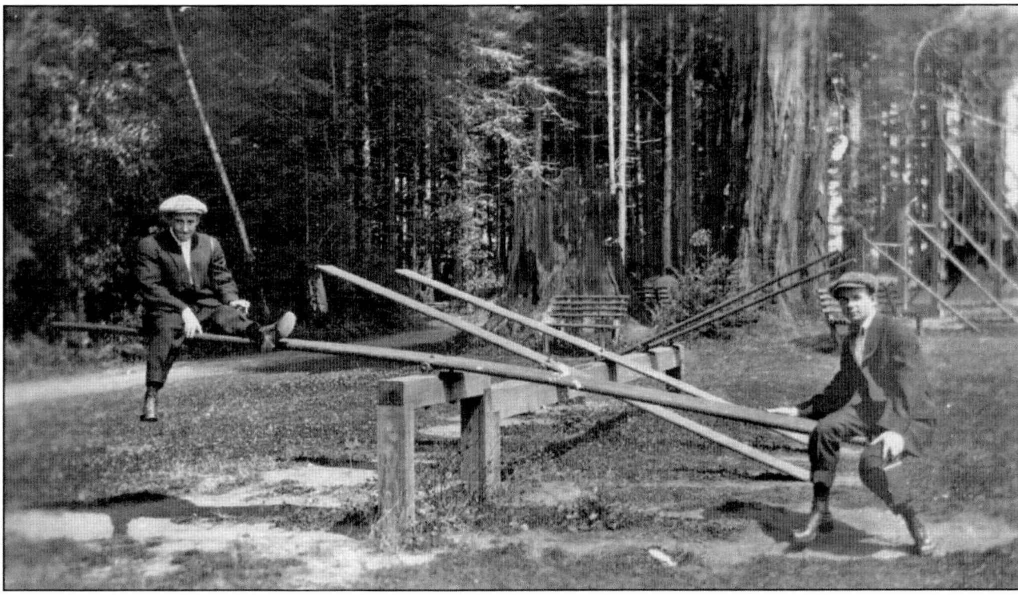

These boys, Winfred Klepper (right) and Colie Campbell, are wearing the newsboy caps popular both for boys and men in the early 20th century. They are shown posing on one of Sequoia Park's teeter-totters. Many play structures have been provided since the park's inception. The oldest were made out of redwood. (Courtesy of the Humboldt County Historical Society.)

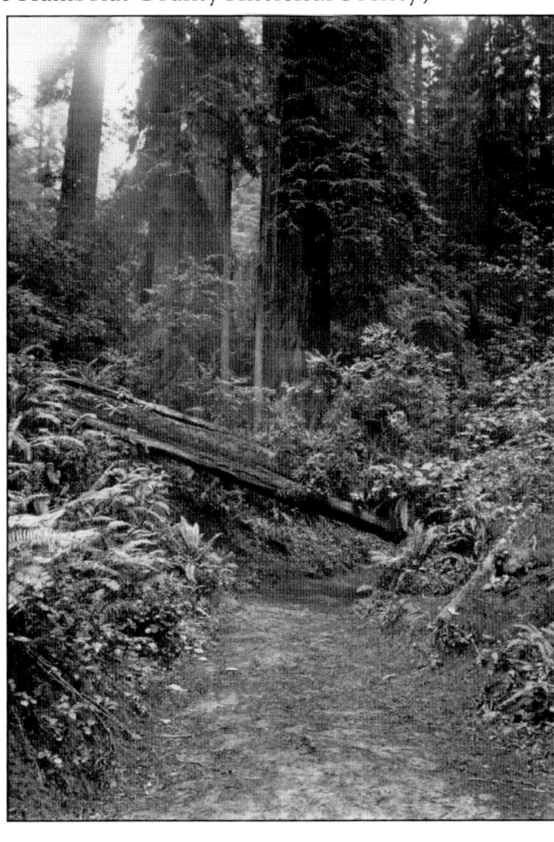

This photograph shows a nurse log in Sequoia Park. Nurse logs provide critical nutrients, water, and shade to other plants and even tree seedlings. Notice that the pictured log is supporting an abundance of ferns and moss. Such fallen logs, once thought of by foresters as debris to be cleared, are now recognized as important habitat for animals and plants. (Courtesy of Humboldt State University.)

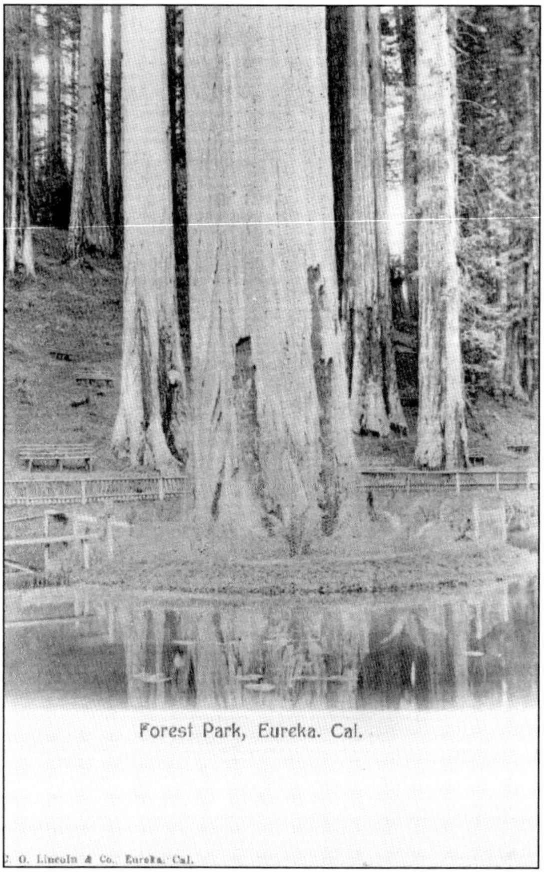

This 1904 postcard shows the ancient redwood tree that stood on Redwood Island in the Sequoia Park duck pond. The giant tree was a park landmark for many years, though it is no longer standing. Although it is not known exactly what year the tree was cut, dated photographs suggest the late 1930s to 1940s. Its demise was inevitable once its roots were submerged. A redwood's shallow root system can extend up to 250 feet and intertwines with the roots of neighboring trees for added stability. (Courtesy of the Clarke Historical Museum.)

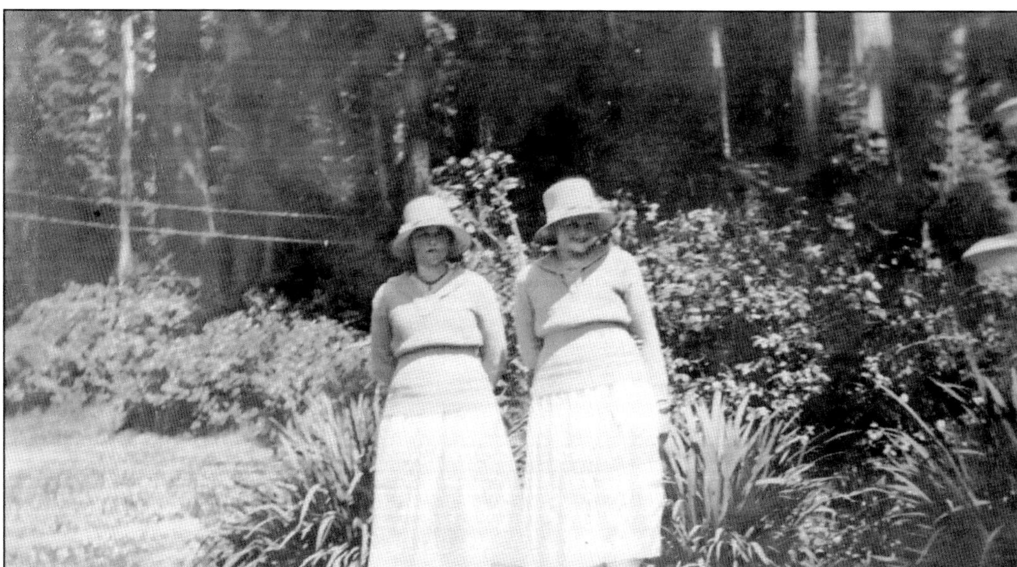

This 1920s photograph shows two unidentified girls posing next to the large three-tiered Victorian fountain at the east end of the valley, near present-day Rhododendron Glen. Strands of lights can be seen in the trees behind them. (Courtesy of the Clarke Historical Museum.)

This postcard shows a small boy posing at the foot of two redwood trees. It is unique within the Sequoia Park postcard genre in its use of the generic name Big Trees. Big Tree was once the common name of the giant sequoia (*Sequoiadendron giganteum*). Giant sequoias, also called Sierra redwoods, are a relative of the coast redwood. They are found in a limited area of the western Sierra Nevada at elevations of 4,000 to 7,000 feet. (Courtesy of the Clarke Historical Museum.)

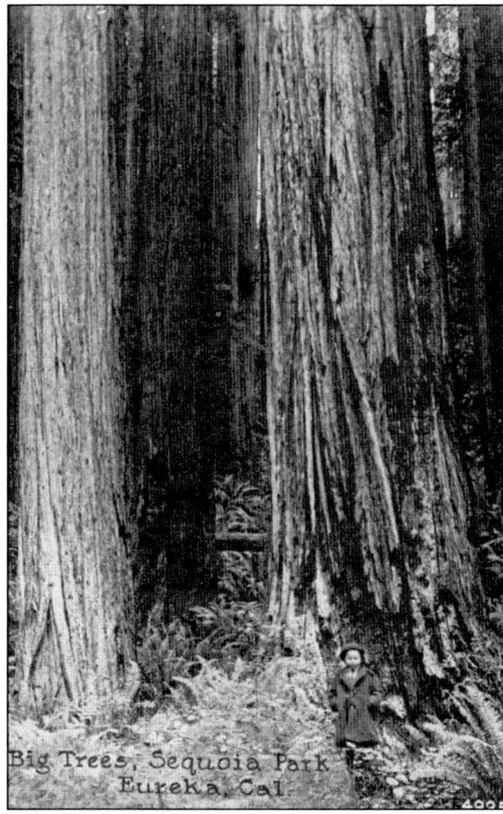

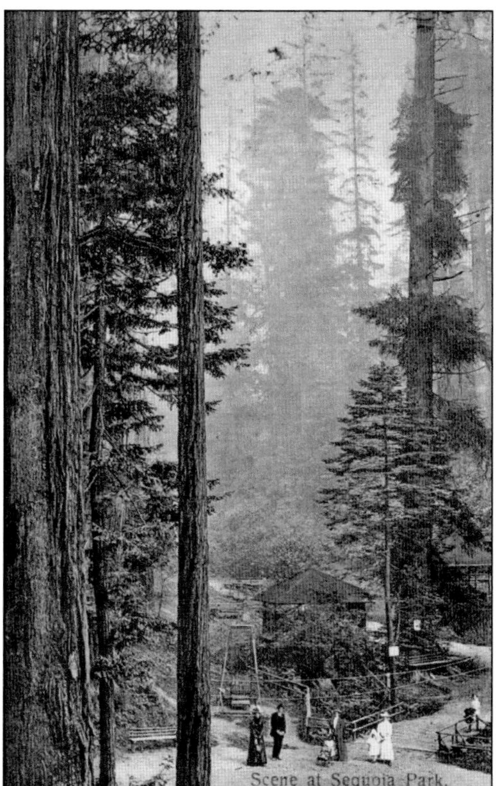

This 1909 postcard entitled Scene at Sequoia Park shows a family visit to the park. The rustic swing near the paths leading to Mirror Lake is also shown. Notice the redwood trees of various ages, including the young redwood in the middle foreground. Varying age trees are an indicator of a healthy old-growth forest. (Courtesy of the Clarke Historical Museum.)

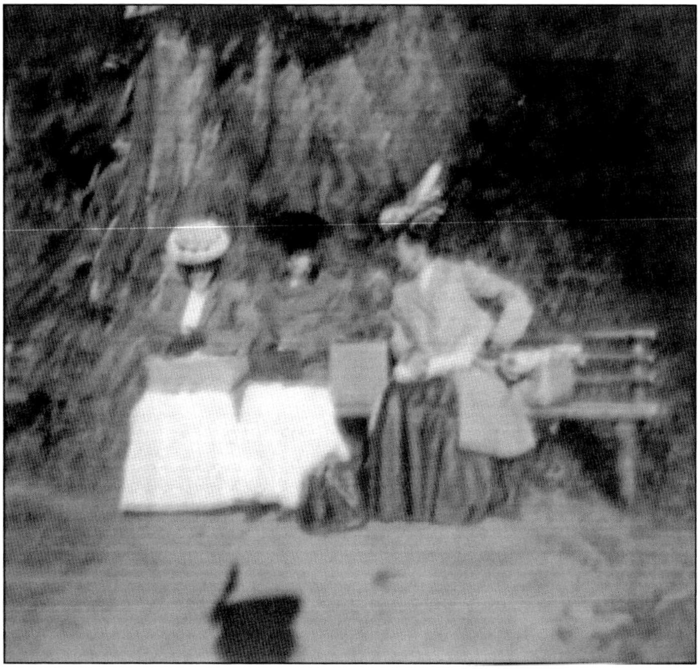

This photograph, obviously by a novice photographer, includes not only the fashionable hats worn by these early-20th-century women subjects, but also the hat of the picture taker. The first mass-market camera, the Brownie, was released in 1900 by the Eastman Kodak Company. By 1905, a folding version of the Brownie cost $5. (Courtesy of the Clarke Historical Museum.)

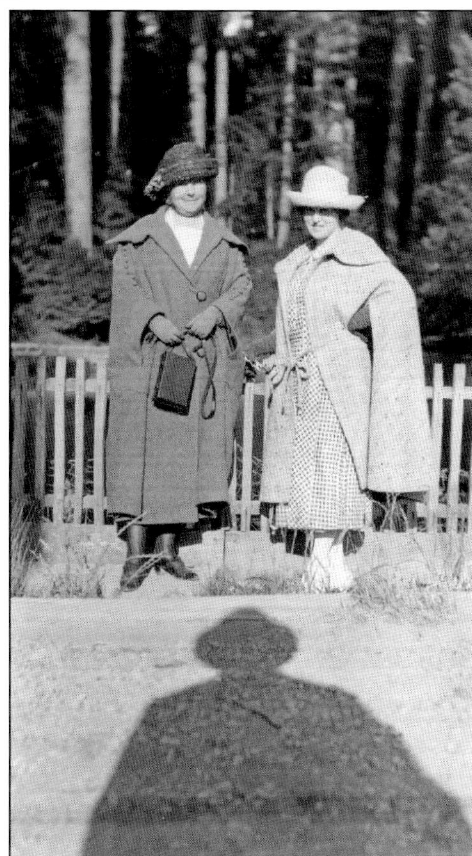

This 1922 photograph of two women standing in front of Mirror Lake in Sequoia Park includes the photographer's long shadow in the image. Notice the cloche hats, fashionable for women at the time. By 1922, the Eastman Kodak Company sold the folding Brownie camera for $9. (Courtesy of the Humboldt County Historical Society.)

From an early Eureka souvenir brochure comes this apt description: "But the chief charm of the place is its appearance of having come fresh from Nature's hands. Nature has previously arranged for the landscape gardening. The large timber—redwood and fir and spruce—furnish the shade." (Courtesy of the Clarke Historical Museum.)

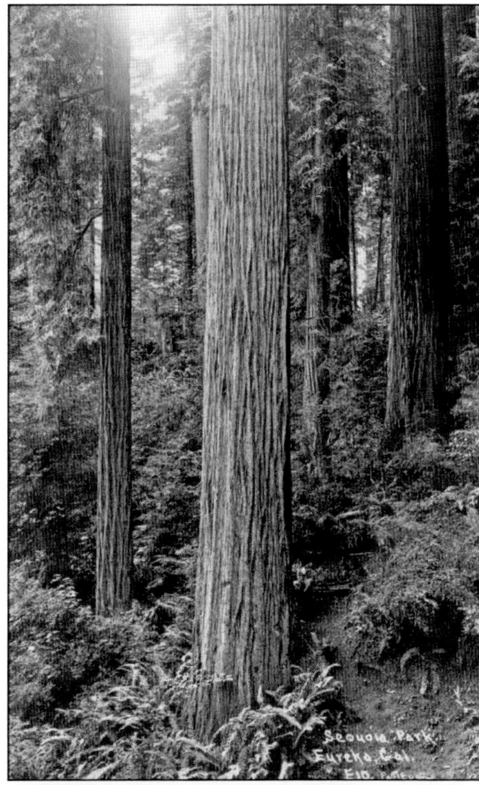

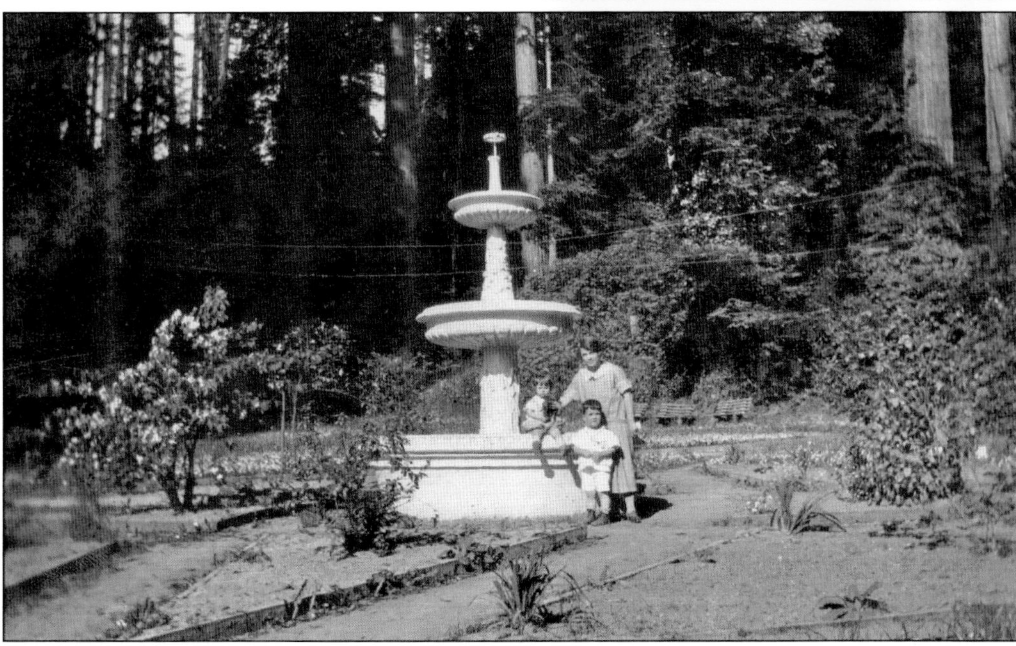

This 1924 photograph identifies the subjects "Bob, Judy, and Mother" and shows them using the three-tiered Victorian fountain as a photographic backdrop. Notice that, though the gardens remain, the fencing from the park's early years appears to have been removed. (Courtesy of the Humboldt County Historical Society.)

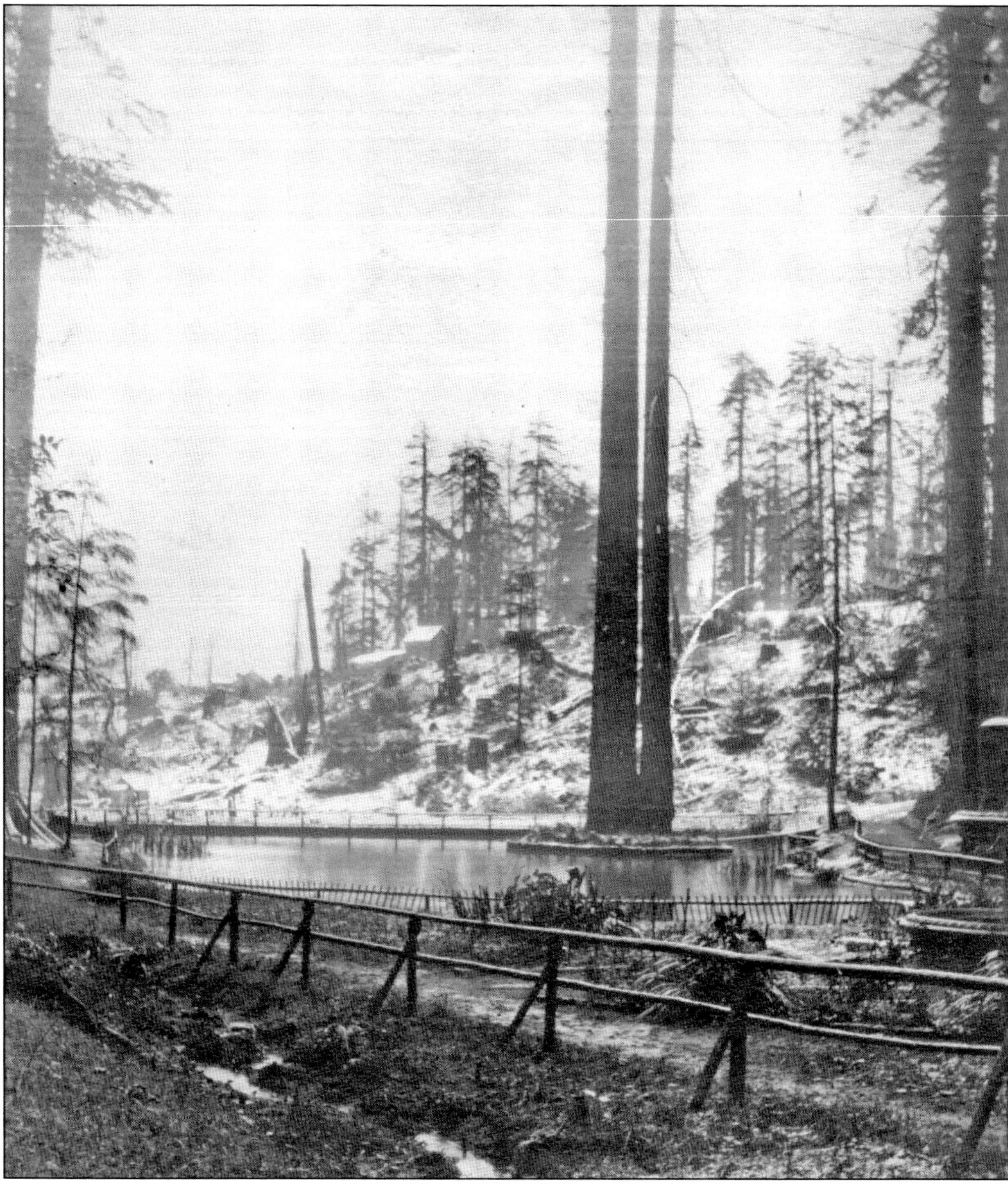

This photograph, possibly taken in the 1930s, shows the results of logging that occurred in the park. Sequoia Park once had a greater number of old-growth redwoods than it does now. The hillside shown has been reforested with second-growth redwoods. The fountain in the right foreground and the placement of the Redwood Island indicate the photographer's northwest-facing vantage point. Keys to a healthy park forest are conserving the remaining trees and planting new ones in areas where trees have fallen because of winter storms. William Hammond Hall, who surveyed, designed, and laid out San Francisco's Golden Gate Park, once said: "Destroy a public building, and it can be replaced in a year. Destroy a woodland park and all the people living at that time will have passed away before its restoration can be effected." (Courtesy of the Humboldt County Historical Society.)

Three

Eureka Gatherings Large and Small

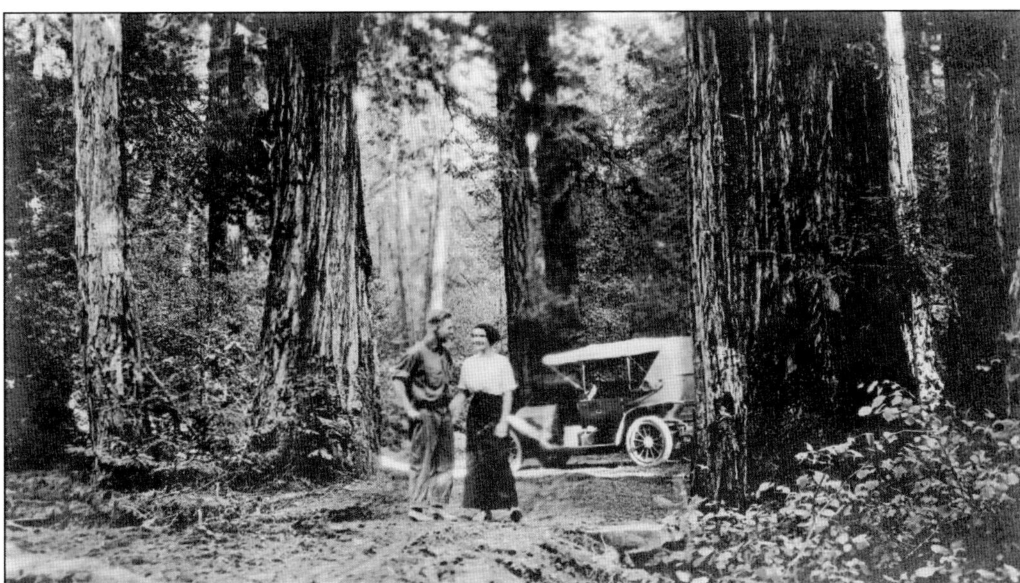

As the bustling center of rural Humboldt County, Eureka has long been an intensely social place. Sequoia Park was an important hub of social activity, particularly during the streetcar era (1903–1940). Fraternal organizations, women's social clubs, and labor organizations used the park as a gathering place. Most importantly, for more than a century, children and their families have enjoyed Sequoia Park's wild, quiet beauty. (Courtesy of the Clarke Historical Museum.)

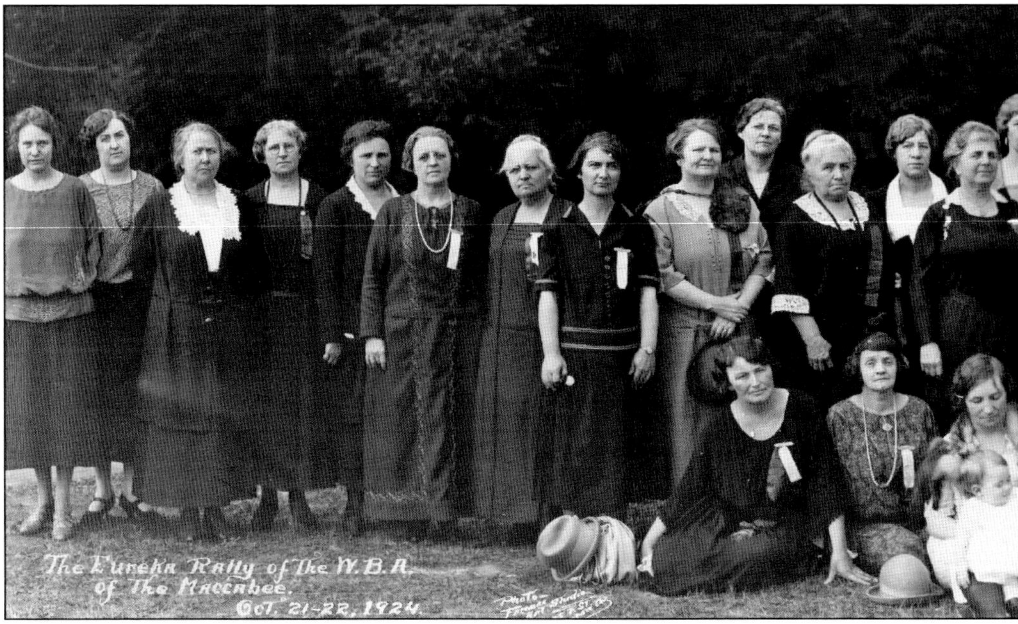

The original photographic print (shown here in three sections) is 39 inches wide and shows the Eureka rally of the Women's Benefit Association (WBA) of the Maccabees that took place in Sequoia Park on October 21–22, 1924. This midweek event (a Tuesday and a Wednesday) was one of many such events that took place in Sequoia Park. Cooking facilities and the log cabin could be reserved in advance for large parties. (Courtesy of the Clarke Historical Museum.)

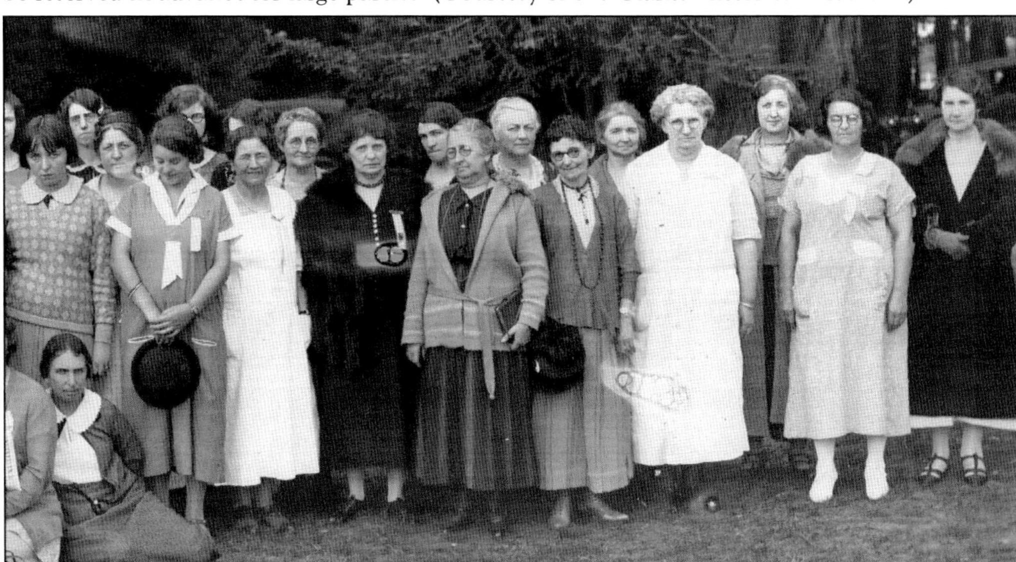

Ladies of the Maccabees (LOTM) was founded in 1890. Under the leadership of a 25-year-old schoolteacher named Bina West, this women's fraternal organization provided life insurance and death benefits to women. West is reported to have once said jestingly that "L.O.T.M. stands for 'Leave Out Those Men,'" and indeed, it became the largest fraternal order controlled exclusively by women. In 1902, it changed its name to the Women's Benefit Association of the Maccabees (WBA). (Courtesy of the Clarke Historical Museum.)

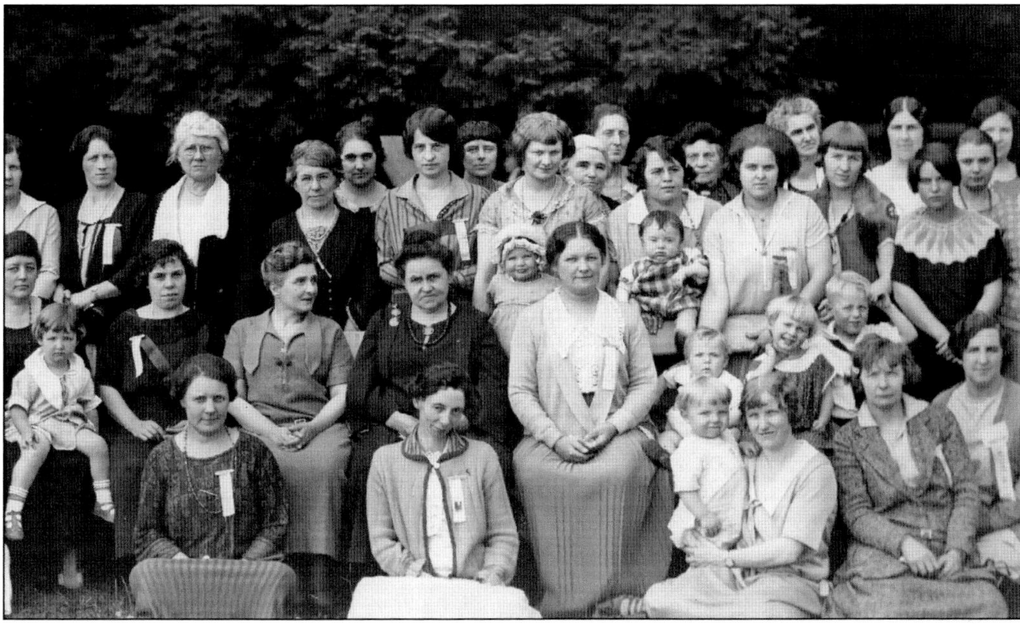

Membership in the WBA of the Maccabees rose to its highest level in 1924 with a total of more than 250,000 members nationwide. It was the first movement of its kind by women and for women that offered life insurance and death benefits. Some of the ribbons that pictured members are wearing say "Santa Rosa," and indeed this event drew members and new initiates from all over northern California. (Courtesy of the Clarke Historical Museum.)

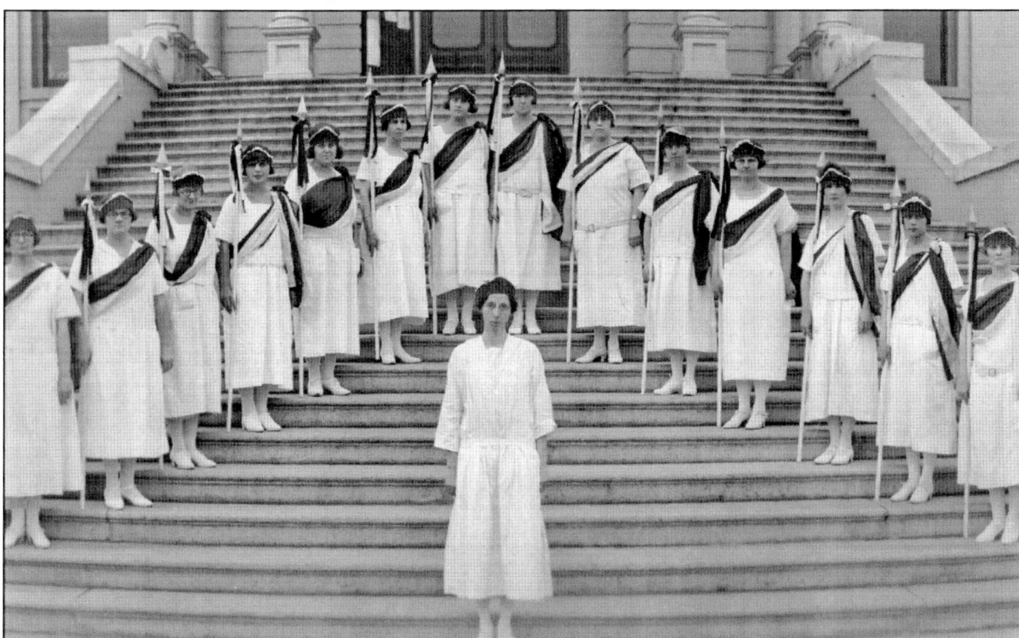

This photograph, taken on December 14, 1924, in front of the Humboldt County Courthouse, shows the WBA Eureka leader (front center) with a group of Gamma Nu initiates. In 1921, the WBA started a youth group called Gamma Nu for the daughters of its members. (Courtesy of the Clarke Historical Museum.)

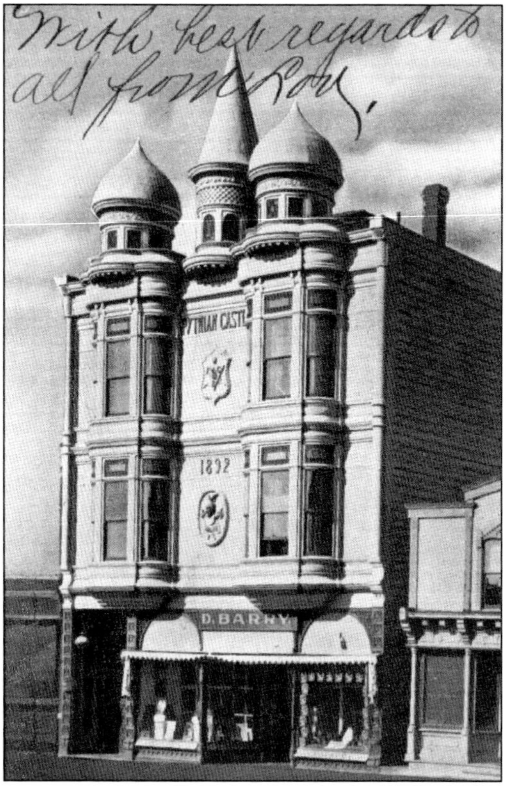

The Knights of Pythias, Lincoln No. 34 Eureka, purchased land in 1886 and built its Byzantine-style Castle Hall in 1892. In 1989, the Castle Hall was purchased by the Lost Coast Brewery and Café. (Courtesy of the Clarke Historical Museum.)

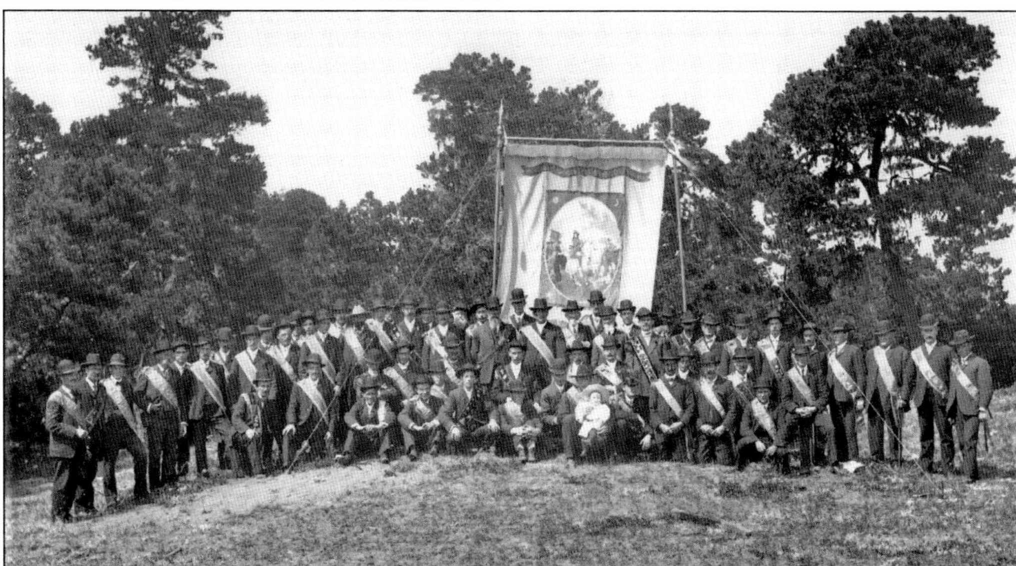

The Loyal Orange Association started in Ireland in 1795 when a group of Protestant loyalists founded a fraternal order in honor of William III, prince of Orange. A Loyal Orangemen lodge was founded in Eureka in 1877, and this photograph was taken in 1908 by R. J. Baker. As shown, full regalia included chains, sashes, medals, dark suits, and bowler hats. On the flag is a representation of William III mounted on his horse beneath degree emblems. (Courtesy of Humboldt State University.)

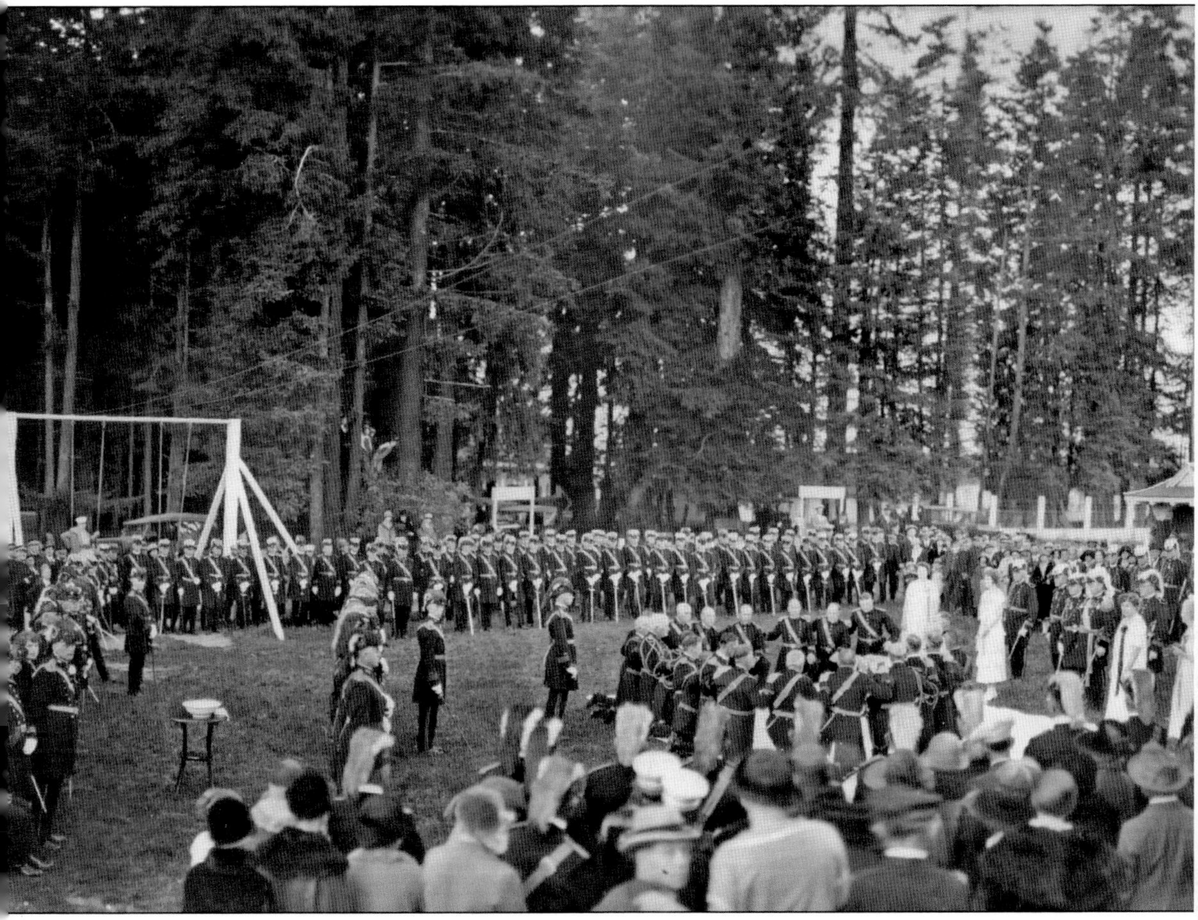

The Knights of Pythias fraternal order was founded in 1864 in Washington, D.C., to aid "worthy Pythians in distress," mainly through insurance benefits such as life and death insurance. The order was once large in Humboldt County. The Humboldt County chapters owned not only a Grand Lodge, which it built in 1892, but also a redwood park on the Van Duzen River called Pythias Park. Around the time of this photograph, the Knights of Pythias in 1921 had more than 31,000 members in the state of California. This image shows a conferral ceremony taking place in the meadow on the east side of Sequoia Park. (Courtesy of the Clarke Historical Museum.)

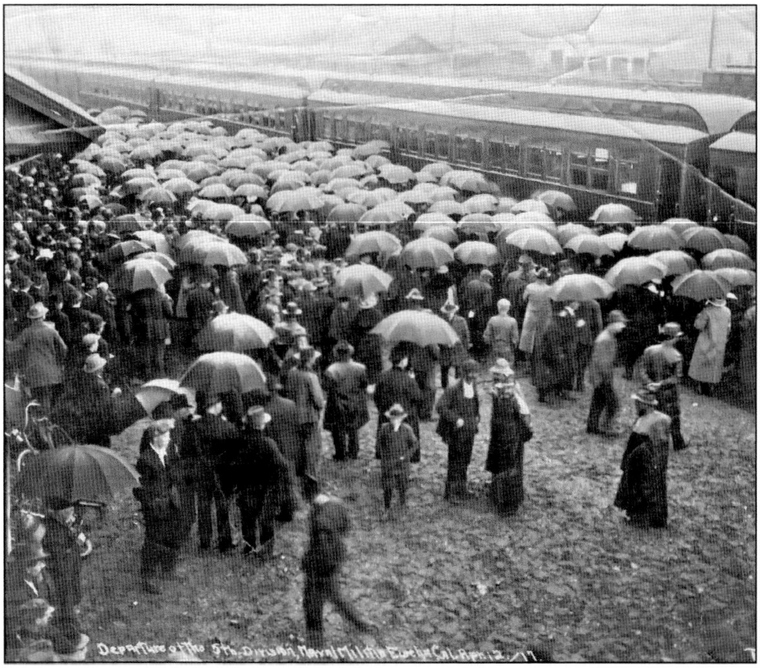

The California Naval Militia was first called into service for the United States on April 6, 1917, with Eureka's 5th Division, commanded by Lt. A. B. Adams. This photograph shows the militia's departure from the Eureka train depot. During wartime, fraternal and labor organizations across the nation saw their numbers decline as men were called up for military service. (Courtesy of the Clarke Historical Museum.)

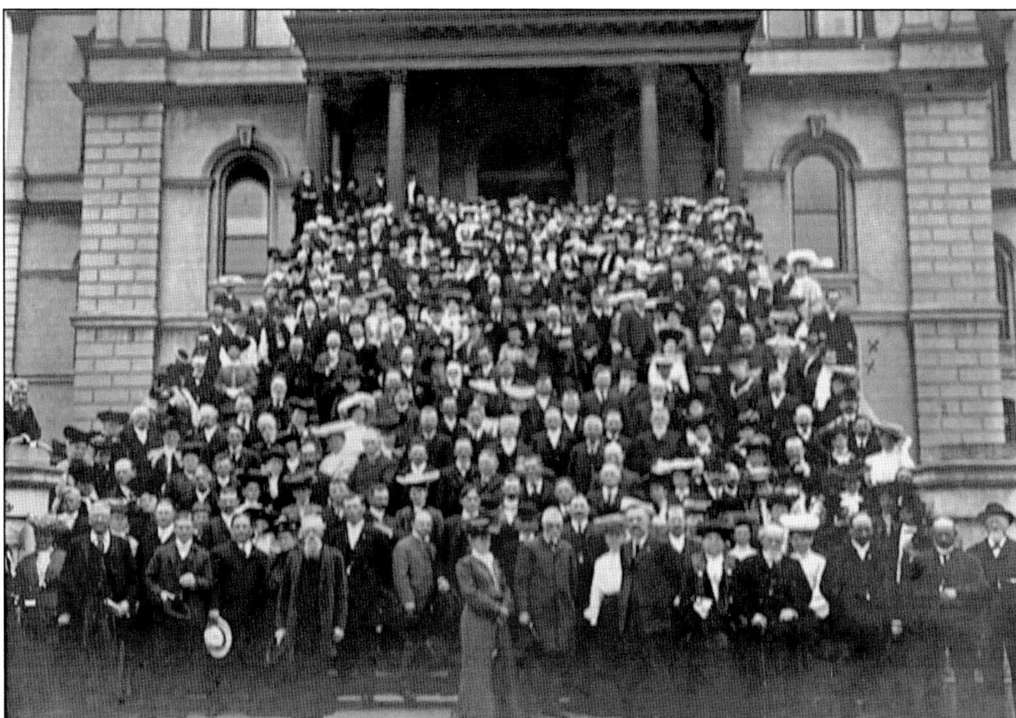

Large gatherings were often held in Sequoia Park if they were less formal or, if they were more formal, on the Humboldt County courthouse steps. This photograph documents the 50th anniversary of the Masonic Lodge of Eureka, 1854–1904. To this day, the Masons are an important part of Eureka civic life. (Courtesy of the Clarke Historical Museum.)

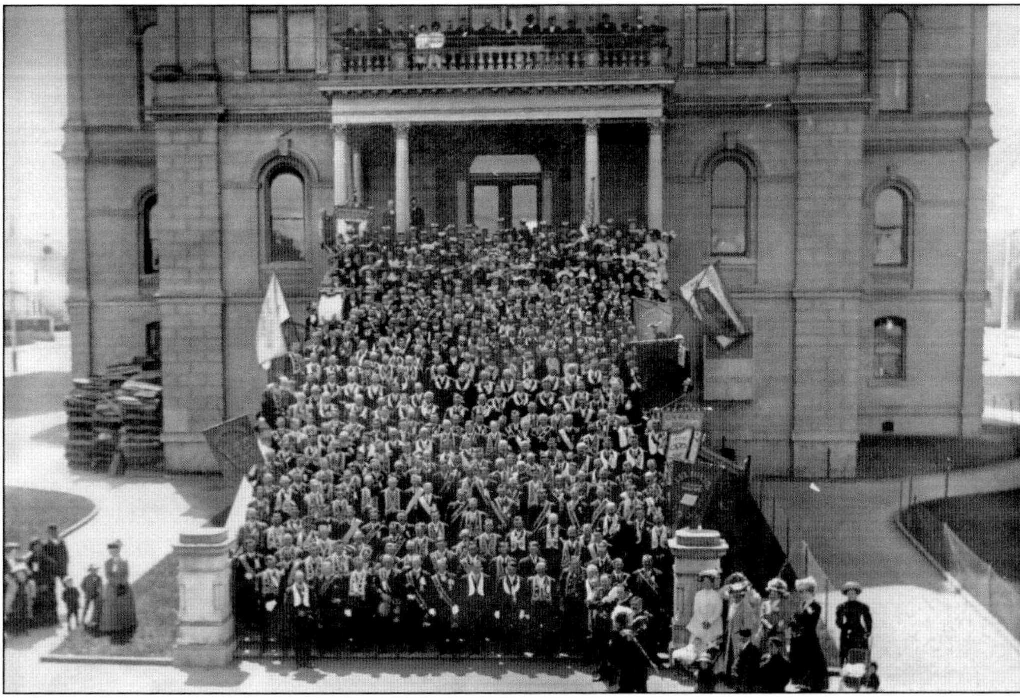

The Eureka lodges (No. 4, No. 77, and No. 221) of the Independent Order of Odd Fellows (IOOF) were some of the earliest established in the state of California. This 1910 photograph shows the 91st anniversary—calculated from the date that the first chapter of the IOOF was established in the United States—from 1819 to 1910. The principal Odd Fellows emblem is the three links, which stand for the virtues of friendship, love, and truth. (Courtesy of the Clarke Historical Museum.)

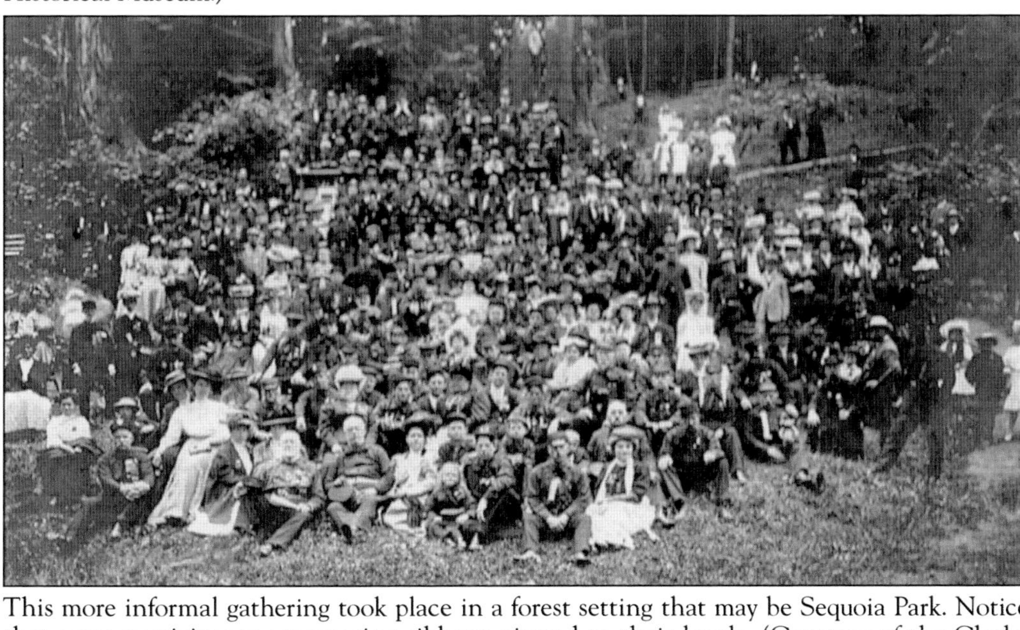

This more informal gathering took place in a forest setting that may be Sequoia Park. Notice that some participants are wearing ribbons pinned to their lapels. (Courtesy of the Clarke Historical Museum.)

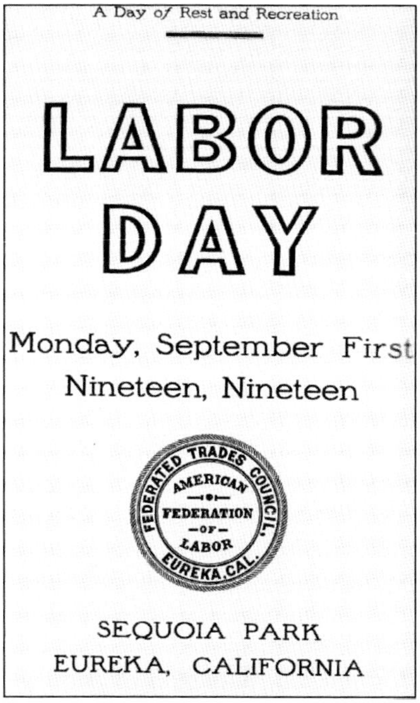

The American Federation of Labor was in its heyday around the time that this advertisement for the 1919 Labor Day festivities in Sequoia Park was published. The label league, the laundry workers, and the telephone operators provided the concessions. (Courtesy of the Clarke Historical Museum.)

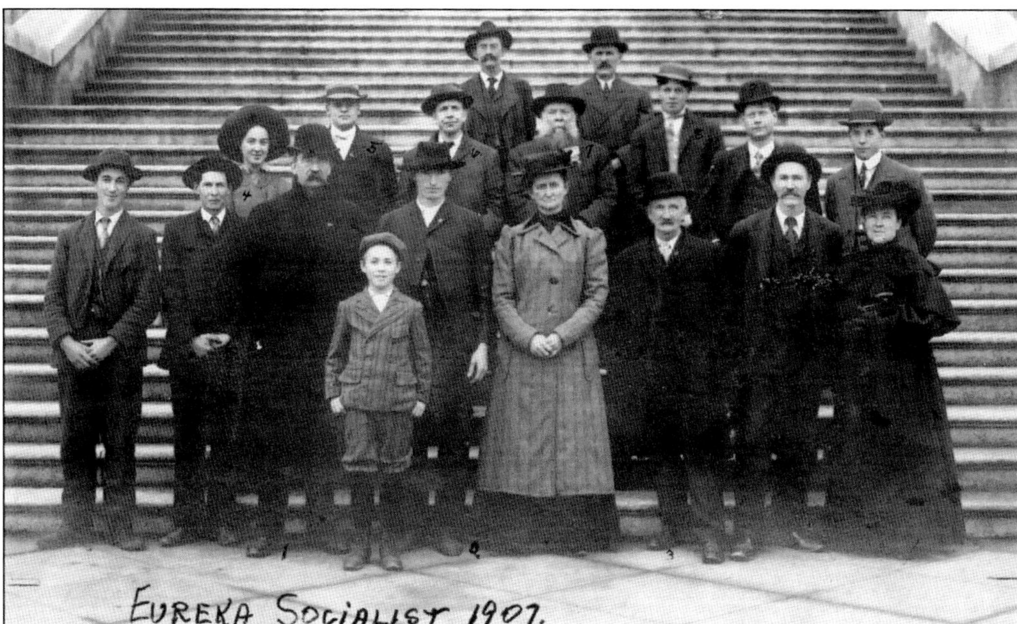

This c. 1907 photograph shows the Eureka Socialists. The tall man in front with the derby hat and long coat is John T. Moore, a sign painter and political activist. To Moore's left are John Messer and his wife, respectively, a hotel cook and restaurant worker. To the left of Mrs. Messer, the man in the overcoat had his own vegetable wagon. R. J. Baker, the photographer, is also shown (no. 5 on photograph). To Baker's left stands George Keeling, a printer, and William Tilley, a junk dealer with a store on Fifth Street. In the derby hat, Joseph Bredsteen is shown (no. 9 on photograph), who was for many years the editor of the *Labor News*. Others pictured are unidentified. (Courtesy of the Humboldt State University.)

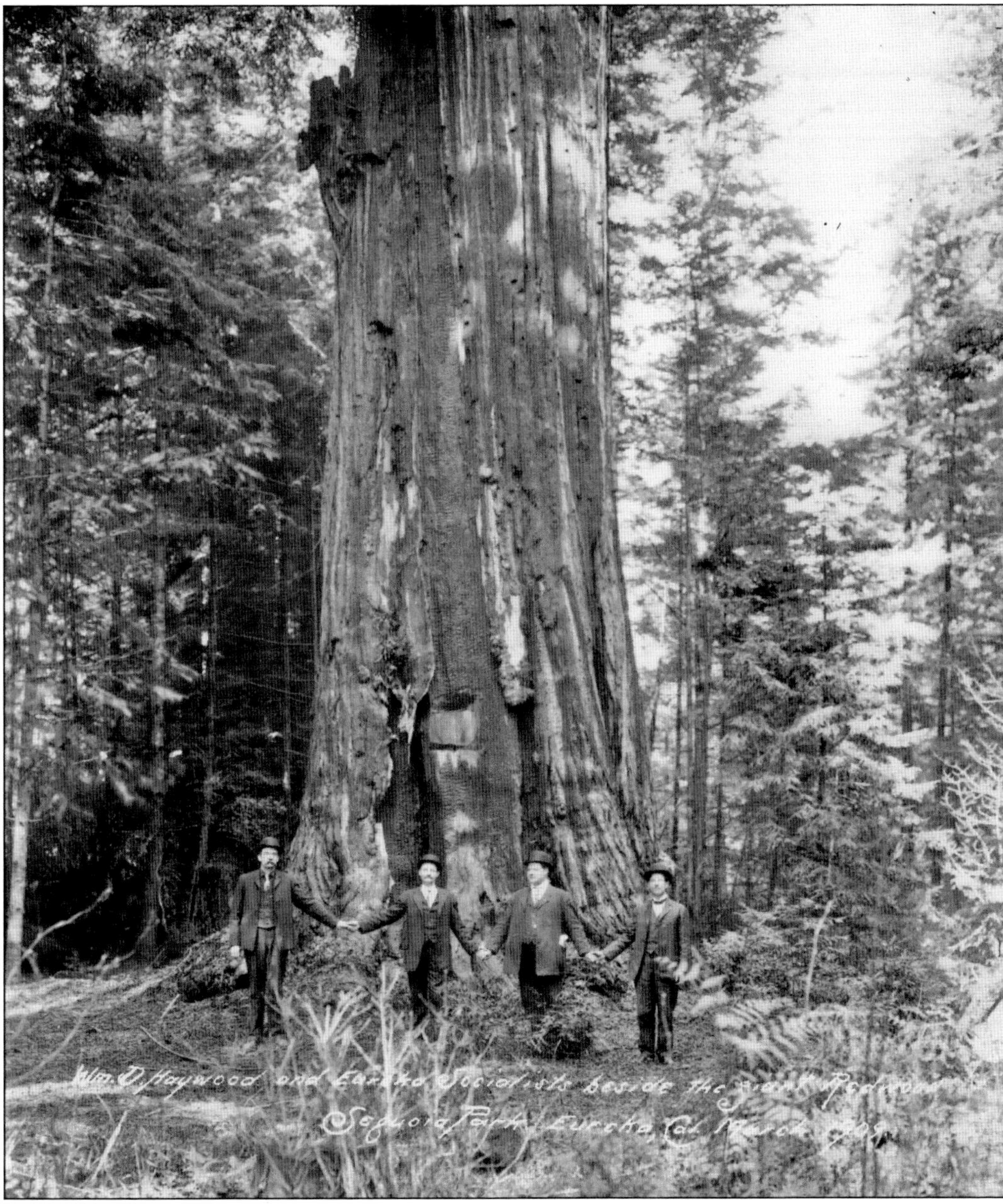

In March 1909, William "Big Bill" Haywood, the ex-miner of Idaho and Industrial Workers of the World (IWW) labor unionist, spoke to large audiences of Socialists at various locations in Eureka, Fortuna, and Arcata. He was a charismatic speaker who spoke in terms of "confederating workers" in order to "emancipate the working class." Formed in 1901, the Socialist Party of America grew steadily until World War I. In May 1908, Haywood was on his way to being nominated as the Socialist candidate for president. He withdrew his name from consideration and supported Eugene V. Debs, who won six percent of the total vote in the 1912 presidential election. In 1916, a few years after Haywood's visit, Debs also visited Eureka, perhaps because Eureka, at the time, enjoyed the leadership of its one and only Socialist mayor, Elijah Falk. R. J. Baker captured this image of Haywood, shown second from the right, and other Socialists standing hand-in-hand in front of one of Sequoia Park's giant redwoods. (Courtesy of Humboldt State University.)

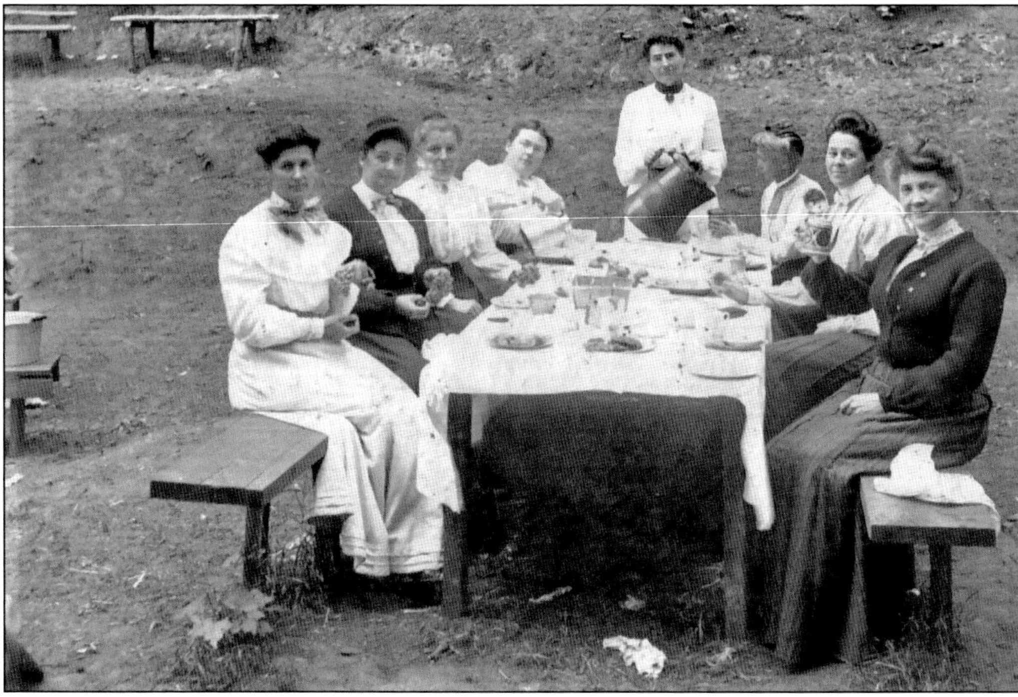

Women's Koffee Klatch gatherings were popular in the late 19th and early 20th centuries. On this photograph's cardboard mount is handwritten: "Sequoia Park: I'm glad I'm livin'." and "It is good to be here." The photograph is dated August 29, 1905. (Courtesy of the Clarke Historical Museum.)

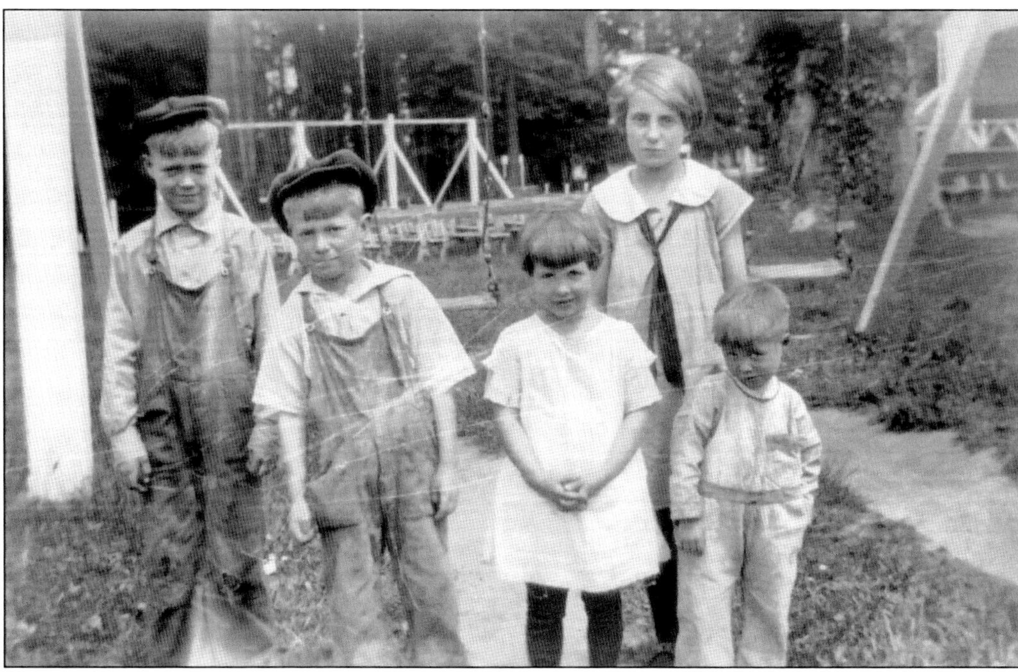

This June 1924 photograph shows the Davenport children in Sequoia Park. From left to right are Wayne, Cledith, Lucile, Ida Mae, and Leo. (Courtesy of the Humboldt County Historical Society.)

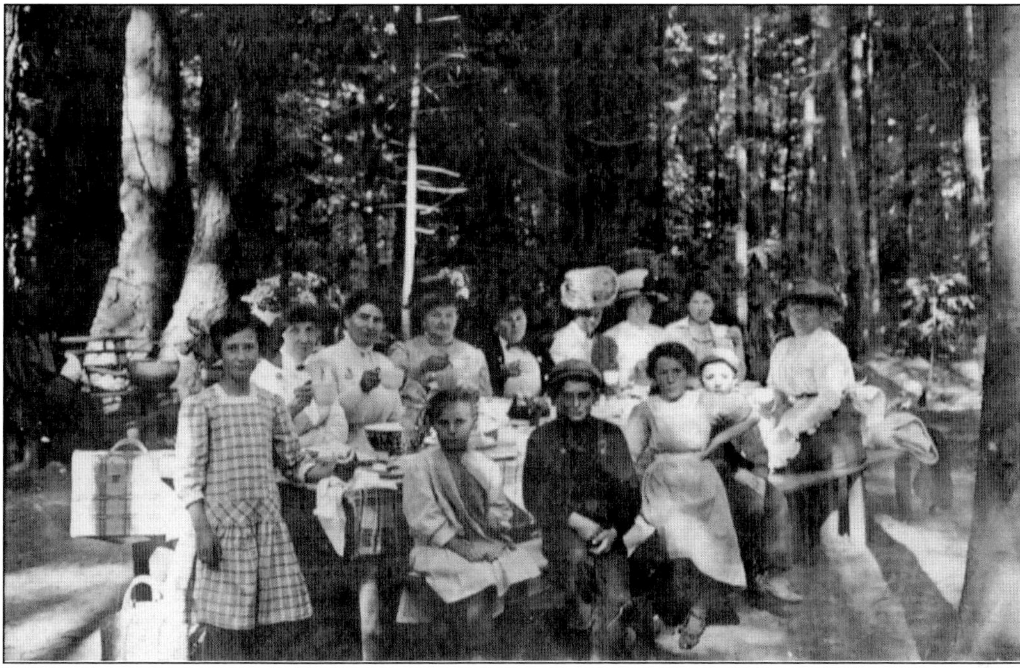

This photograph shows a women's Koffee Klatch gathering that took place in Sequoia Park in 1910. (Courtesy of the Clarke Historical Museum.)

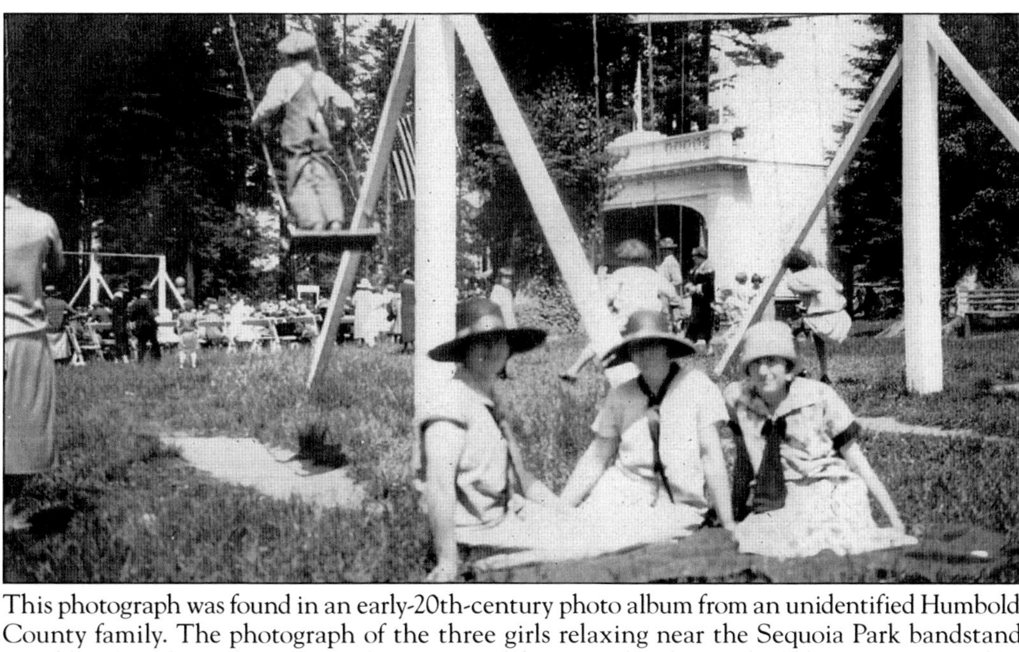

This photograph was found in an early-20th-century photo album from an unidentified Humboldt County family. The photograph of the three girls relaxing near the Sequoia Park bandstand, possibly taken during an Independence Day celebration, also shows a little boy swinging and his nearby mother. (Courtesy of the Humboldt County Historical Society.)

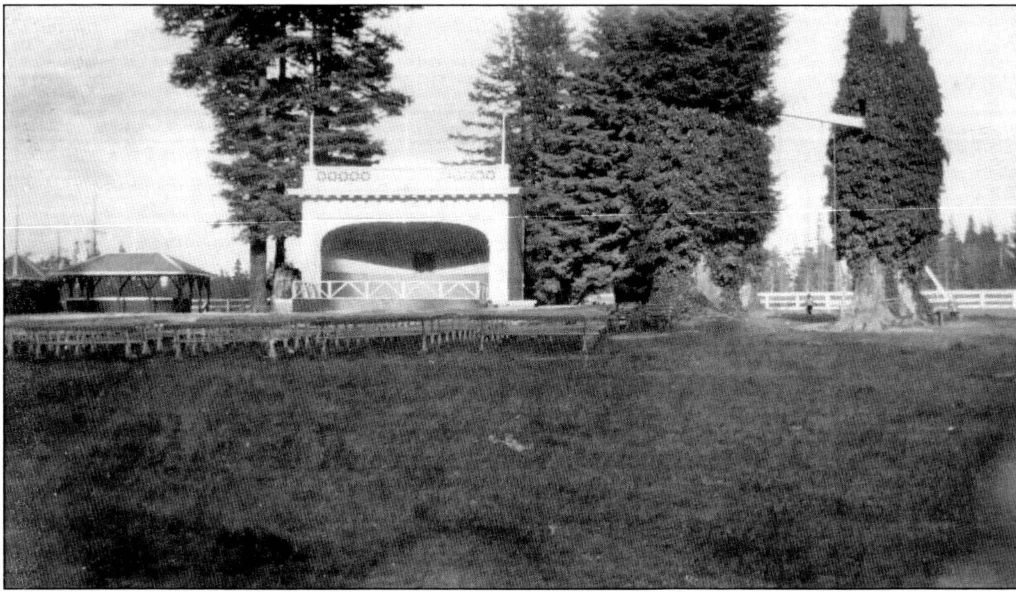

This shell-type bandstand was used nearly every weekend during its time. In the right of the photograph, notice the unusual swing set formed by the careful placement of a steel bar high up between two tall redwoods. These swings allowed for extremely thrilling—and some would say dangerous—heights. The swing set was eventually removed due to safety regulations. (Courtesy of the Humboldt County Historical Society.)

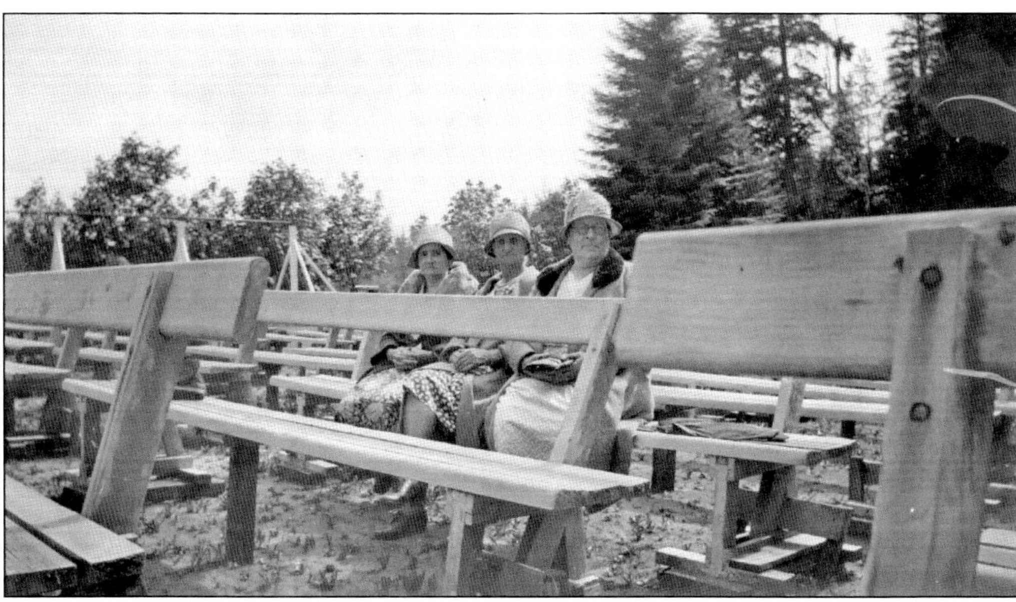

These three unidentified women sit patiently while waiting for other concertgoers to arrive. Although the photograph is undated, the women's clothing suggests the 1920s or 1930s. (Courtesy of the Clarke Historical Museum.)

This photograph shows a May Day program being performed at Sequoia Park. In the 1920s, the May Day (May 1) festivities would draw Eureka grade-school children and their teachers. May Pole dances were performed by the different schools. Reportedly, since May 1 also marked the opening of trout season, some of the kids would leave the bandstand area to go trout fishing in the old canal. (Courtesy of the Humboldt County Historical Society.)

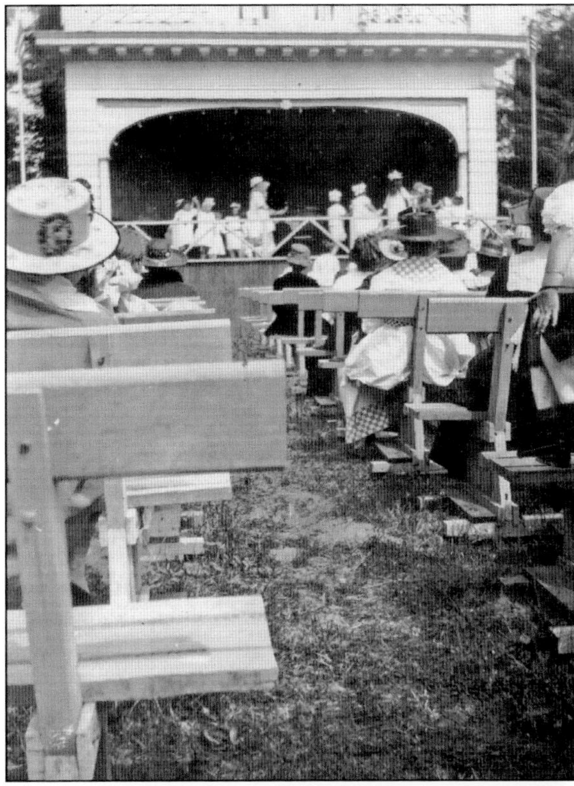

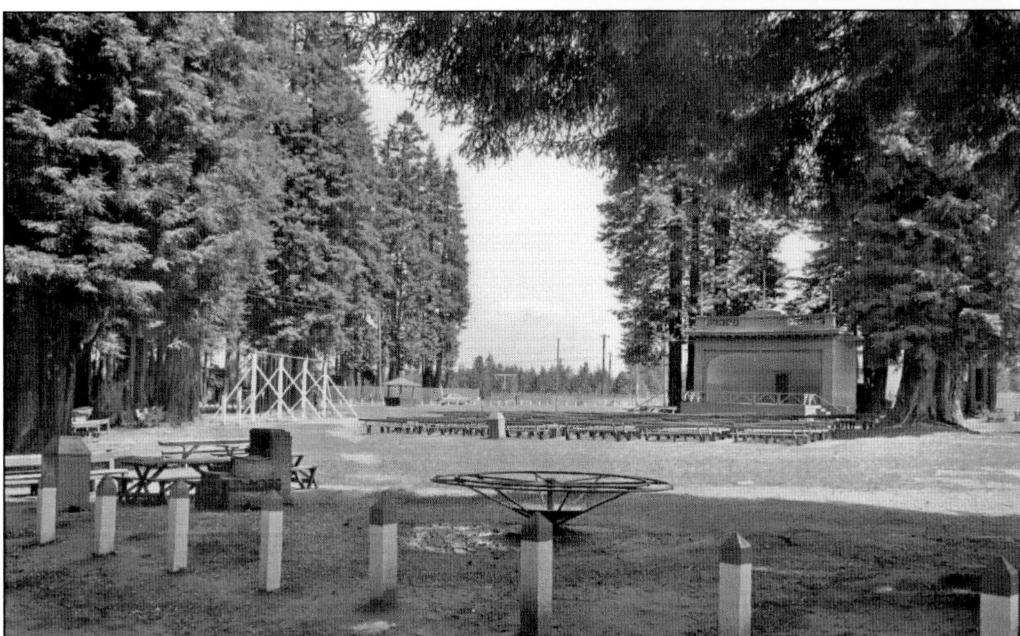

This wide-view photograph of the Sequoia Park bandstand, swings, and children's playground was taken by Eureka Chamber of Commerce photographer Kenny Kilburn. (Courtesy of the Humboldt County Historical Society.)

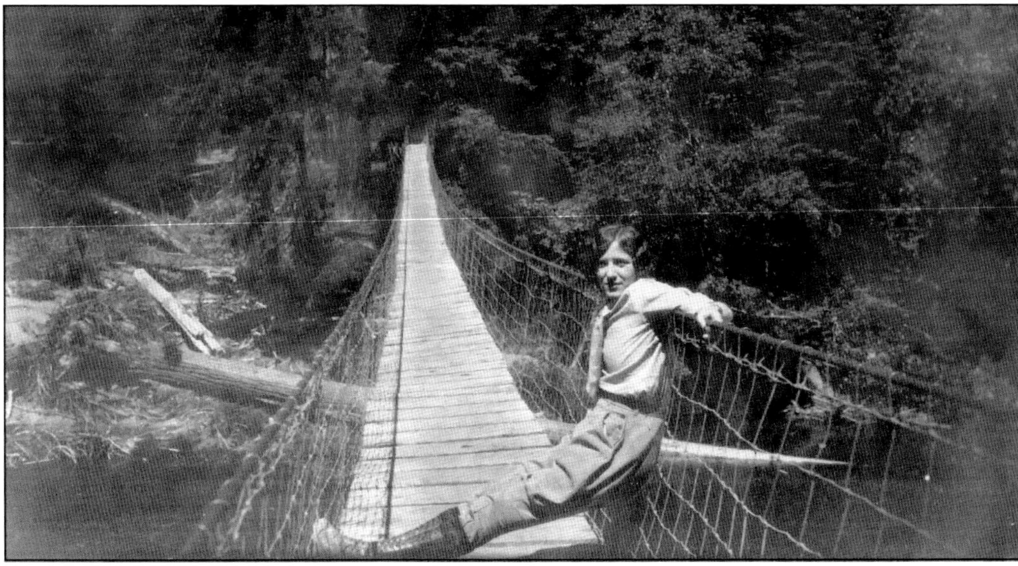

This 1920s photograph of an adolescent girl in a scout uniform shows her posing on a suspension bridge. Suspension bridges were common in Humboldt County in the days prior to automobile bridges and were used by pedestrians, mule trains, and horsemen across the county. (Courtesy of the Humboldt County Historical Society.)

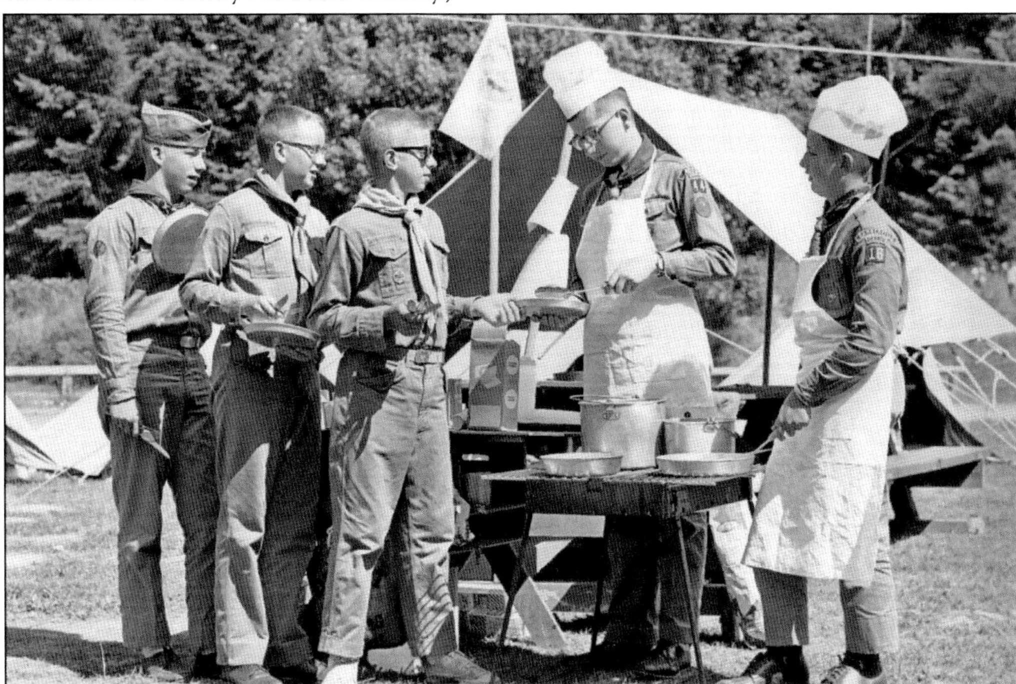

The World Organization of the Scout Movement started in August 1907 and has had a long history in Humboldt County. Many Eagle Scout projects help to make Sequoia Park a better place, such as the one recently completed by Brian Butler of Eureka Troop No. 54, in which he led the construction of a fence and picnic area at Sequoia Park. (Courtesy of the Clarke Historical Museum.)

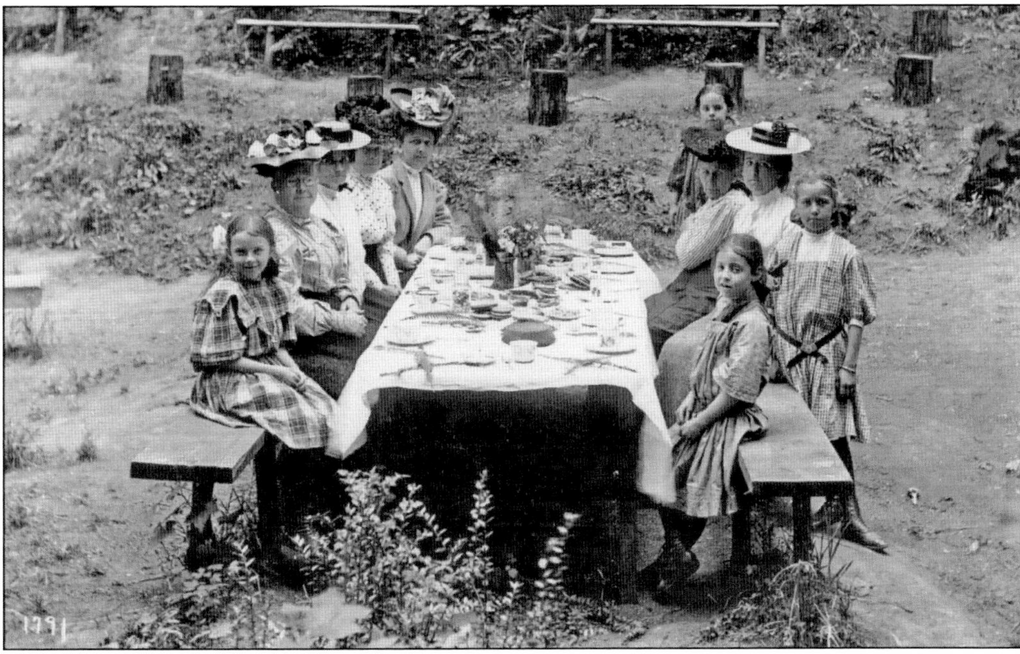

This photograph, taken in Sequoia Park in 1907 by R. J. Baker, shows the Baker family having a picnic. The photographer's wife, Edith Frost Baker, is identified as the woman seated at the end of the table on the left. Others are unidentified. Edith and her family owned property just east of Briceland and near Miranda. (Courtesy of the Humboldt County Historical Society.)

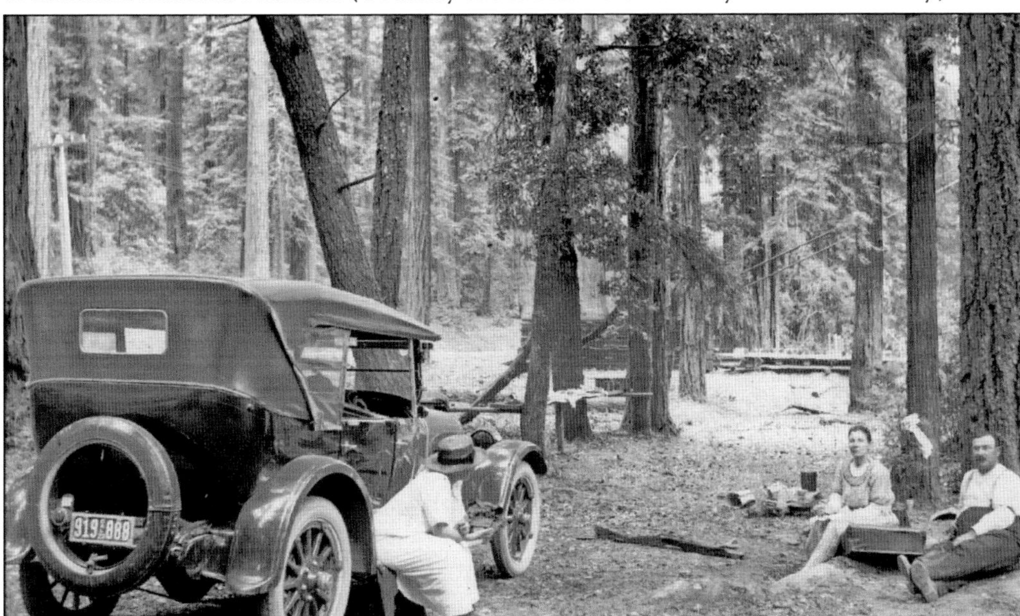

As automobiles became more widely available in Humboldt County, they increasingly made an appearance in park photographs. This one shows Mrs. William McDade sitting on the car's running board. Her husband, William McDade, and Mrs. E. F. Pettingill sit at the base of a redwood. E. F. Pettingill was a contributor to *Marbury's Favorite Flies and Their Histories*, a fly-fishing natural history published in 1892. (Courtesy of the Clarke Historical Museum.)

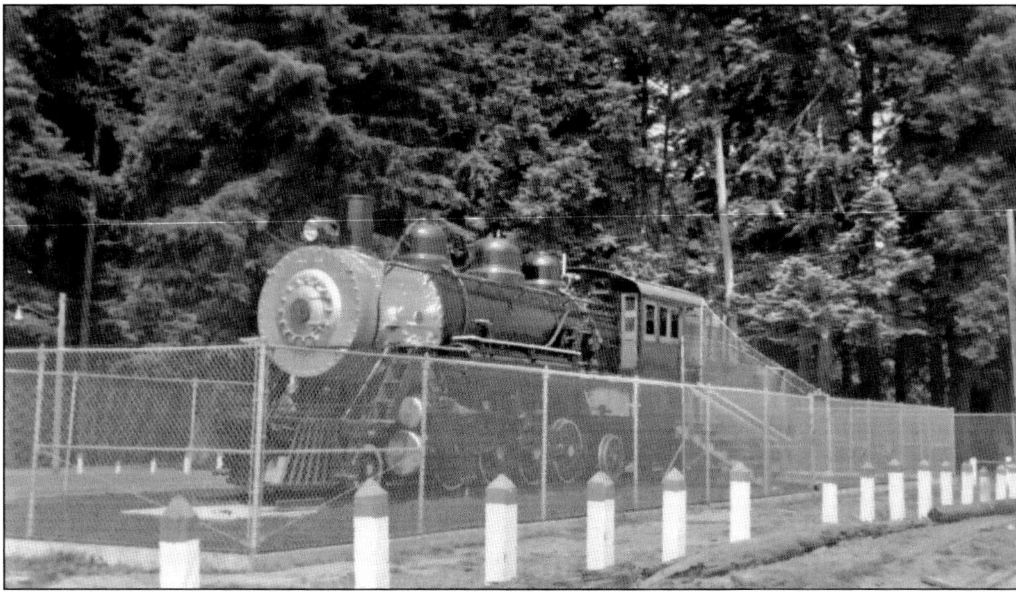

"Big George" was the name given to the Baldwin locomotive that delighted Sequoia Park visitors for nearly 20 years. The locomotive, No. 15, was originally built in 1916 and served on the Hammond Redwood Lumber Company Railroad between Samoa and Crannell from 1941 to 1960. It was the last steam locomotive to operate on the line. It was given to the City of Eureka in 1960 by the Georgia Pacific Corporation, the successor of Hammond Lumber Company, before being donated to the Northern Counties Logging Interpretive Association in 1979. (Courtesy of the Humboldt County Historical Society.)

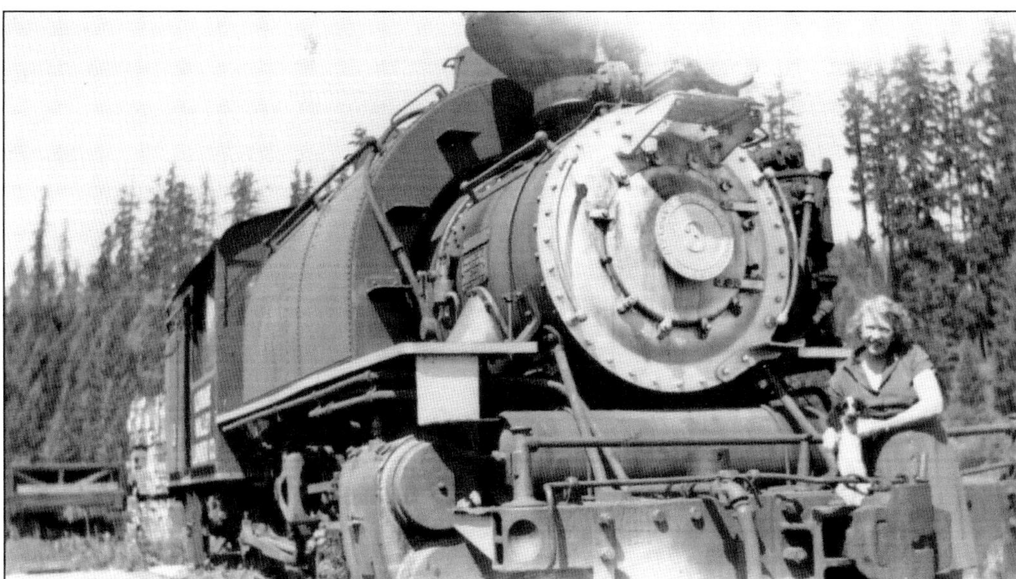

This young woman and her dog, posing in front of a large steam locomotive made by the American Locomotive Company, are testament to the importance of rail transportation in Humboldt County in the late 19th and early 20th centuries. (Courtesy of the Clarke Historical Museum.)

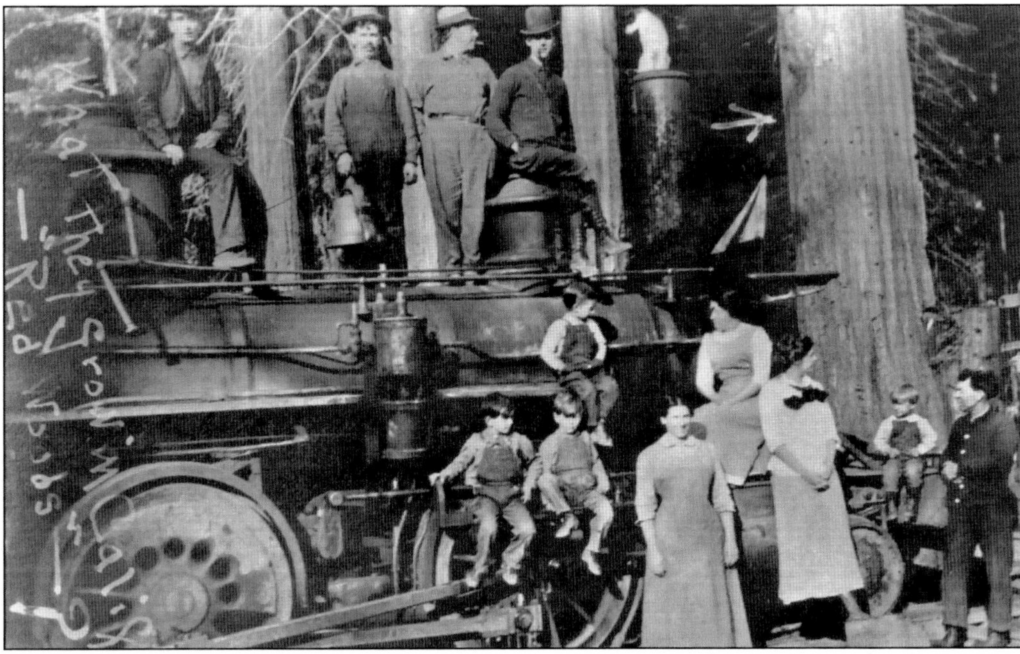

This photograph of a family on a logging train's locomotive recalls that loggers and camp staff and their families would ride the lumber company rails into the main Humboldt County towns at the end of the workweek and return the same way. One young woman, a cook at the Northern Redwood Lumber Company in 1926, reported that the train ride from Eureka to the logging camp at Korbel took two hours. (Courtesy of the Clarke Historical Museum.)

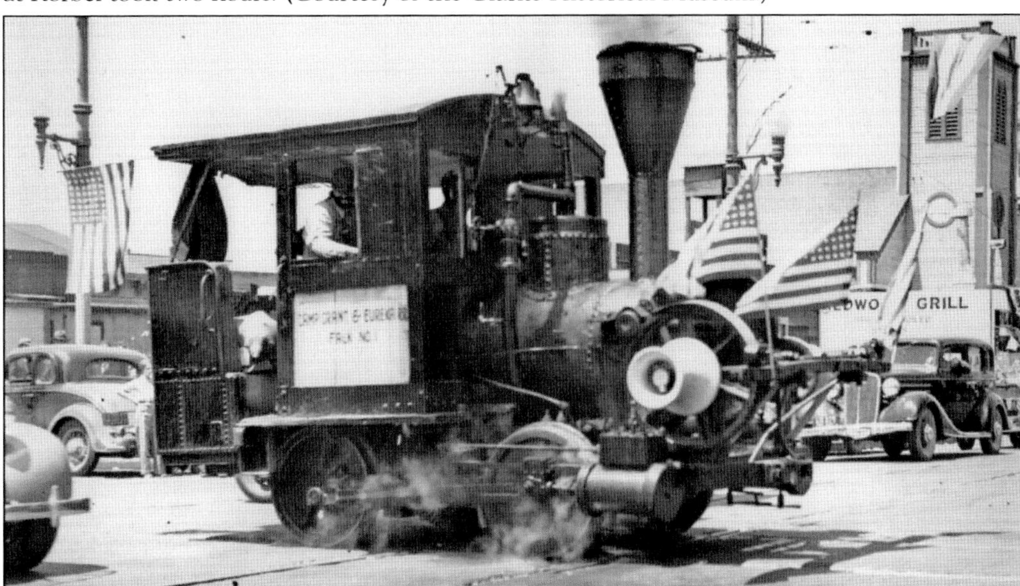

The Falk No. 1 wood-powered gypsy locomotive was purchased by N. H. Falk of the Elk River Mill and Lumber Company in 1884. It was put to work hauling logs over a 3-mile railroad for the Falk Mill. When it was retired from service, a group of Eurekans joined together to use the locomotive in the Days of General Grant Celebration in 1936. The gypsy's progress in downtown Eureka on that day is shown in this photograph. (Courtesy of the Humboldt County Historical Society.)

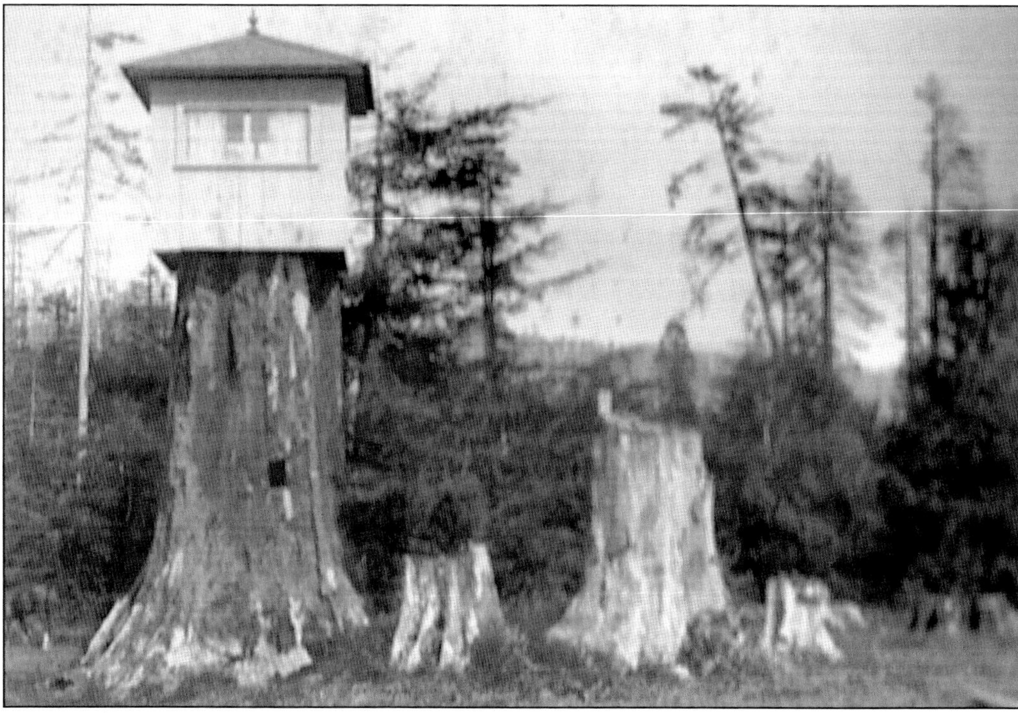

Stumps like these were often left behind by early logging operations because of the difficulties involved in removing them. The typical land-use progression was from virgin forest, to stump-covered parcels for sale, to housing developments. As this photograph shows, some householders put stumps to ingenious uses rather than clearing them. (Courtesy of the Clarke Historical Museum.)

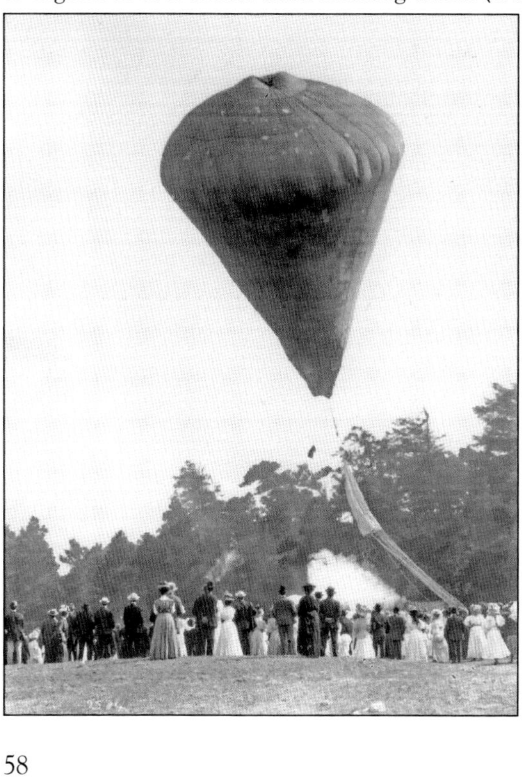

This photograph was taken by R. J. Baker in 1909. It shows George Sousa's hot air balloon at a Humboldt County park, possibly New Era Park. The balloonist and his helpers would build a large bonfire so that the smoke and heat could be piped in to fill the balloon, held by ropes at four corners. When the balloon inflated sufficiently, the intrepid balloonist would climb aboard and ascend skyward. (Courtesy of Humboldt State University.)

Noted on the front of this 1915 photograph is "Grandpa Lander and Alice in Sequoia Park." The large stump, shown surrounded by young redwoods, illustrates a redwood cathedral of trees where one "mother" tree sprouts numerous "child" trees, eventually forming a cathedral of giants around the matriarch. (Courtesy of the Humboldt County Historical Society.)

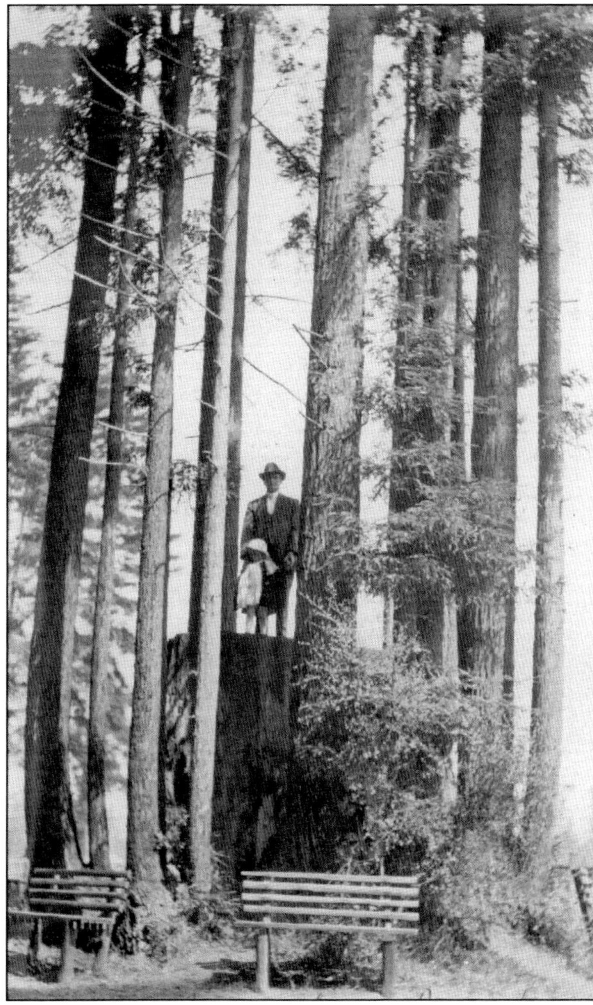

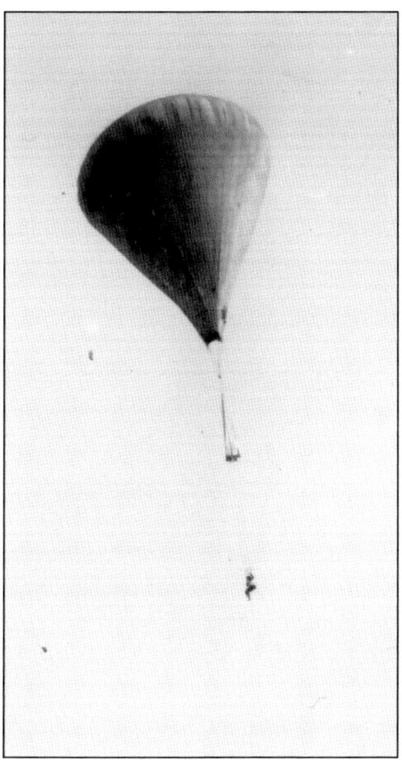

This photograph shows George Sousa's hot air balloon aloft, a major Sunday attraction at New Era Park. Once his balloon reached a certain height, the balloonist would open his parachute and make his way back to earth. Although Sousa's flights in Humboldt County were safely conducted, he was killed on a descent in southern California when his chute failed to open. (Courtesy of Humboldt State University.)

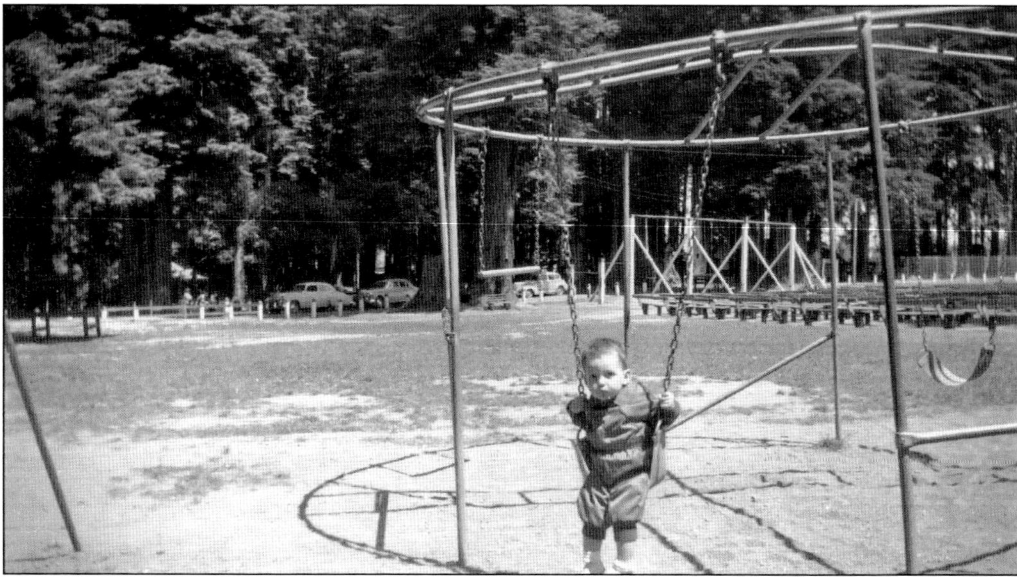

The children's playground in Sequoia Park has undergone many changes over the years as play structures aged or safety regulations required changes. (Courtesy of the Clarke Historical Museum.)

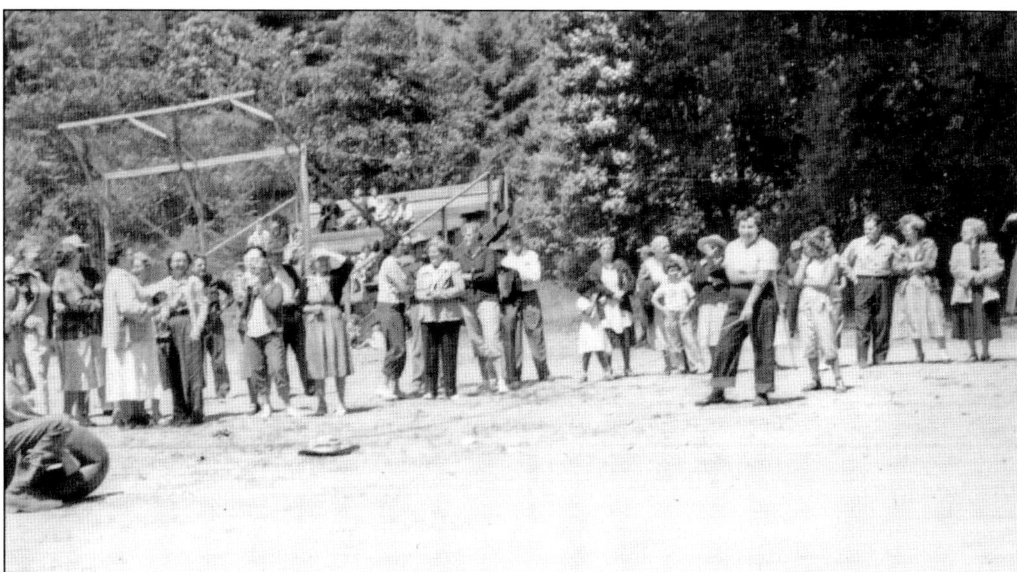

This softball game took place either in Sequoia Park or across the street in the baseball diamond next to the National Guard armory. (Courtesy of the Clarke Historical Museum.)

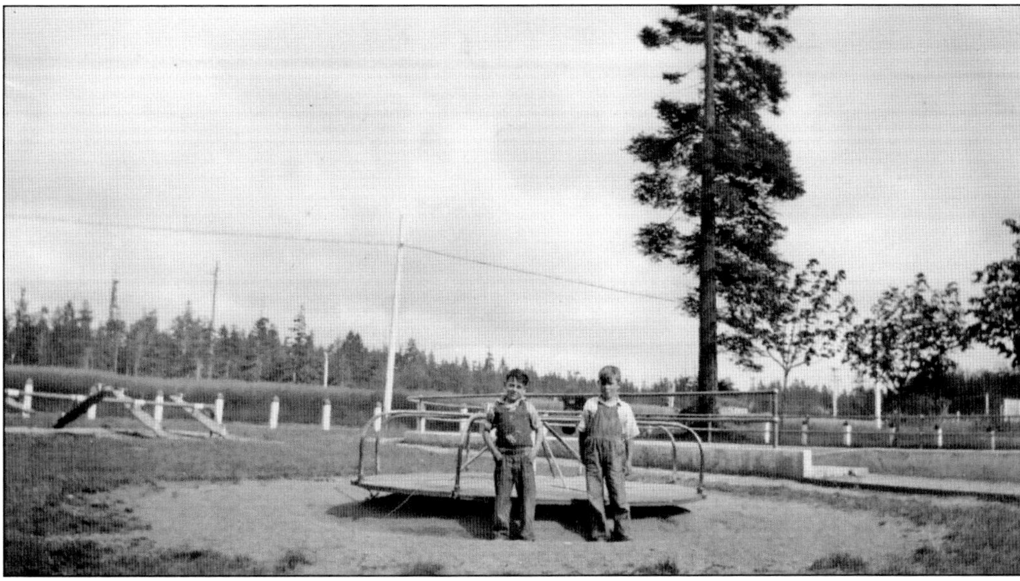

This rare east-facing view of the area beyond Sequoia Park shows the huge inventory of second-growth timber prior to the massive residential development of the 1950s and 1960s. (Courtesy of the Clarke Historical Museum.)

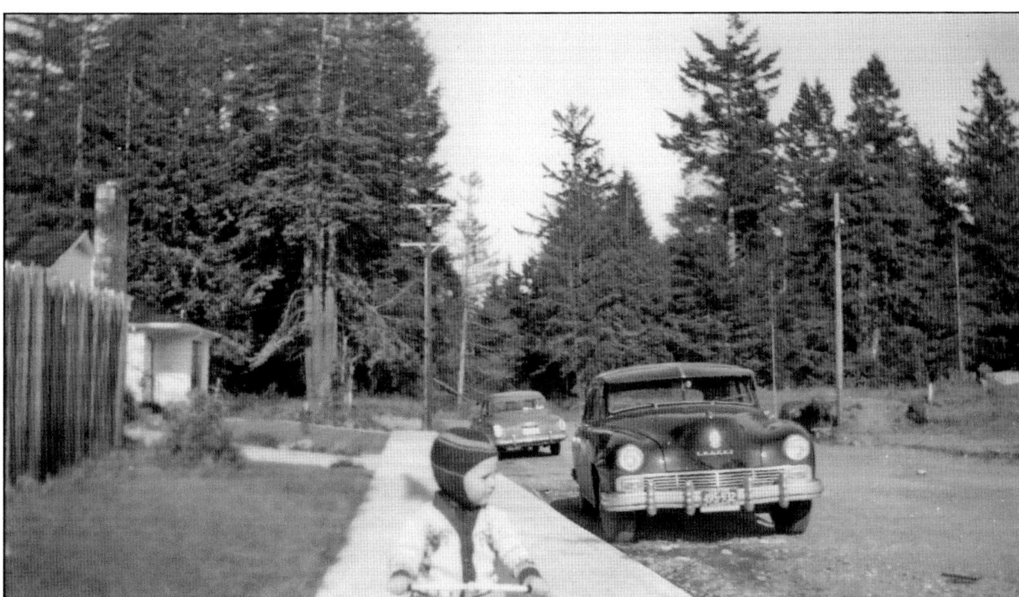

This 1950s photograph shows an unidentified child riding a tricycle near Sequoia Park. (Courtesy of the Clarke Historical Museum.)

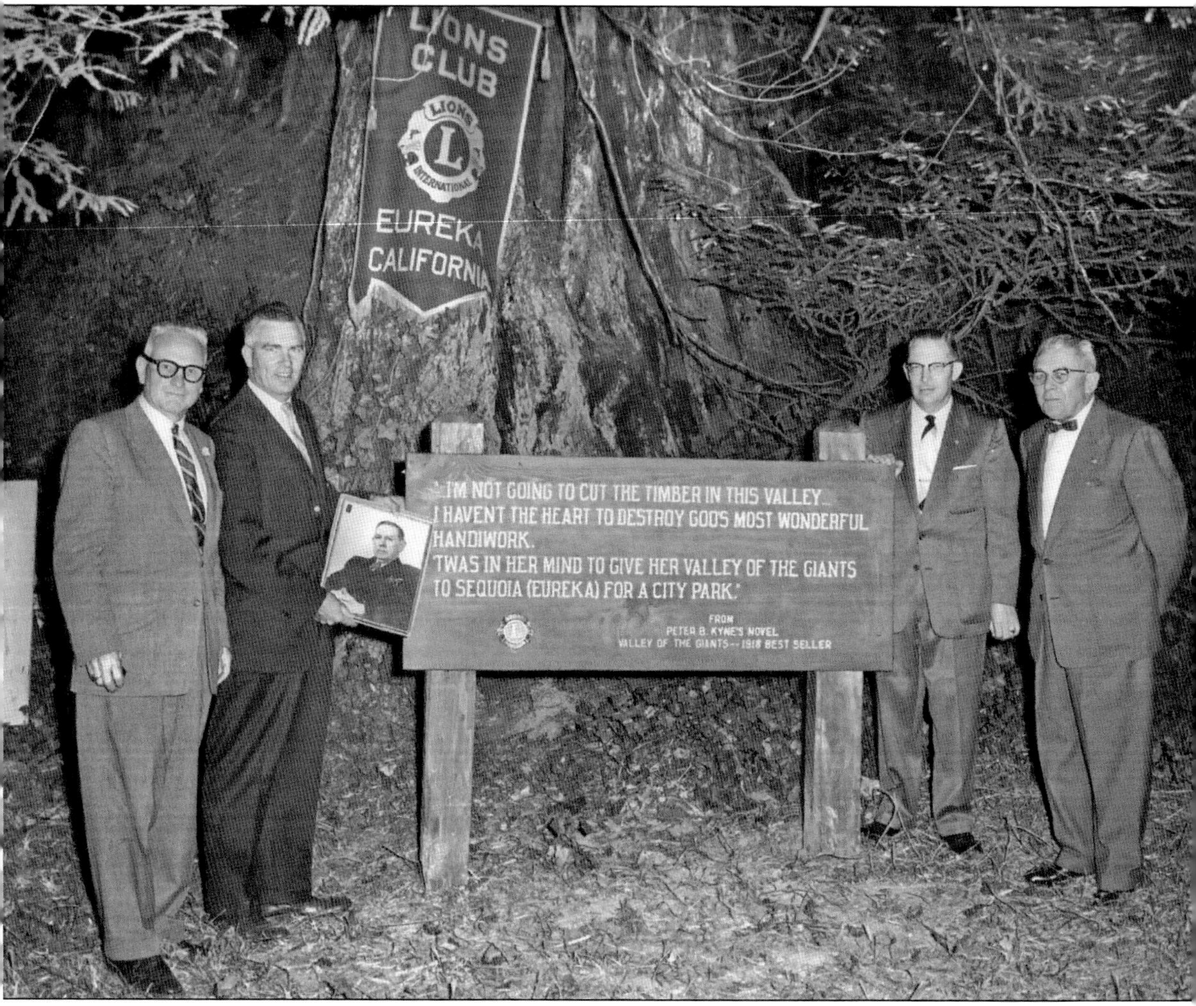

Pictured from left to right are Eureka mayor Oscar Swanlund, Burton Spear, an unidentified man, and T. P. Carlson at the dedication of the Peter B. Kyne plaque in Sequoia Park, which stands today near Rhododendron Glen on the east side of the duck pond. The wooden plaque commemorates the popular author Peter B. Kyne, who in 1918 published a bestselling novel, *The Valley of the Giants*. He was inspired to write the novel by his earlier visit to Humboldt County. It is the story of a Eureka pioneer and timber baron whose young wife wishes to save a favorite patch of redwood forest for future generations to enjoy as a city park. The wife dies in childbirth, and the man fights to honor her wishes and protect his beloved's valley of the giants. Kyne based his novel on the real intrigues of early Humboldt's competing timber barons. The plaque's inscription reads: "I'm not going to cut the timber in this valley. I haven't the heart to destroy God's most wonderful handiwork. Twas' in her mind to give her Valley of the Giants to Sequoia (Eureka) for a city park." (Courtesy of the Clarke Historical Museum.)

Four

SEQUOIA PARK ZOO

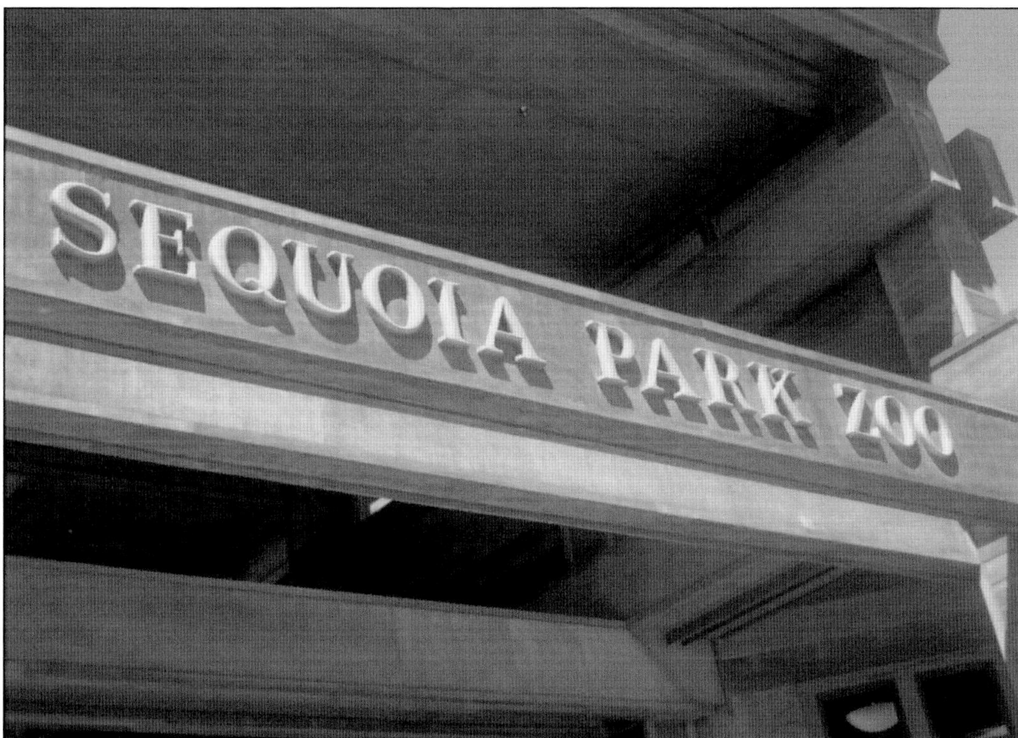

Built in 1907, the Sequoia Park Zoo is the oldest zoo in the state of California, and the smallest accredited zoo in the nation. The early Sequoia Park Zoo is described beautifully in a 1911 souvenir brochure: "On the eastern portion of the park, all level and cleared ground, is found the animal pens. Here deer and elk and other animals native to this county find a home, less in extent to be sure, but upon the same ground over which they roamed before the coming of man. Here also are birds both native and foreign. Little by little the colony of tame-wild things is growing, and it will not be many years at the present rate until we have a very creditable menagerie." Sequoia Park Zoo serves as a valuable recreational and educational resource for more than 10 counties in northwestern California. It is the only accredited zoological park on the Pacific Coast between San Francisco and Portland. (Courtesy of Christian V. Pennington.)

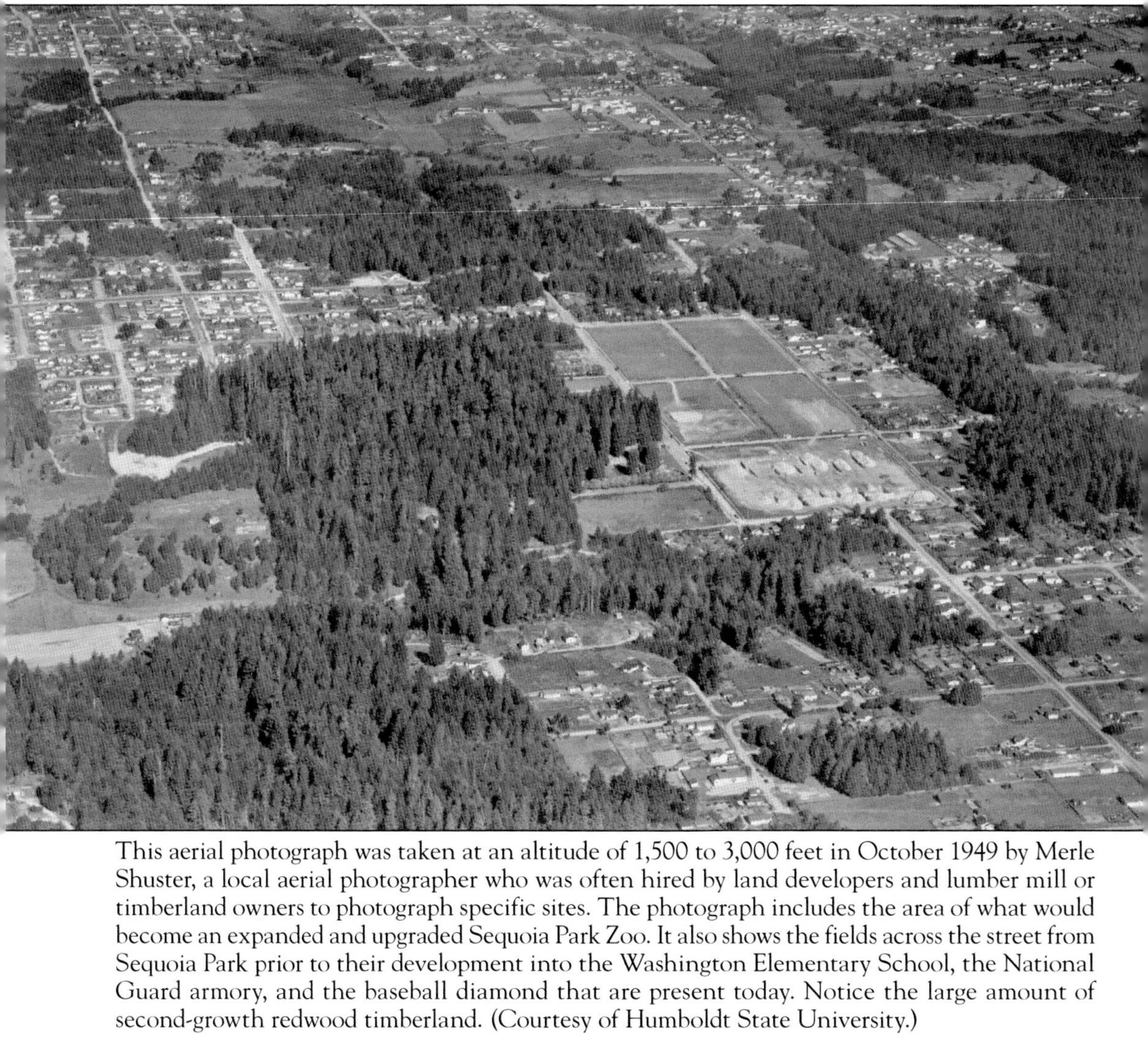

This aerial photograph was taken at an altitude of 1,500 to 3,000 feet in October 1949 by Merle Shuster, a local aerial photographer who was often hired by land developers and lumber mill or timberland owners to photograph specific sites. The photograph includes the area of what would become an expanded and upgraded Sequoia Park Zoo. It also shows the fields across the street from Sequoia Park prior to their development into the Washington Elementary School, the National Guard armory, and the baseball diamond that are present today. Notice the large amount of second-growth redwood timberland. (Courtesy of Humboldt State University.)

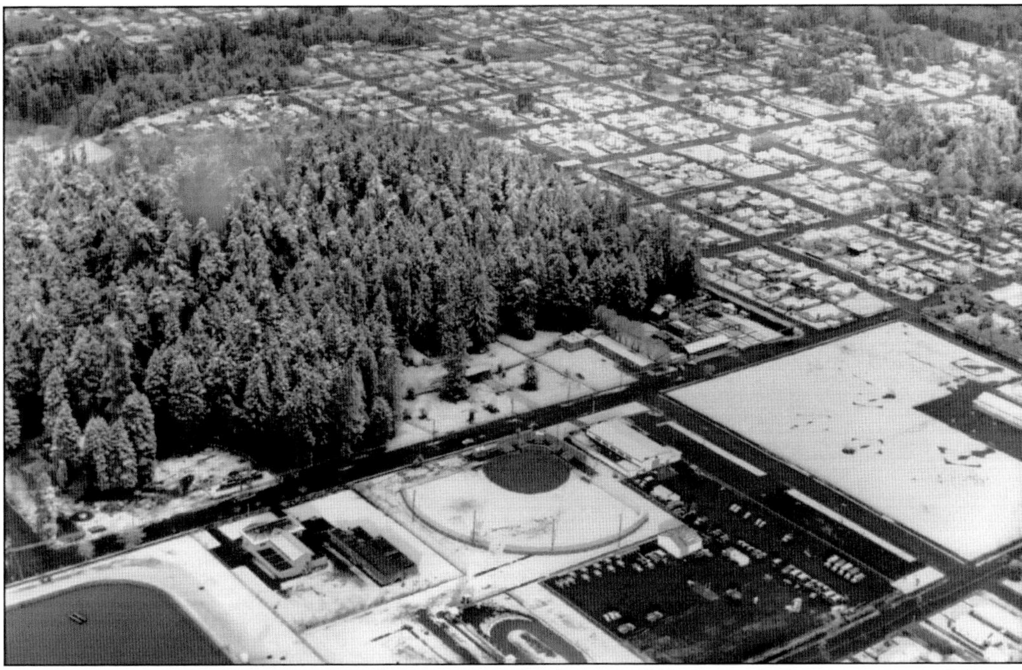

This 1960 aerial photograph, taken during a rare Eureka snowfall, shows the huge amount of change in the area during the development boom of the 1950s. During this time, the Sequoia Park Zoo was located as shown in the middle right of the photograph. The beautiful structures that animal residents and zoo visitors enjoy today had not yet been built. Notice the small patch of fog to be found above the duck pond within Sequoia Park. (Courtesy of Humboldt State University.)

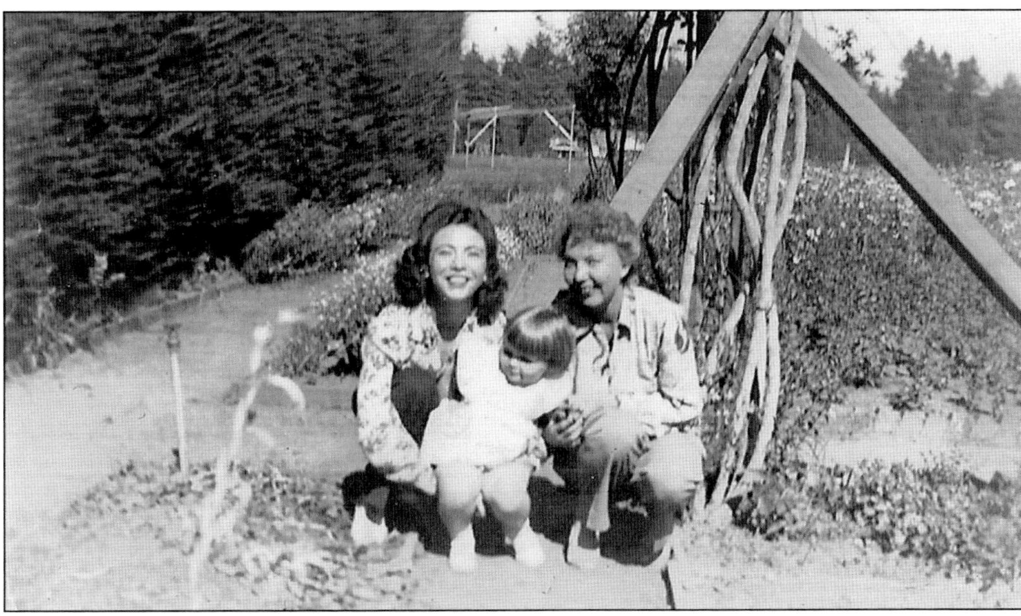

This photograph was taken in July 1944 in front of the big hedge on the east side of what is today the Sequoia Park Zoo. Pictured are local Eureka historian Arlene Hartin as a child with family friend Cora Miller (left) and her aunt Helen Codding Sundfor (right). (Courtesy of Arlene Hartin.)

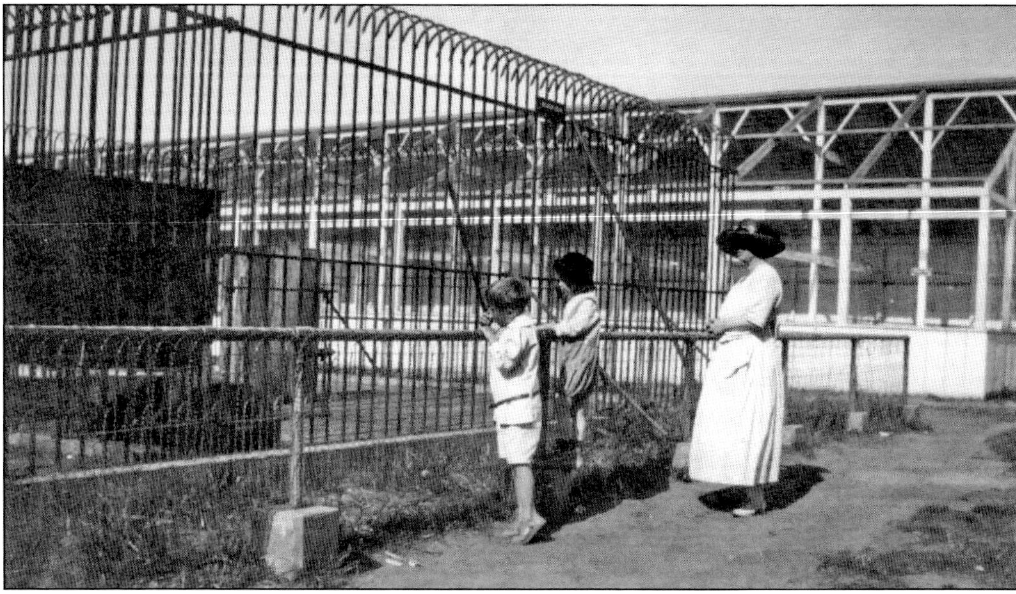

The Sequoia Park Zoo in the early years housed its animals in cages such as this one. These children and their mother peer at the black bear as exhibited around 1920. (Courtesy of the Humboldt County Historical Society.)

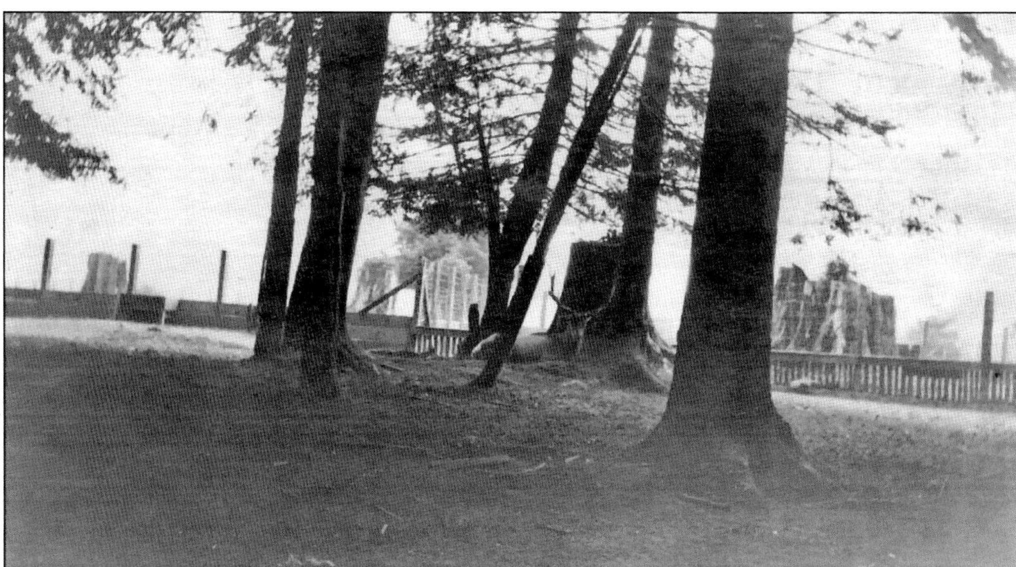

This elk buck is enclosed in the old elk paddock surrounded by large redwood stumps. The elk paddock was renovated in 1983. (Courtesy of the Humboldt County Historical Society.)

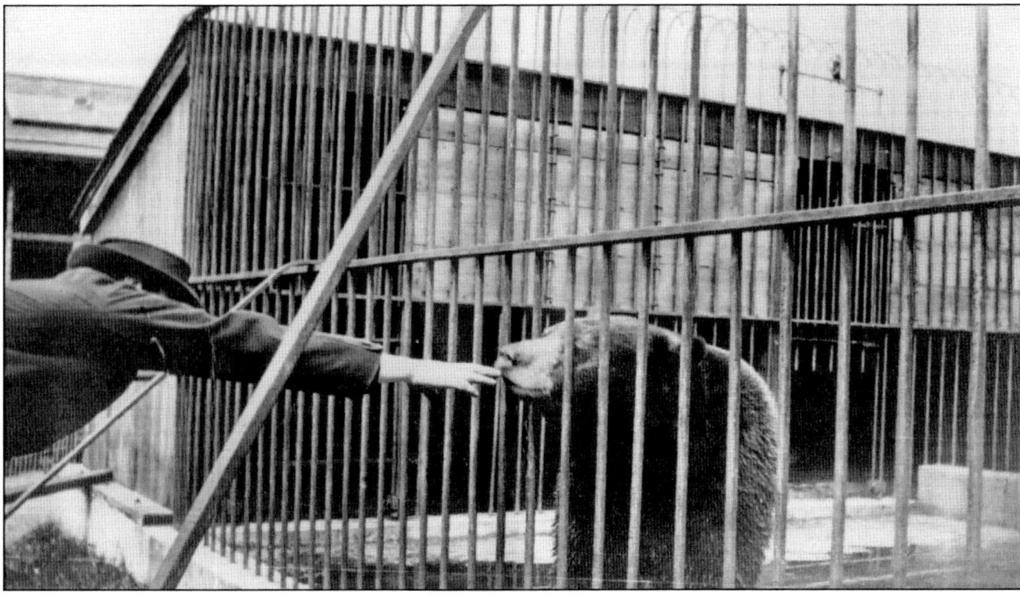

Today cages like this one have been replaced by natural enclosures, and visitors are advised not to touch the black bears or other animals. Black bears are not aggressive, but as with all wild animals, they warrant caution. This album photograph is dated 1913. (Courtesy of the Clarke Historical Museum.)

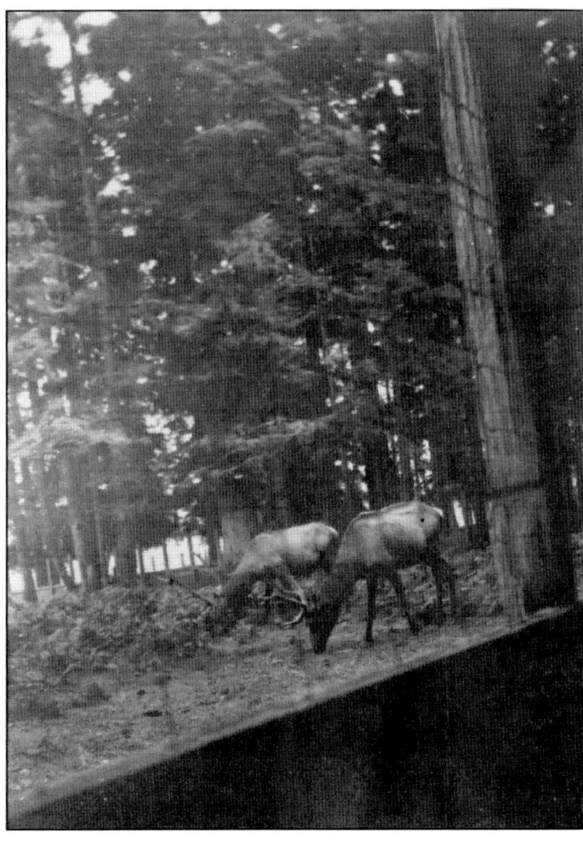

For many years, the Sequoia Park Zoo had an elk paddock; however, elk are native to the redwood region, including the Sequoia Park forest. Roosevelt elk once ranged widely in the north coast region but are now mostly restricted to Redwood National and State Parks, where they are protected. (Courtesy of the Humboldt County Historical Society.)

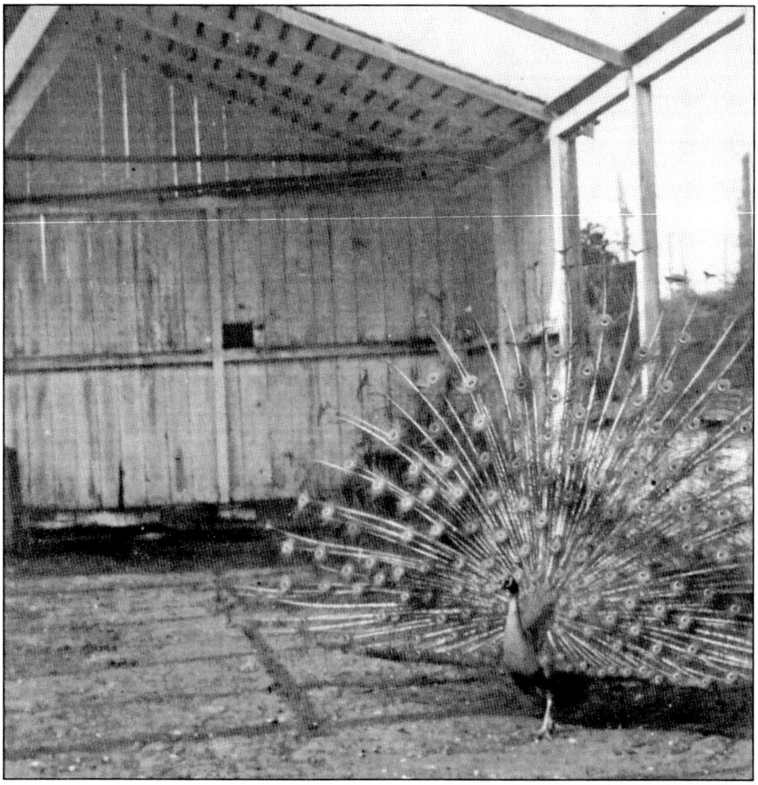

The peacock is shown here with tail feathers on full display, which is said to be an act of courtship. The building shown is the 1920's aviary, which was replaced by the new Nancy Hilfiker Aviary in 1992. (Courtesy of the Humboldt County Historical Society.)

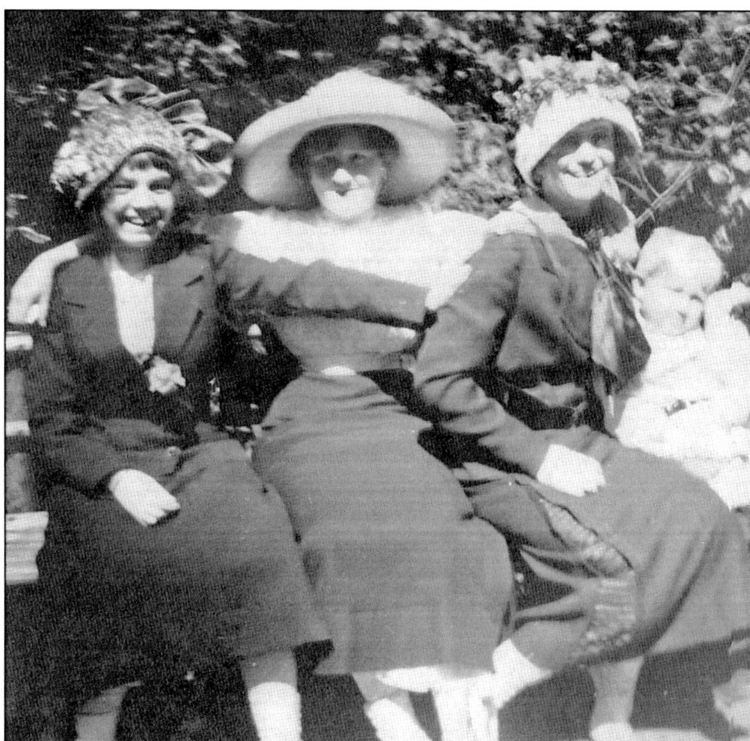

These three young women (identified only as Leona, Irene, and Mary) visited the Sequoia Park Zoo around 1913. The adjacent photograph in the same album shows a young woman wearing men's clothing, which suggests that perhaps these girls are wearing costumes. (Courtesy of the Clarke Historical Museum.)

This redwood stump house is a representative in miniature of the whimsical nature of early artistic redwood building styles from the early 20th century. At the base of the structure lies a gray stone memorial. The memorial honors the extraordinary bravery of a local soldier in World War II, Robert M. Viale, who covered a live grenade with his own body to save others in his unit—his final act. (Courtesy of Dione F. Armand.)

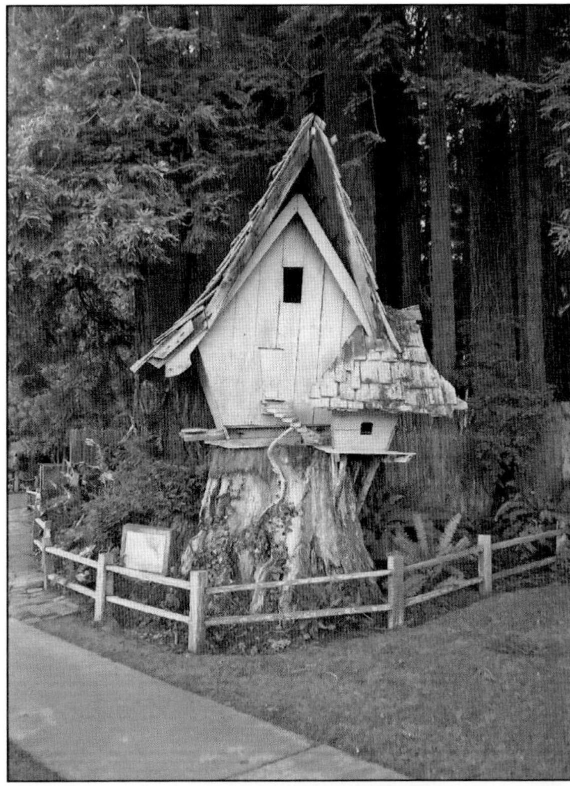

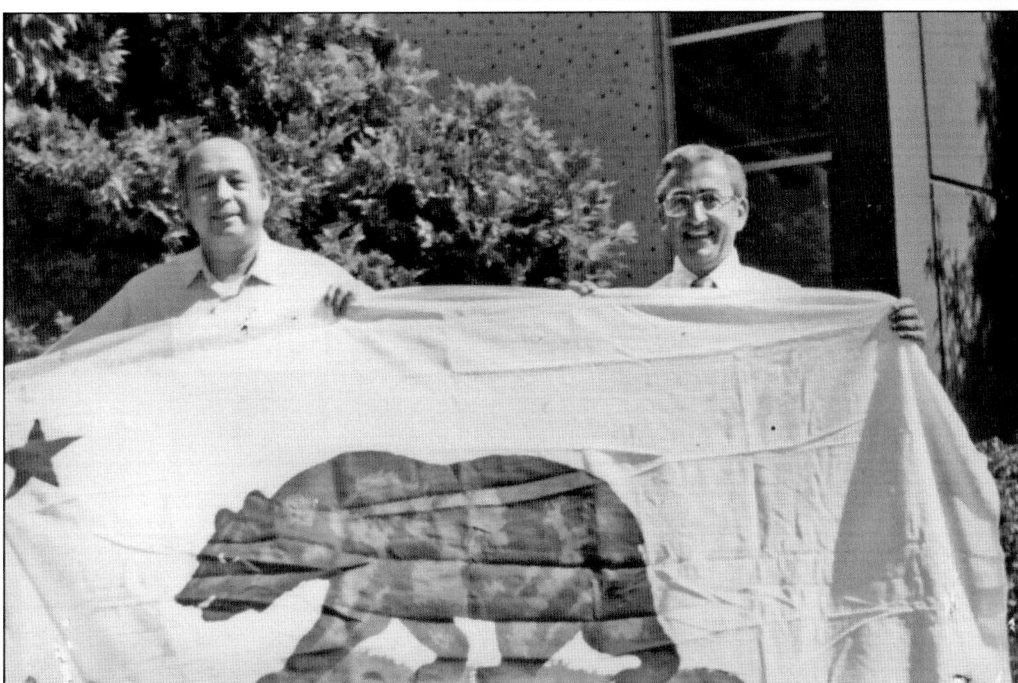

Eureka mayor Sam Sacco and Jerome Coleras receive the State of California Republic flag at the Sequoia Park Zoo on September 9, 1979. (Courtesy of the Clarke Historical Museum.)

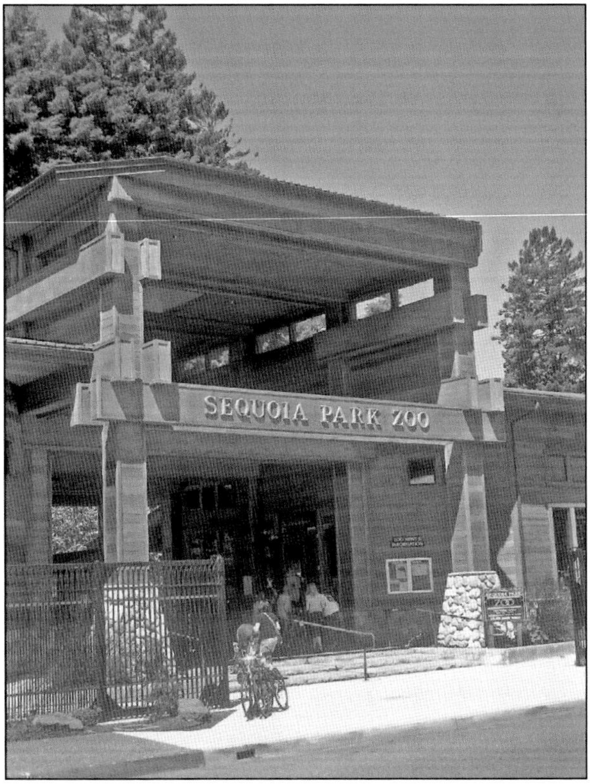

In 2003 and 2004, the Sequoia Park Zoo opened its multipurpose entrance pavilion, including a new gift shop, café, interpretive center, and lecture hall. The new pavilion is part of the master plan drafted in 1993, which aims to improve zoo facilities for residents and visitors alike. (Courtesy of Christian V. Pennington.)

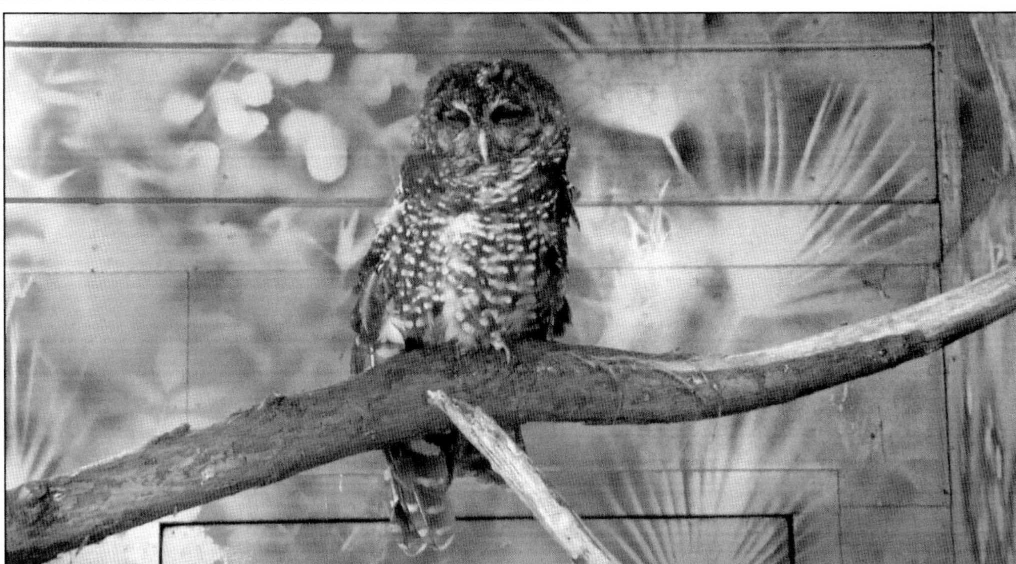

Spotted owls like this one require the branch platforms and cavities found exclusively in old-growth redwood and Douglas fir forests in order to nest. Spotted owl numbers have declined due to excessive logging, particularly the resulting forest fragmentation. They have been listed as an endangered species since 1990. This spotted owl, named Luna, was rescued by the Humboldt Wildlife Care Center after an injury and now makes her home at the Sequoia Park Zoo. (Courtesy of Christian V. Pennington.)

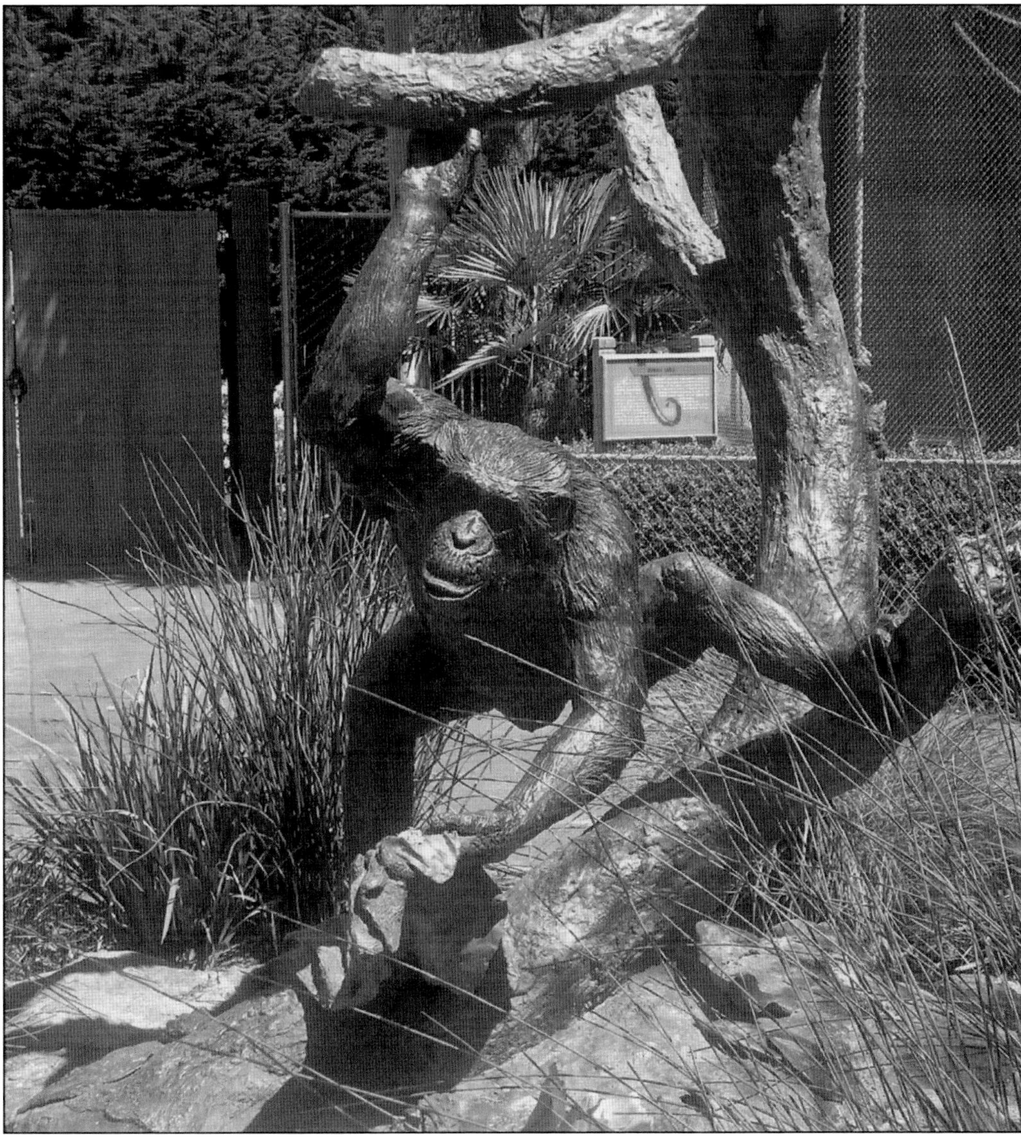

Bill the Chimp became a household name in Humboldt County during his 50-year residence at Eureka's Sequoia Park Zoo. In July 1957, local children sent in their pennies, nickels, and dimes during a weeklong fund-raising drive to raise $350—the price of buying "Bill the Champ of Chimps" from the Polack Brothers Circus, a traveling circus in operation from 1944 to 1961. Ten days after the fund-raising drive, the community gathered for a reception to welcome the zoo's newest resident. Eureka mayor Oscar Swanlund offered the chimp a key-shaped cookie, which Bill then ate from the top of his new house. Eleven years old at the time of his arrival, young Bill was known for his rambunctious behavior. In his later years—Bill was 60 when he passed away on June 26, 2007—he was famous for his paintings, which were sold for many years at the zoo and were featured on the *Late Show with David Letterman*. Shortly after World War II, when Bill was born, the number of chimpanzees in Africa was estimated in the millions. Today there are an estimated 150,000 remaining worldwide. This cast bronze commemorative statue of Bill was commissioned by Rob and Cherie Arkley and created by sculptor Yannis Stefanakis. (Courtesy of Christian V. Pennington.)

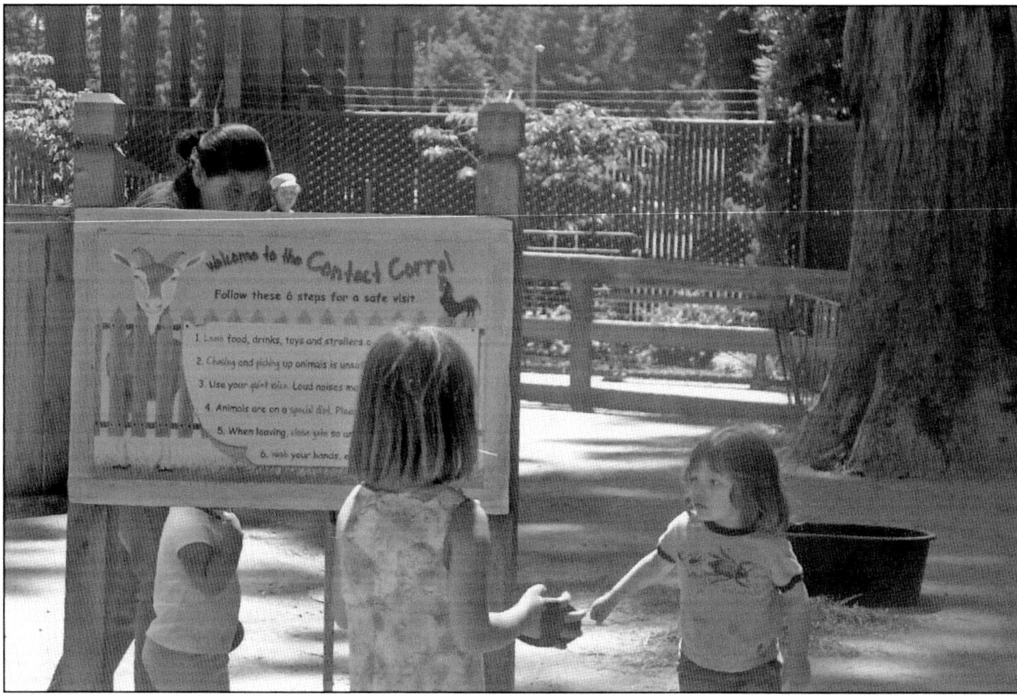

The Barnyard area enables children to meet many animals that are typically found in and around a barnyard. Donkeys, sheep, goats, alpacas, rabbits, and chickens are just a few of the animals that make their home at the Sequoia Park Zoo. (Courtesy of Christian V. Pennington.)

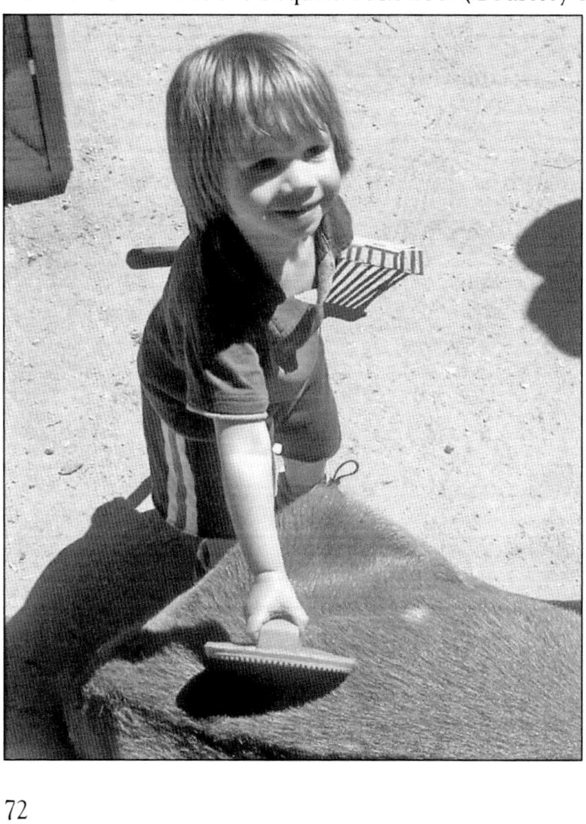

Children such as young Henry Pennington can groom the goats and sheep in the Sequoia Park Zoo Contact Corral. (Courtesy of Christian V. Pennington.)

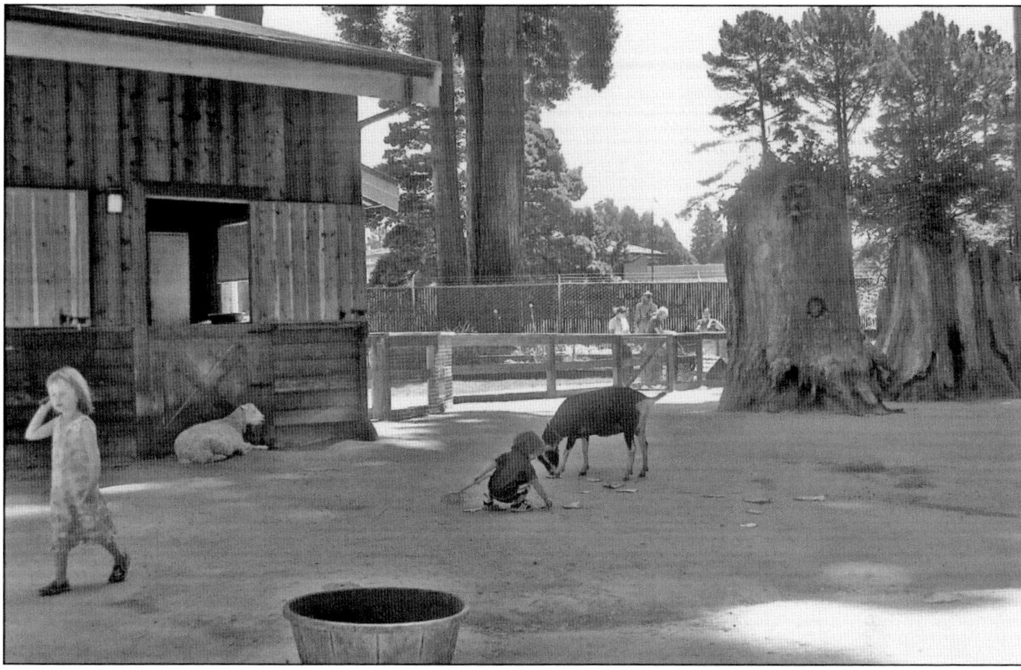

The five-acre Sequoia Park Zoo is unique in being the only zoo in the world in a redwood forest setting. The Barnyard and Contact Corral children's area are shown here surrounded by soaring redwoods and the huge stumps of the ancient trees logged in the 19th century. (Courtesy of Christian V. Pennington.)

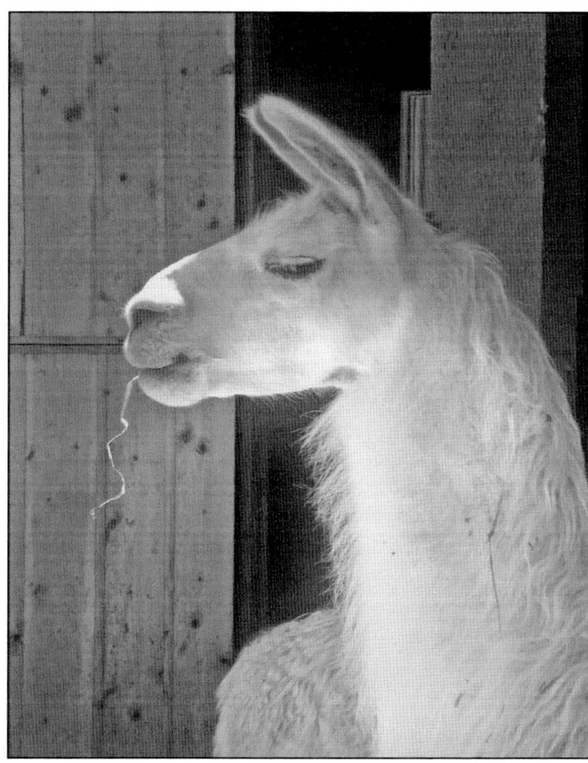

The mission of the Sequoia Park Zoo is "to inspire wonder, understanding, and respect for the natural world by providing fun, rewarding, educational experiences that encourage meaningful connections between animals, humans, and our environment." The opportunity to interact with this alpaca in the Barnyard is one example of the zoo's commitment to fostering a sense of human interconnection with animals. (Courtesy of Christian V. Pennington.)

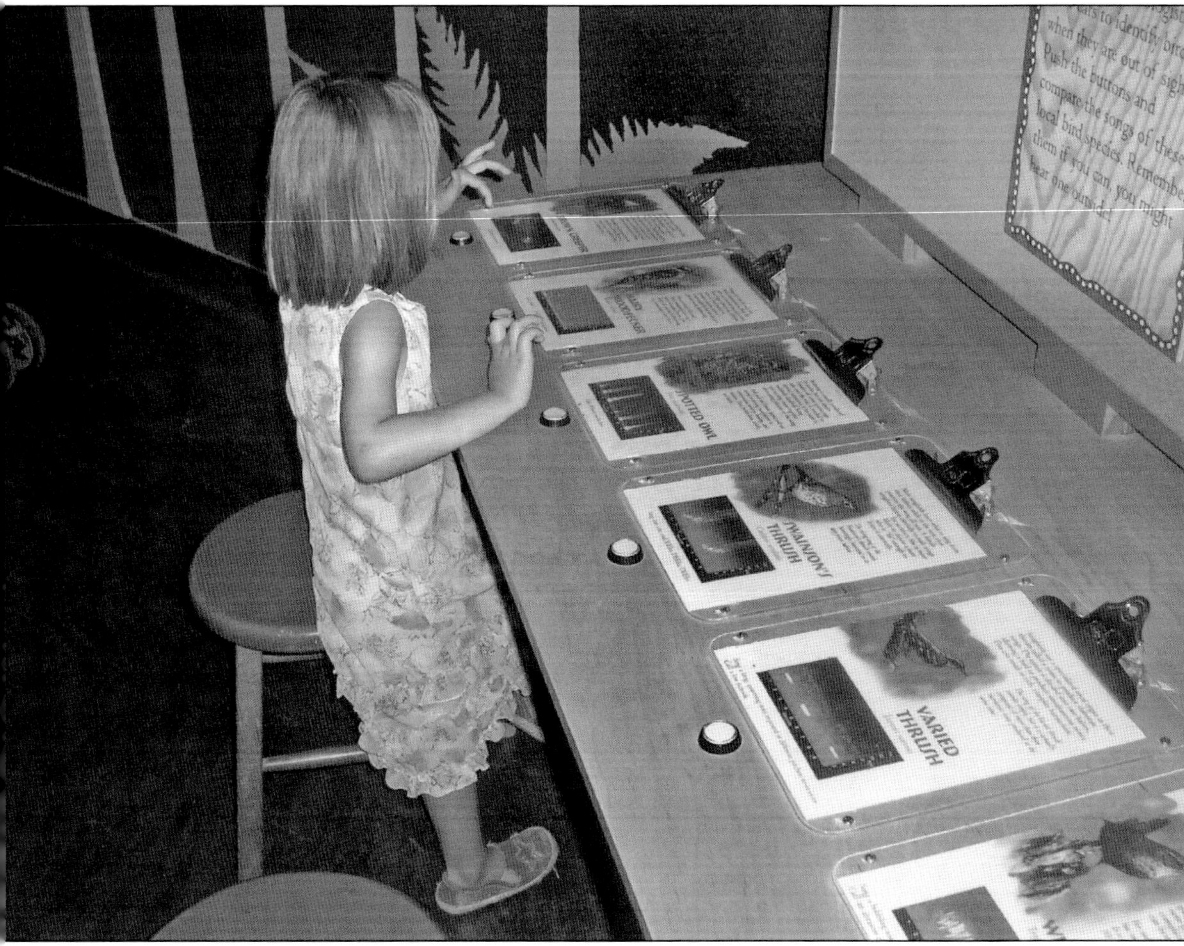

Lucy Pennington is shown exploring the Secrets of the Forest exhibit at the Sequoia Park Zoo. The Secrets of the Forest tells the story of the complex local ecosystem of the coast redwood forests of northern California and the hidden creatures that live there. (Courtesy of Christian V. Pennington.)

Five

Sequoia Park by Trolley Car

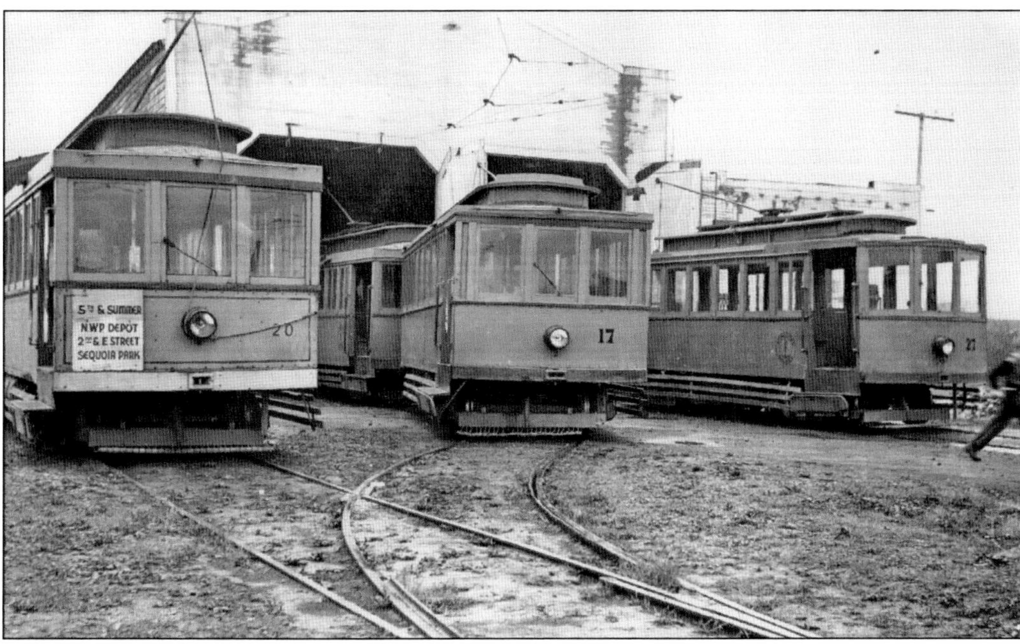

It is no accident that the heyday of Sequoia Park and the era of the electric trolley car in Eureka overlap with near perfect precision. At the time of its inception, Sequoia Park—located near the city's southeastern boundary—was beyond the area of already developed land. Most people did not own cars, and the trolley cars were an easy and inexpensive way to ride out to the park. Much of the town would ride the trolley cars out to Sequoia Park on any given weekend. The festive and communal nature of the trolley car can still be enjoyed in San Francisco. However, in Eureka, as in most cities across the nation, the trolley car era came to an end. (Courtesy of the Humboldt County Historical Society.)

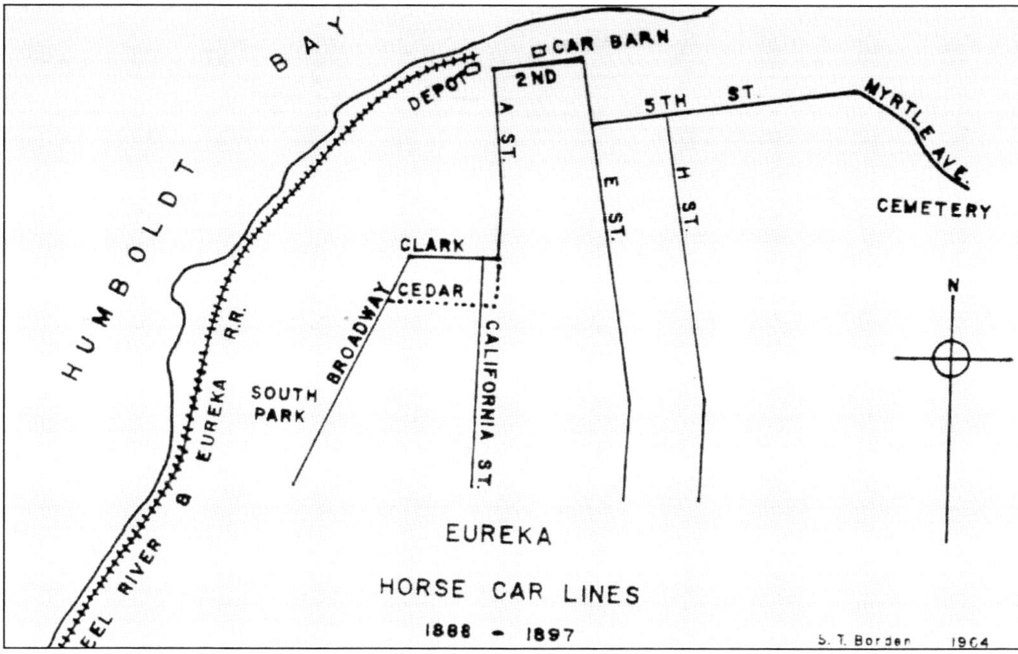

This map shows the horse-drawn streetcar lines from 1888 to 1897. Intra-city public transport started in 1888 with horse-drawn cars. Initially, there were three miles of tracks, six cars, and 25 horses. The fare was 5¢. About 700 people rode the horse-drawn cars daily out of a city population of just under 5,000 people. (Courtesy of the Humboldt County Historical Society.)

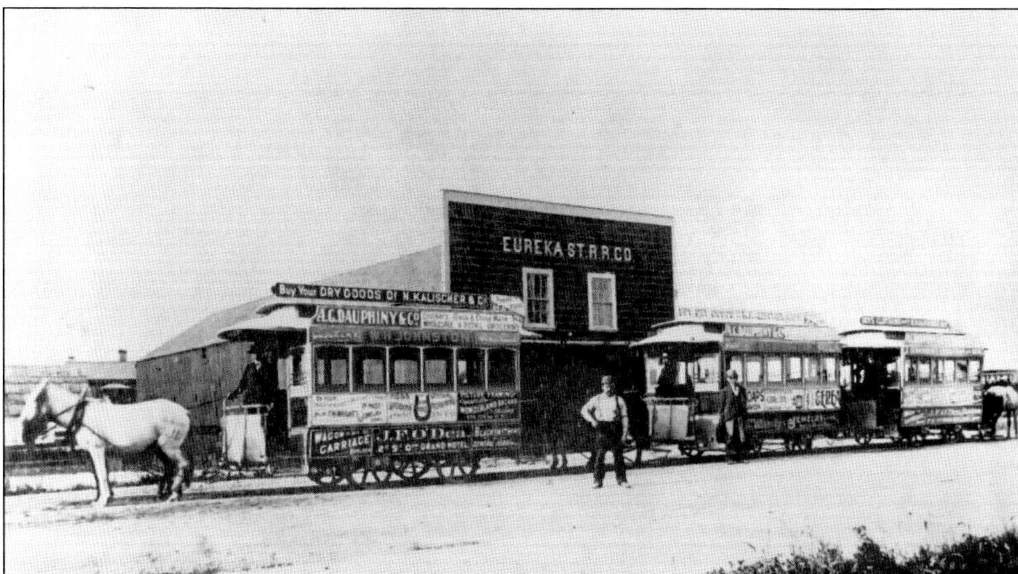

Eureka's first streetcar system was run by the Eureka Street Rail Road Company and used horse-drawn rail cars. When the principal railway owner, R. M. Fernald, died in 1897, the company encountered financial trouble, and the horses had to be sold. Shown here is a horse-drawn railcar festooned with local advertisements in front of the company office on First Street. The man in the foreground is identified as Jack Zientara. (Courtesy of the Clarke Historical Museum.)

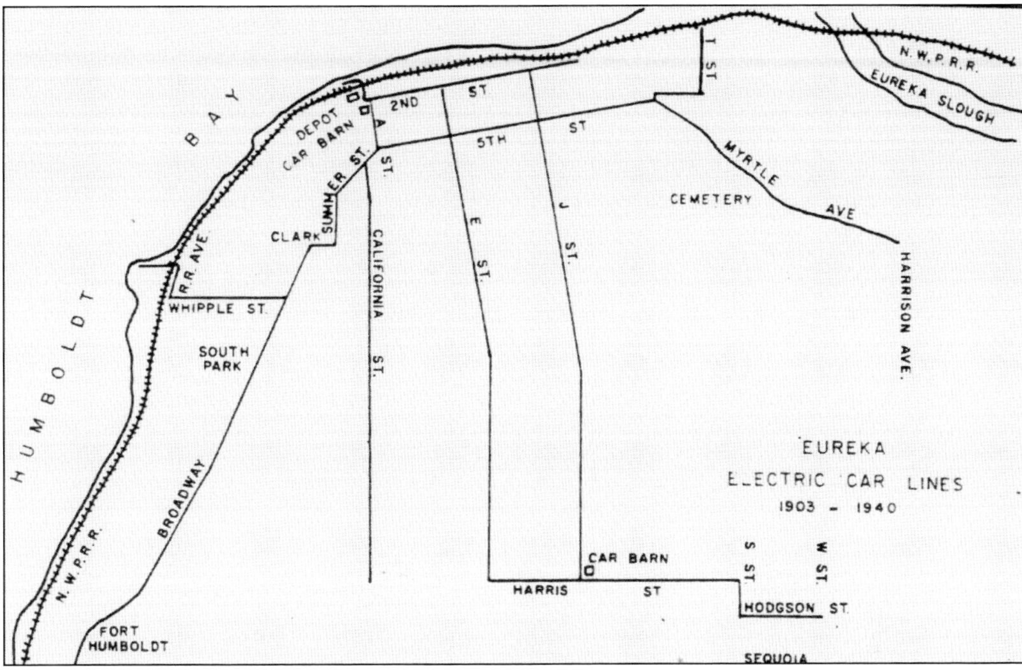

This map shows the electric streetcar lines from 1903 to 1940. The Humboldt Transit Company was incorporated on July 31, 1903, with an authorized capital stock of $1 million by J. C. Bull Jr., president; George W. Henderson, vice president; C. P. Cutten, secretary; R. W. Bull; and J. C. Bull, with the Bank of Eureka as treasurer. The company was to pay a franchise tax of three and one third percent to the city and five and one quarter percent to the state. On August 13, 1903, Henderson transferred the franchise to the company. (Courtesy of the Humboldt County Historical Society.)

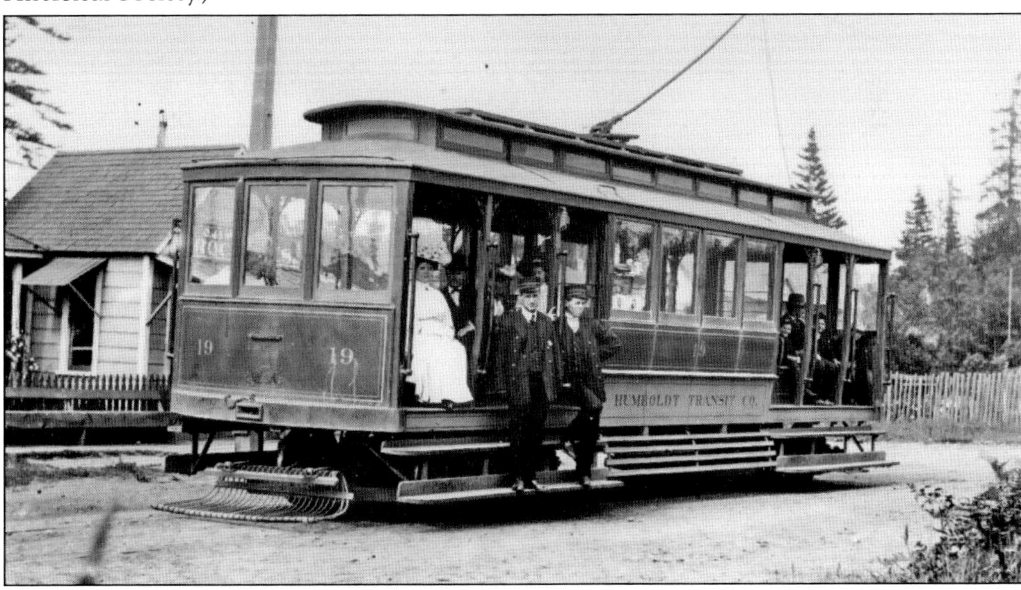

Sequoia Park was the southern terminus of the trolley car line bearing its name. This photograph was taken around 1906 at the corner of W and Harris Streets on the line serving Sequoia Park. (Courtesy of the Clarke Historical Museum.)

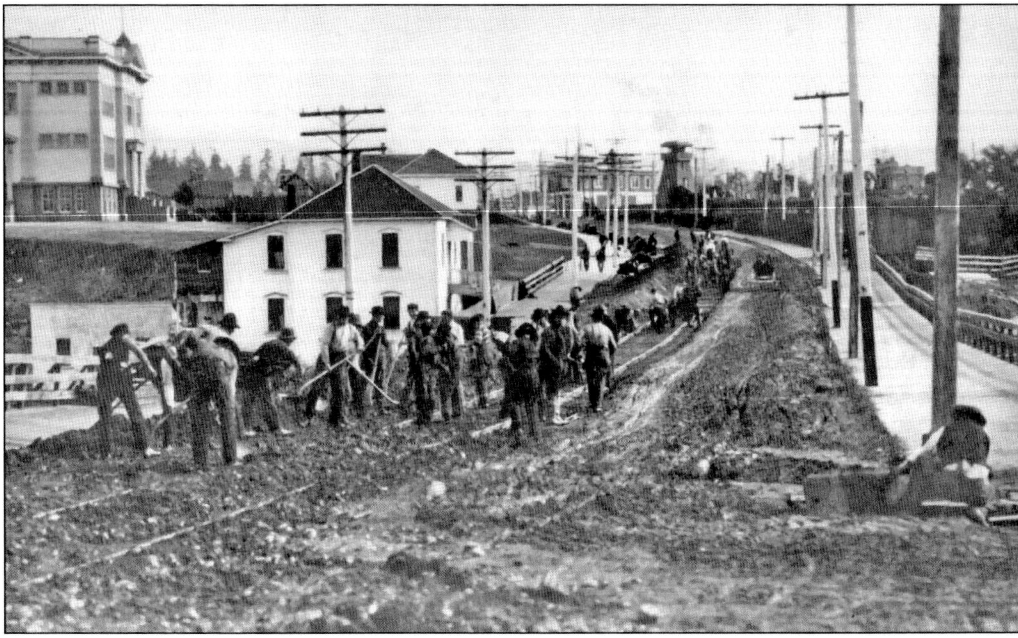

This photograph shows men laying the rails for the Myrtle Avenue trolley car line at Myrtle Avenue and Seventh Street in 1907. (Courtesy of the Humboldt County Historical Society.)

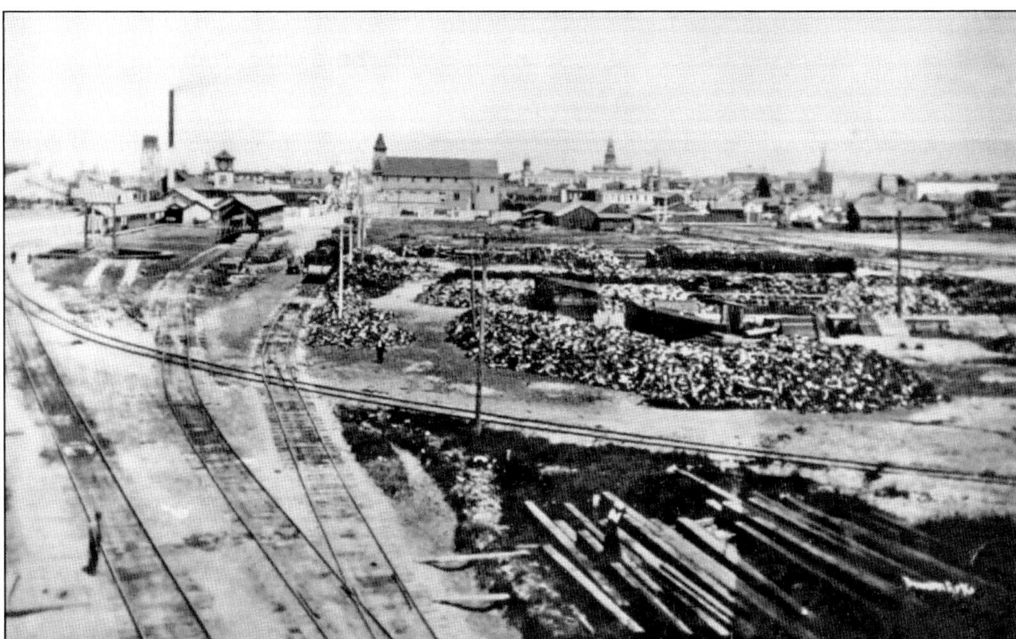

The Eureka railway depot and carbarn for the trolley cars was located at the foot of A and Second Streets. The railroad station is shown on the left, and the carbarn is in the center of the photograph. (Courtesy of the Humboldt County Historical Society.)

This Eureka Street railway time table shows the frequency and schedule of the various trolley car lines. The Sequoia Park line is not shown. Gene Lytle shared his memories of a time when there was no manner of switching to the Sequoia Park line without transferring. A direct line to Sequoia Park was later added. (Courtesy of the Humboldt County Historical Society.)

EUREKA STREET RAILWAY TIME TABLE

This Time Table is computed to apply to Cars when FOUR are running, generally on Holidays and Days of Celebration. When TWO Cars are running the figures marked with an * will apply.

DEPOT.		CEMETERY.		SOUTH PARK	
*7:40 A. M.	4:43 P. M.	*8:03 A. M.	5:00 P. M.	*8:05 A. M.	5:02 P. M
8:00 "	*5:00 "	8:20 "	*5:18 "	8:22 "	*5:20 "
*8:20 "	5:17 "	*8:40 "	5:35 "	*8:44 "	5:37 "
8:40 "	*5:35 "	9:00 "	*5:53 "	9:02 "	*5:55 "
*9:00 "	5:53 "	*9:18 "	6:10 "	*9:19 "	6:12 "
9:17 "	*6:10 "	9:35 "	*6:28 "	9:37 "	*6:30 "
*9:35 "	6:27 "	*9:52 "	6:45 "	*9:54 "	6:47 "
9:52 "	*6:45 "	10:09 "	*7:03 "	10:11 "	*7:05 "
*10:09 "	7:02 "	*10:26 "	7:20 "	*10:28 "	7:22 "
10:25 "	*7:20 "	10:43 "	*7:38 "	10:45 "	*7:40 "
*10:43 "	7:37 "	*11:00 "	7:55 "	*11:02 "	7:57 "
11:00 "	*7:55 "	11:17 "	*8:13 "	11:19 "	*8:15 "
*11:17 "	8:12 "	*11:34 "	8:30 "	*11:36 "	8:32 "
11:34 "	*8:30 "	11:51 "	*8:48 "	11:53 "	*8:50 "
*11:51 "	8:48 "	*12:08 P. M.	9:05 "	*12:10 P. M.	9:07 "
12:08 P. M.	*9:05 "	12:25 "	*9:23 "	12:27 "	*9:25 "
*12:25 "	9:23 "	*12:42 "		*12:44 "	
12:43 "	*9:40 "	1:00 "		1:01 "	
*12:59 "		*1:17 "		*1:18 "	
1:17 "		1:33 "		1:35 "	
*1:33 "		*1:50 "		*1:52 "	
1:50 "		2:07 "		2:09 "	
*2:07 "		*2:24 "		*2:26 "	
2:24 "		2:41 "		2:43 "	
*2:41 "		2:58 "		*3:00 "	
2:58 "		*3:15 "		3:17 "	
*3:15 "		3:33 "		*3:35 "	
3:32 "		*3:50 "		3:52 "	
*3:50 "		4:08 "		*4:10 "	
4:07 "		*4:25 "		4:27 "	
*4:25 "		4:43 "		*4:45 "	

H STREET DIVISION

Connecting with the Main Line at the corner of Fifth and H streets. The time being the same for Two or Four Cars. Time computed showing when Car leaves the corner of Fifth and H streets

7:27 a. m.	12:12 p. m.	5:22 p. m.
8:07 "	15:46 "	5:57 "
8:47 "	1:20 "	6:32 "
9:22 "	1:54 "	7:07 "
9:56 "	2:28 "	7:42 "
10:30 "	3:02 "	8:17 "
11:04 "	3:37 "	8:52 "
11:38 "	4:12 "	9:27 "
	4:47 "	

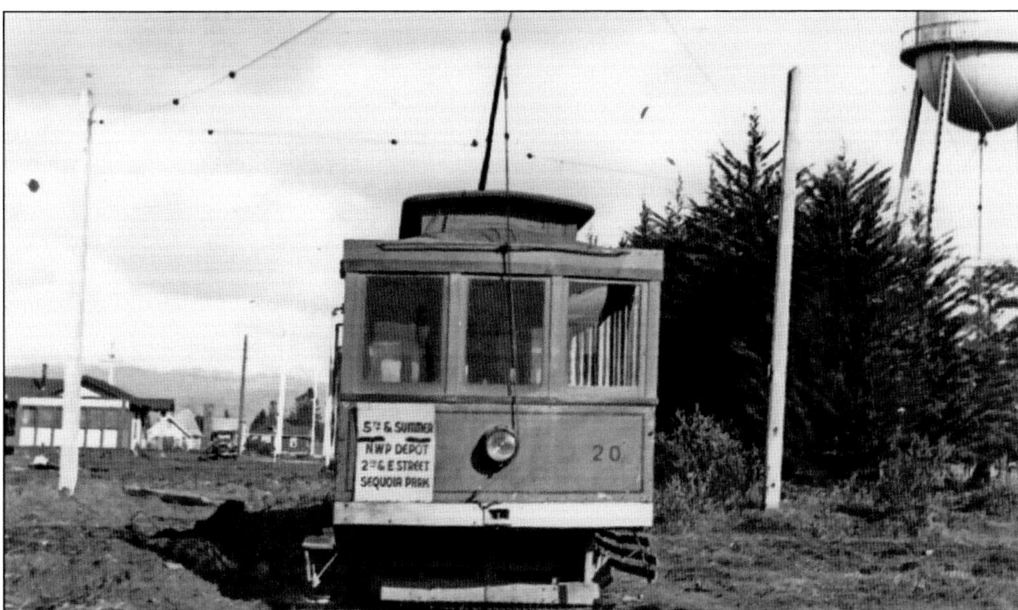

This photograph shows the Sequoia Park trolley car No. 20 heading toward Sequoia Park and going past the old Eureka water tower on Harris Street. The water tower shown predates both the 1950 water tower and the 500,000-gallon water tower that currently provides water for more than half the population of Eureka. (Courtesy of the Humboldt County Historical Society.)

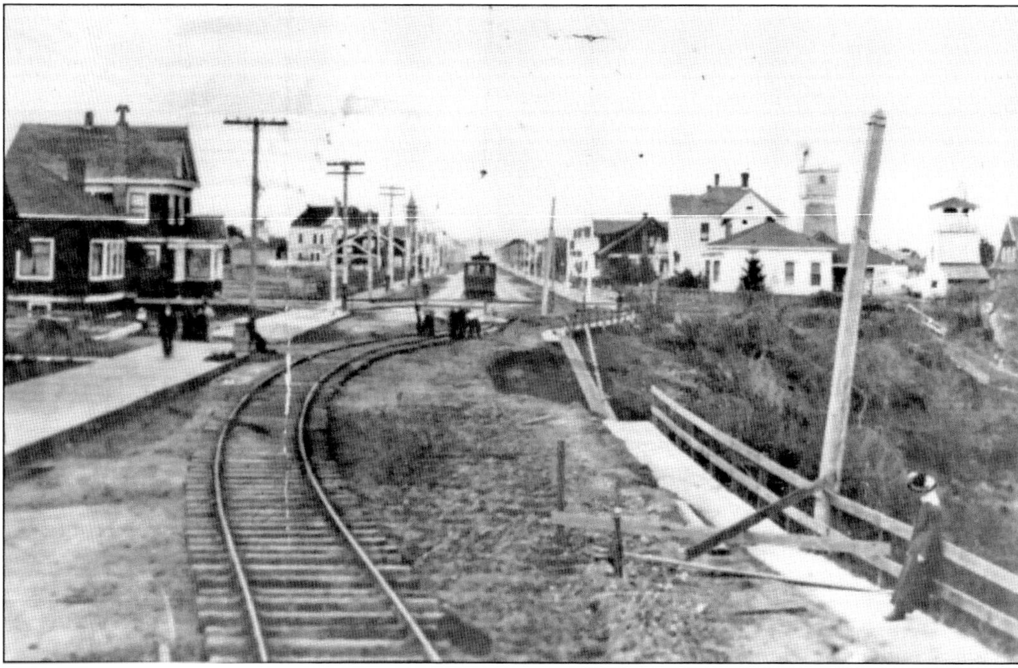

This 1911 photograph shows the J Street slip-out between Sixteenth and Seventeenth Streets in Eureka. (Courtesy of the Humboldt County Historical Society.)

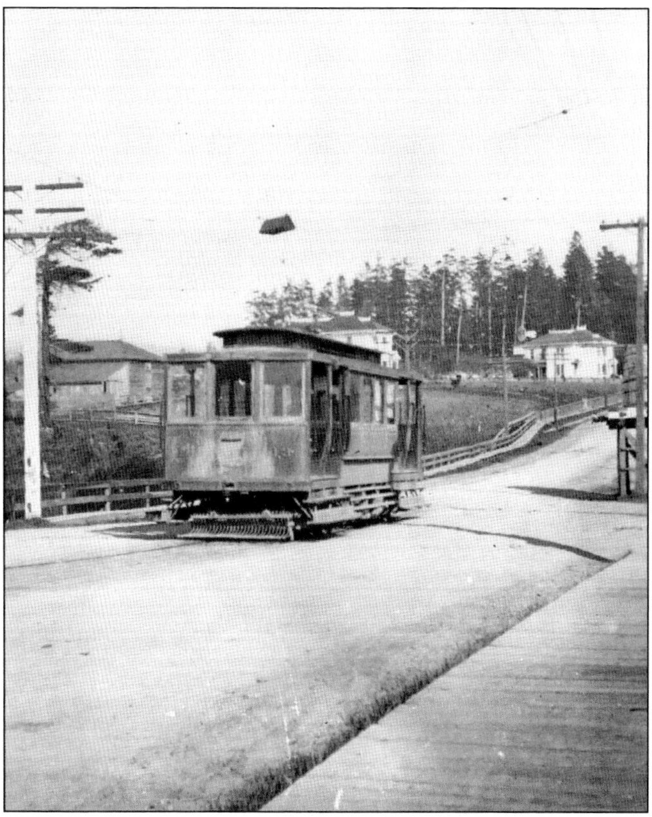

Gene Lytle shared his memories of the traffic before the installation of the Myrtle Avenue trolley car line (shown) as having "consisted of beautifully harnessed two- and four-horse teams drawing freight wagons into town, and men riding bicycles to and from work." (Courtesy of the Clarke Historical Museum.)

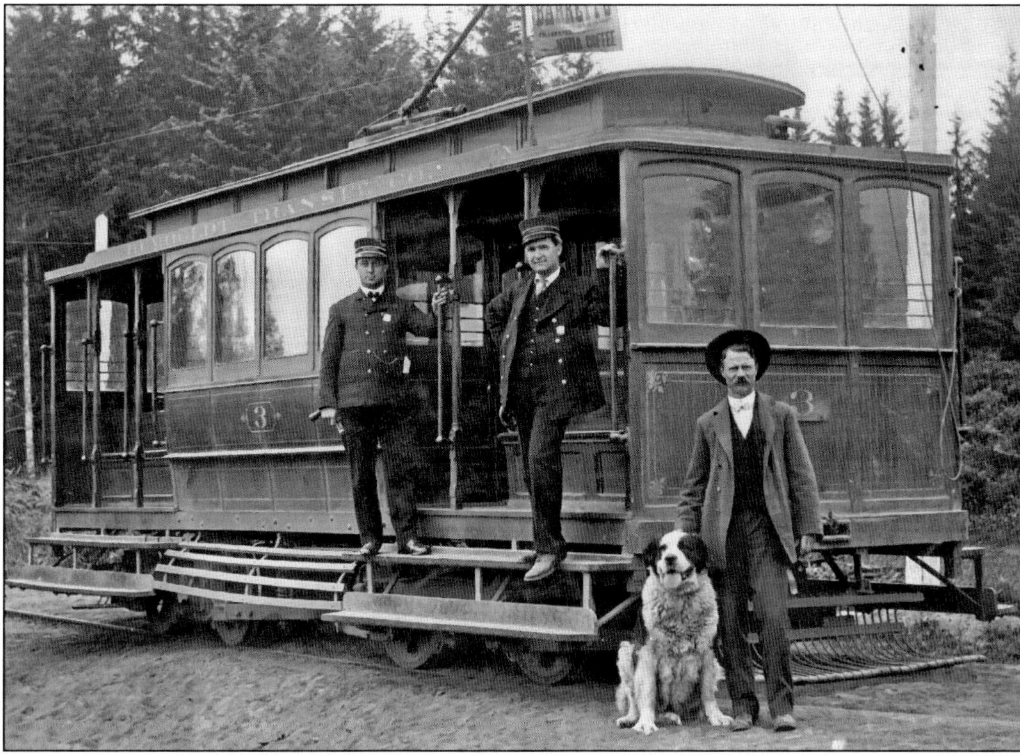

Eureka's trolley cars were purchased used from San Francisco and Sacramento. The men in this photograph are identified as Louis Brown, William Ward, and Frank Wornell and his dog Jack. (Courtesy of the Clarke Historical Museum.)

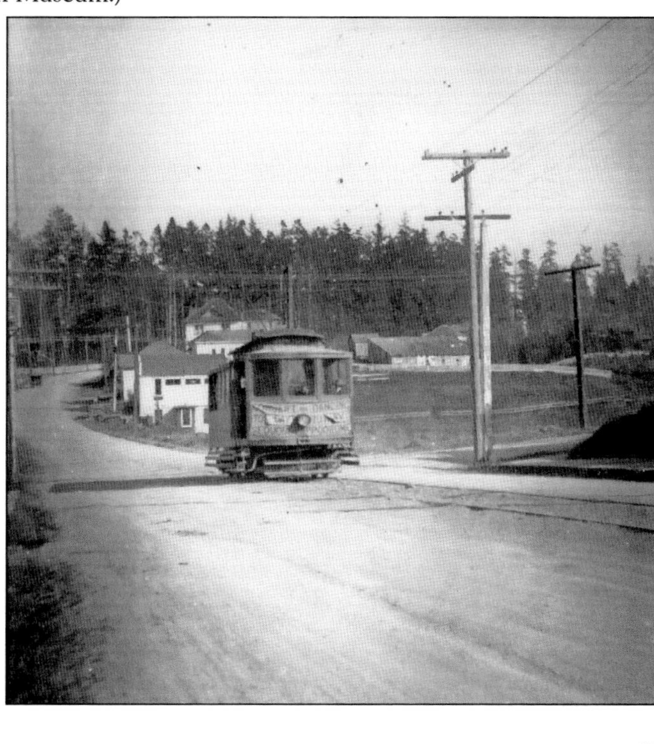

This trolley car makes its way up Myrtle Avenue in the 1920s. Redwoods can be seen in the background. (Courtesy of the Clarke Historical Museum.)

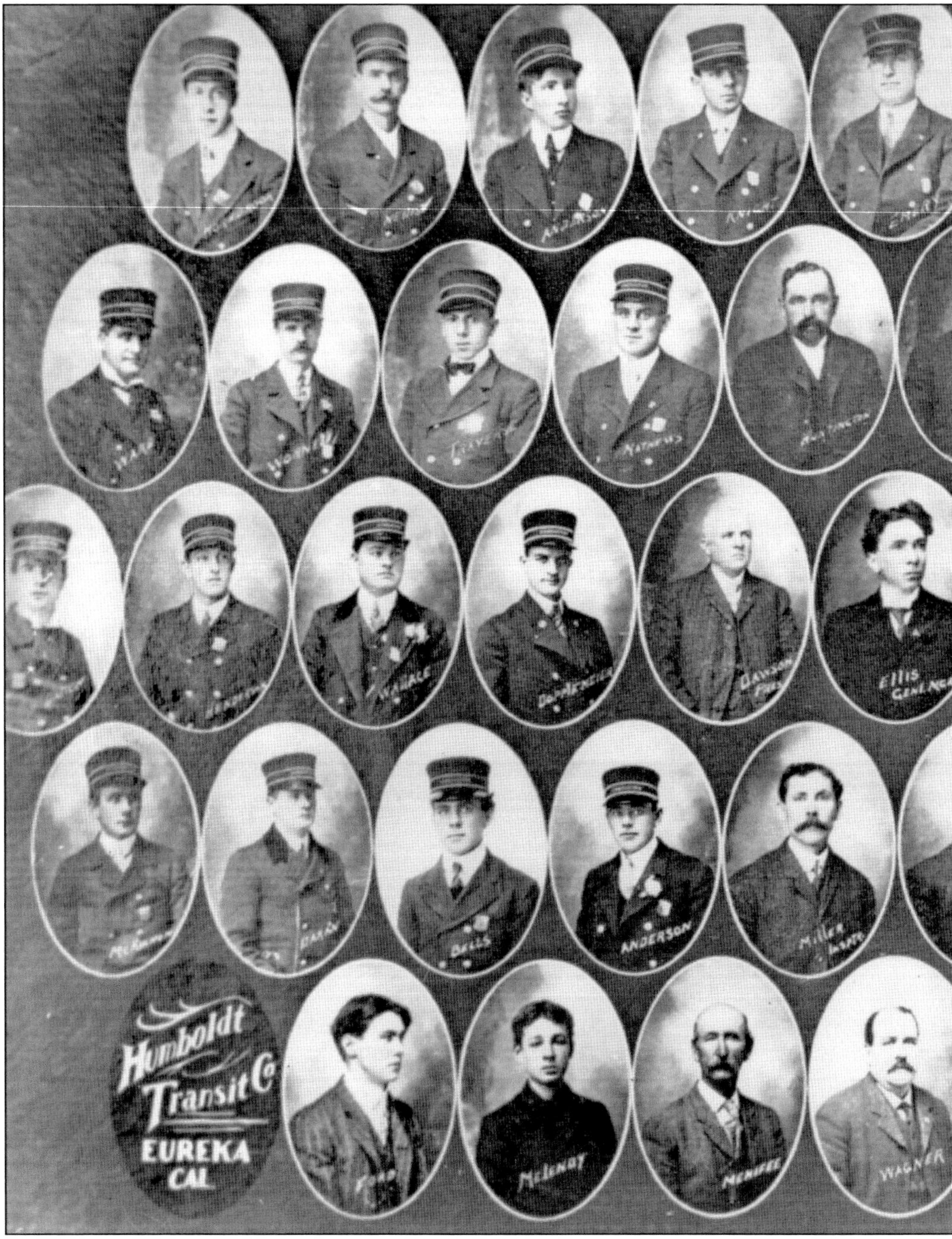

This composite portrait of the men who worked for the Humboldt Transit Company in 1905 was taken by R. J. Baker. The firm's trolley cars operated in all sections of the city: F Street line to Sequoia Park; J Street line to Harris Street; Myrtle Avenue line to Harrison Avenue; and Fifth Street line to Second and T Streets. (Courtesy of the Humboldt County Historical Society.)

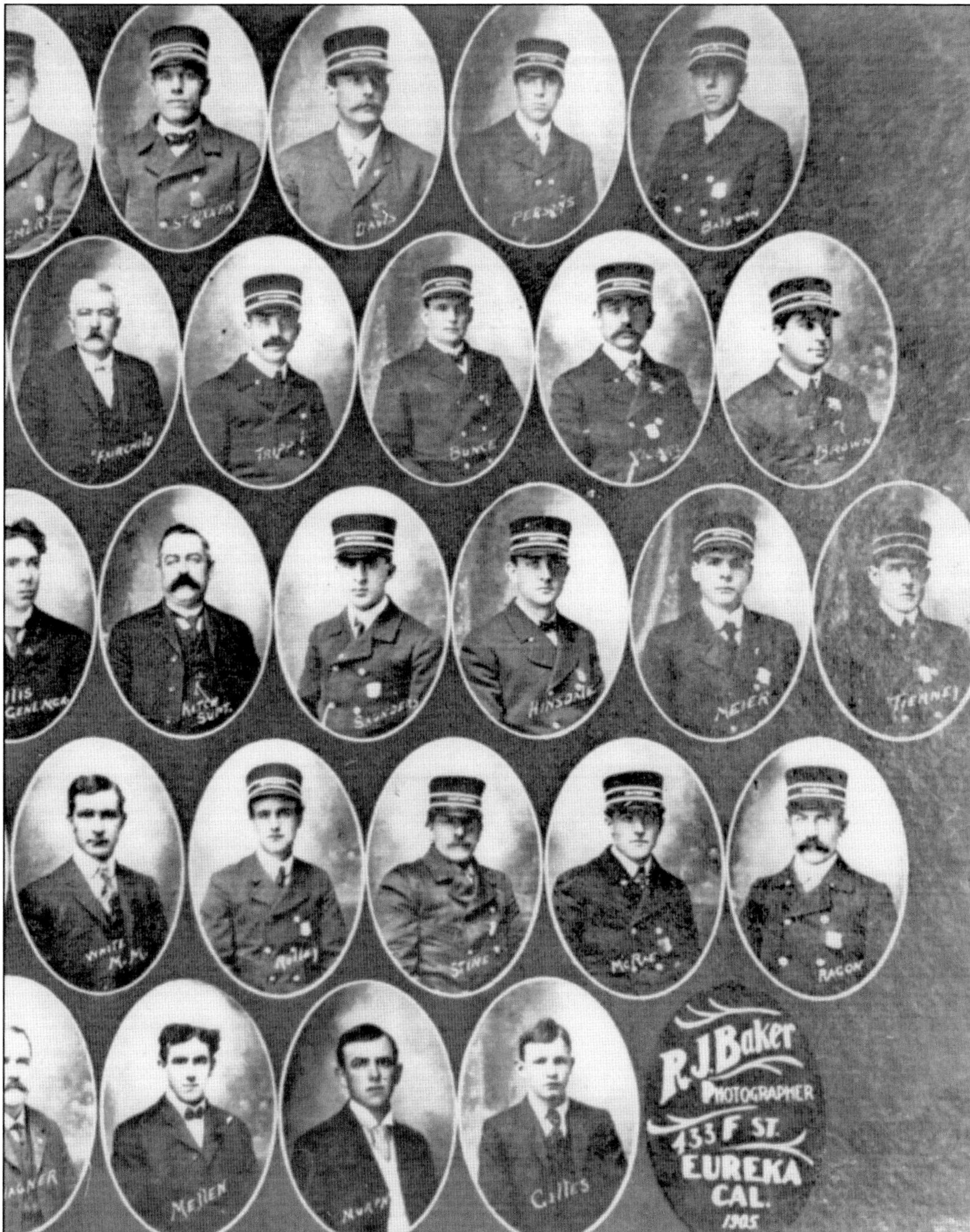

Hugh Jones (not shown) remembers that around the time this photograph was taken in 1905 there were not more than 30 automobiles in Eureka. Cars were an expensive novelty, and the main modes of personal transport were walking, bicycling, and riding the trolley cars. He also recalls that in the old days everyone would listen for the trolley bell ringing. (Courtesy of the Humboldt County Historical Society.)

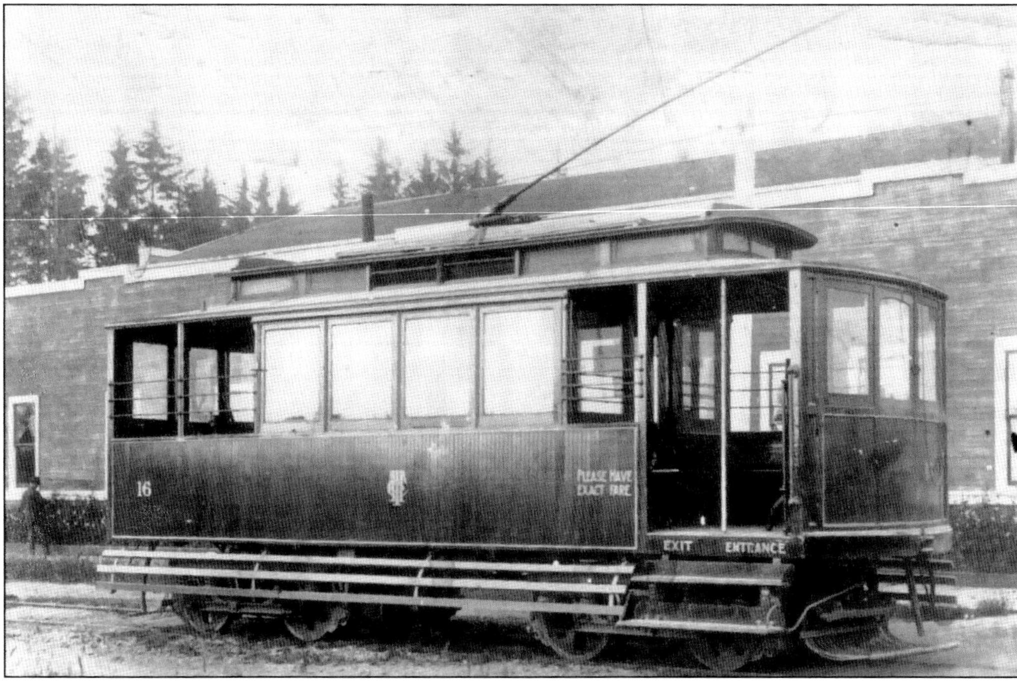

This old-style streetcar, No. 16, is shown parked outside of the old Sequoia Auditorium directly adjacent to Sequoia Park. The auditorium, which burned down in 1926, was a popular dance hall and later a skating rink. (Courtesy of the Clarke Historical Museum.)

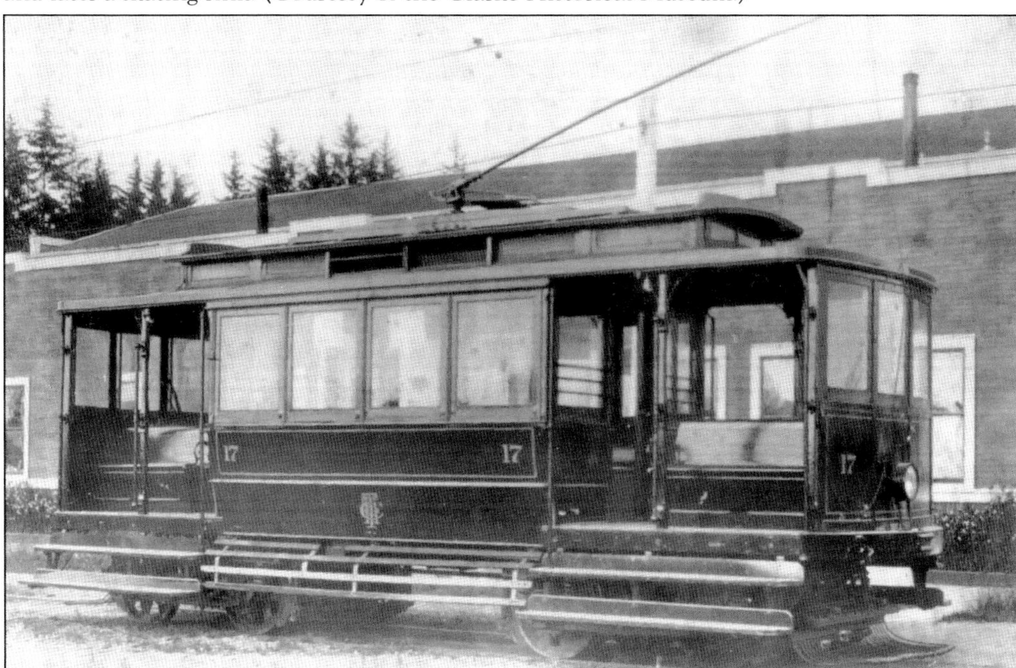

This photograph shows Humboldt Transit No. 17 in a company photograph used to illustrate the car's appearance prior to rebuilding. Notice the open-side design of the trolley car. (Courtesy of the Humboldt County Historical Society.)

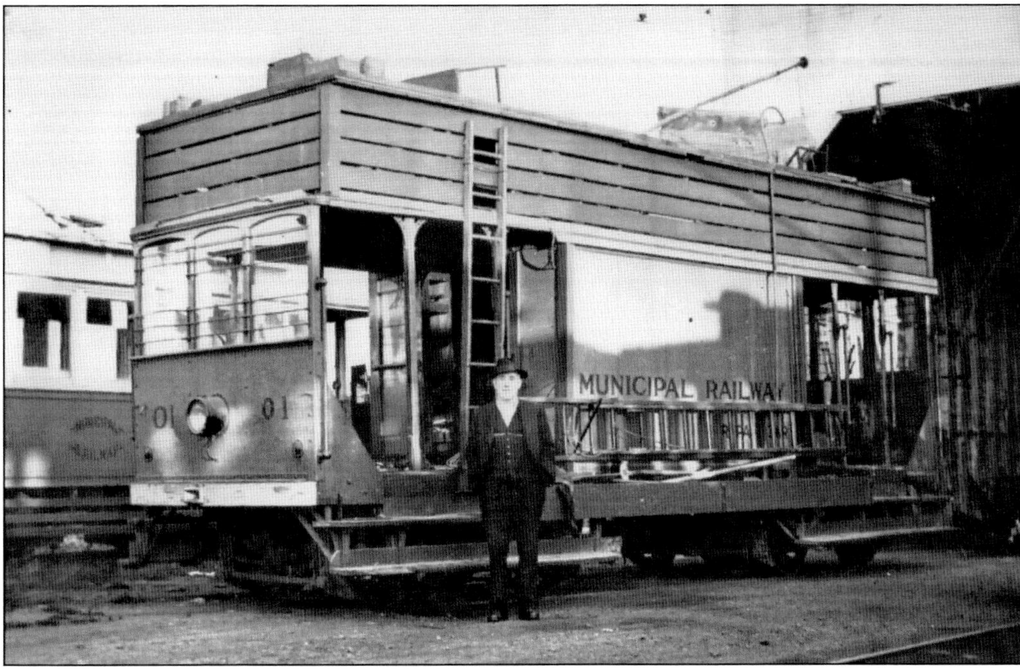

There were many design variations of trolley cars. The models most conducive to picnics were run on the weekends on the Sequoia Park line. This one is shown with George Beattie in front of it. (Courtesy of the Humboldt County Historical Society.)

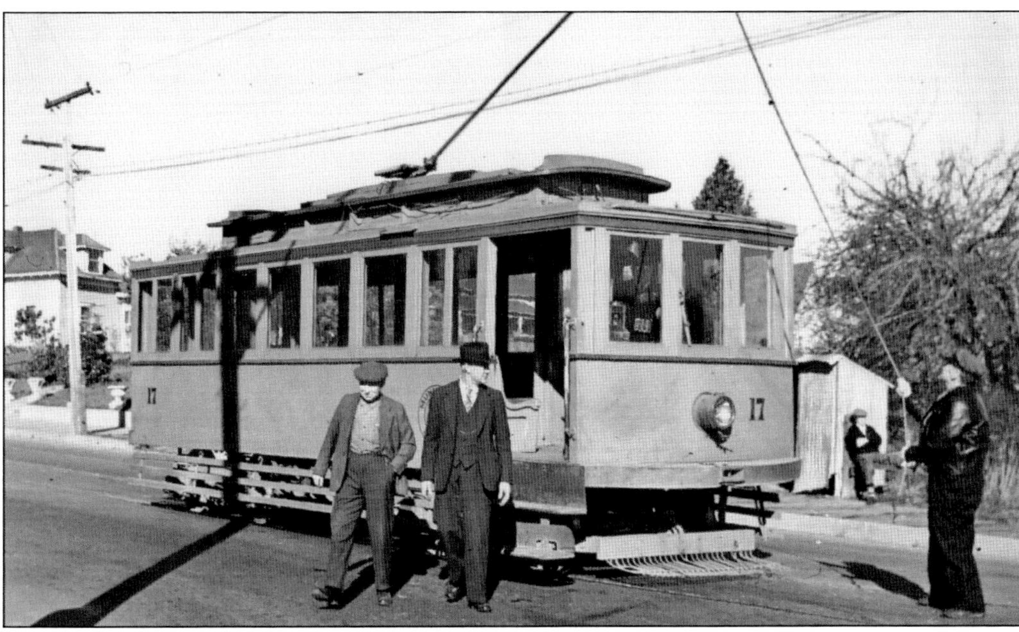

This 1940 photograph taken at Myrtle and Harrison Avenues shows another closed-design trolley car and the motorman preparing to turn the car around to make its return journey. (Courtesy of the Humboldt County Historical Society.)

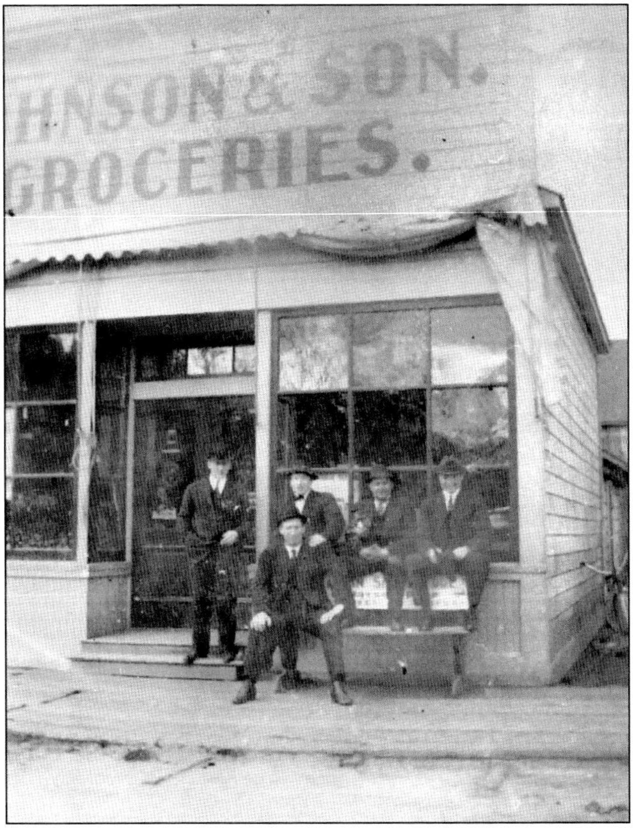

This photograph was taken at the terminus of the Sequoia Park line at Hodgson and W Streets. The second man from the left is Charles "Chas" Johnson, son of Ole Johnson, who originated the store. Chas was the uncle of Fred Penoli, who was the son of Johnny Penoli, a streetcar conductor. (Courtesy of the Humboldt County Historical Society.)

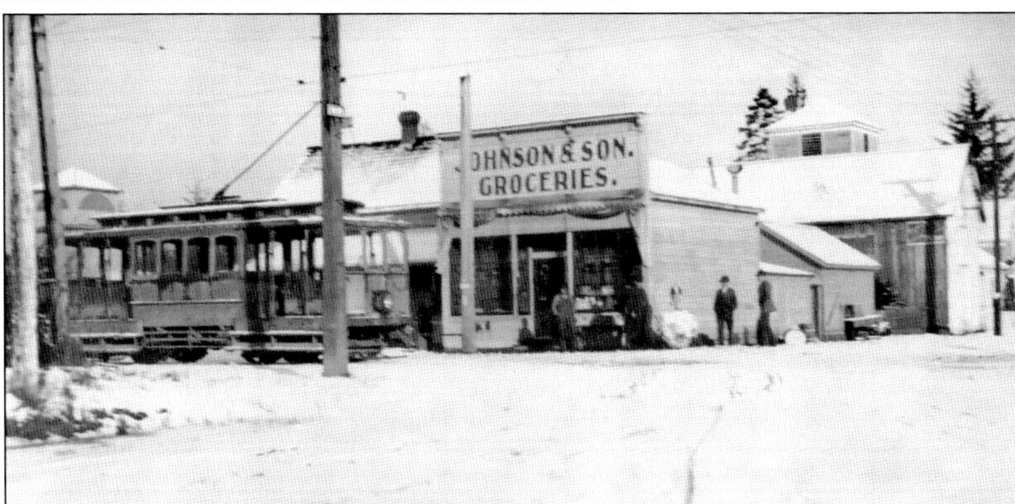

This photograph, taken after a rare Eureka snowfall, shows Johnson and Son Groceries at Sequoia Park. Independent, family-run grocery stores were once a common sight. Horel Smith, who worked for the transit company off and on for 20 years, remembers an attempted robbery at the Johnson and Son store. A passerby apparently scared the would-be robbers away. He also remembers the time that tracks greased by pranksters caused his streetcar to plunge into the Johnson and Son garden beds. (Courtesy of Humboldt State University.)

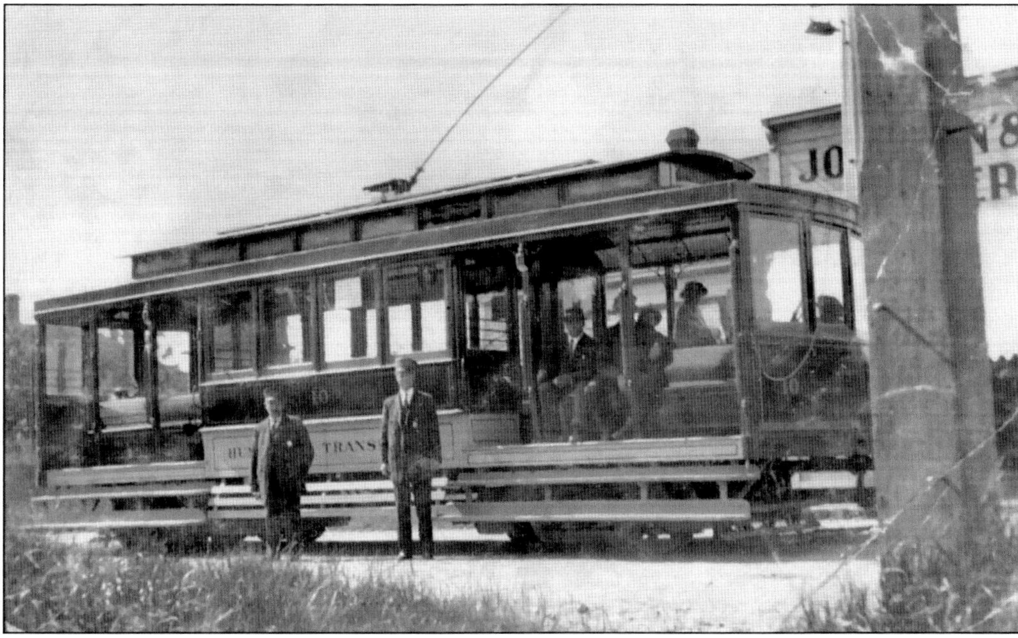

The first open cross-bench car run by Humboldt Transit Company was purchased secondhand from a company in Sacramento. These cars were especially popular for weekend picnickers and were often used on the Sequoia Park line. Shown here is conductor Frank Wornell at left. (Courtesy of the Humboldt County Historical Society.)

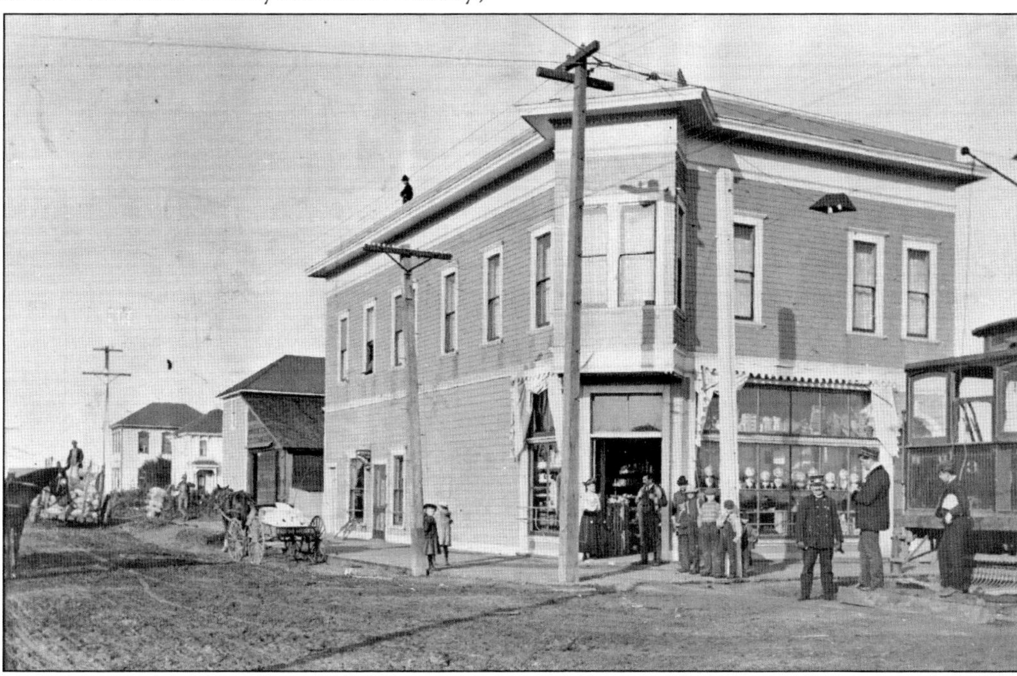

This photograph shows unpaved California Street in 1915. In the doorway is Christian Nick Jensen, who built the grocery store across California Street on the northeast corner. Humboldt Transit Company employees Stine and Bells are shown on the right. (Courtesy of the Humboldt County Historical Society.)

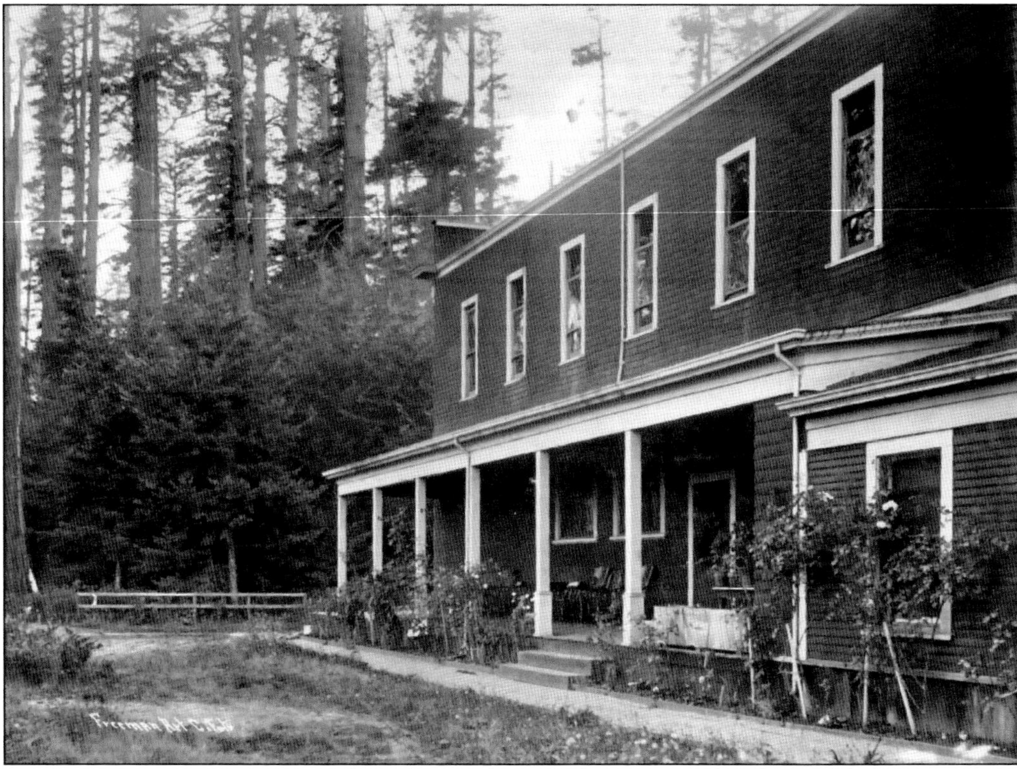

This early-20th-century photograph shows the Sequoia Tavern adjacent to Sequoia Park. The tavern was once the main drinking establishment in the neighborhood. (Courtesy of the Clarke Historical Museum.)

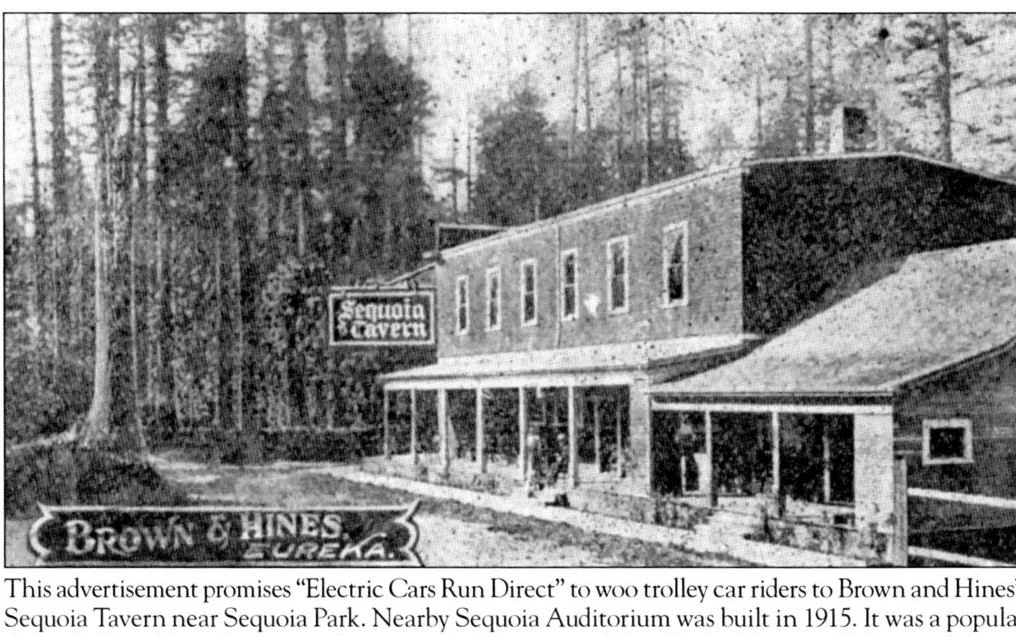

This advertisement promises "Electric Cars Run Direct" to woo trolley car riders to Brown and Hines's Sequoia Tavern near Sequoia Park. Nearby Sequoia Auditorium was built in 1915. It was a popular dance hall and later became a skating rink. (Courtesy of the Clarke Historical Museum.)

This photograph shows a playbill for the Sequoia Auditorium. On July 9, 1926, a huge blaze destroyed the building. The fire threatened the entire park area, and it took firemen five hours to prevent the fire from spreading to the nearby redwoods. The damage done by the fire, not including the giant redwoods consumed at the edge of the park, was estimated at the time to be $15,000. The alleged cause of the early morning fire was a cigarette left burning in a resting room after skating had ended shortly after 10:00 the night before. (Courtesy of the Humboldt County Historical Society.)

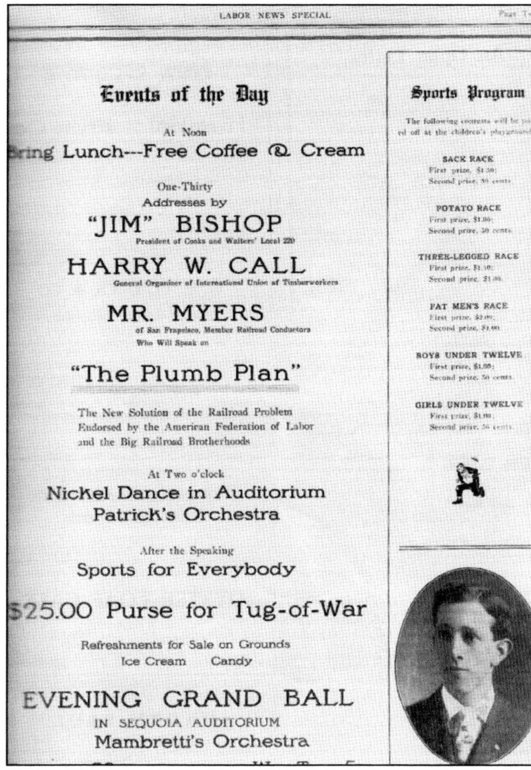
LABOR NEWS SPECIAL

Events of the Day

At Noon

Bring Lunch---Free Coffee & Cream

One-Thirty

Addresses by

"JIM" BISHOP

President of Cooks and Waiters' Local 220

HARRY W. CALL

General Organizer of International Union of Timberworkers

MR. MYERS

of San Francisco, Member Railroad Conductors

Who Will Speak on

"The Plumb Plan"

The New Solution of the Railroad Problem

Endorsed by the American Federation of Labor

and the Big Railroad Brotherhoods

At Two o'clock

Nickel Dance in Auditorium

Patrick's Orchestra

After the Speaking

Sports for Everybody

$25.00 Purse for Tug-of-War

Refreshments for Sale on Grounds

Ice Cream Candy

EVENING GRAND BALL

IN SEQUOIA AUDITORIUM

Mambretti's Orchestra

Sports Program

The following contests will be pulled off at the children's playgrounds:

SACK RACE

First prize, $1.50;

Second prize, 50 cents.

POTATO RACE

First prize, $1.00;

Second prize, 50 cents.

THREE-LEGGED RACE

First prize, $1.50;

Second prize, $1.00.

FAT MEN'S RACE

First prize, $2.00;

Second prize, $1.00.

BOYS UNDER TWELVE

First prize, $1.00;

Second prize, 50 cents.

GIRLS UNDER TWELVE

First prize, $1.00;

Second prize, 50 cents.

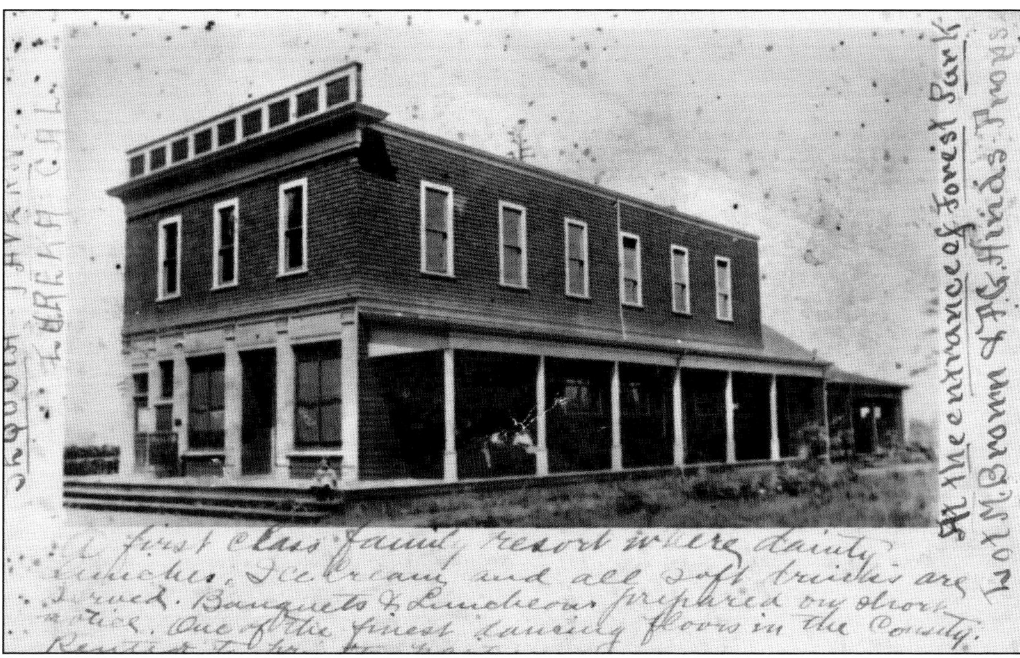

This pre-1907 Sequoia Tavern postcard offers the following description: "A first class family resort where dainty lunches, ice cream, and all soft drinks are served. Banquets and luncheons prepared on short notice. One of the finest dancing floors in the county. Rented to private parties. At the entrance of Forest Park." (Courtesy of Humboldt State University.)

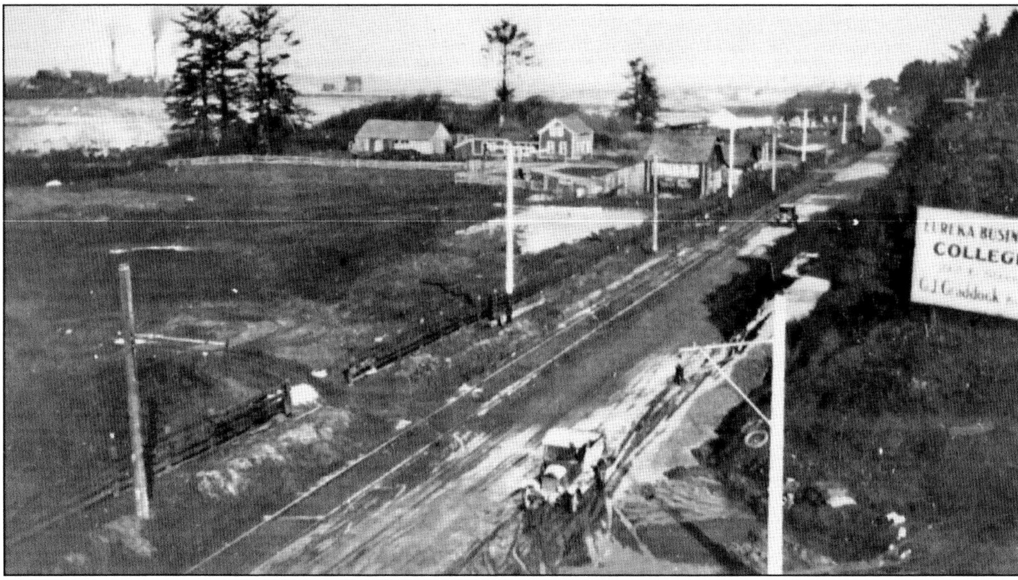

This December 1926 photograph shows Broadway at Henderson Street. Hap Waters remembers a story about this stretch of road where the trolley car line traveled the wrong way for traffic traveling southbound down Broadway. One Saturday night during the Prohibition era, the Broadway streetcar, on its final night's run, was knocked off its track by a motorist. The collision remained a mystery until a Ferndale farmer confided in his mechanic at Harper's Ford Garage. The farmer thought the vehicle was a car, traveling the wrong way with only one headlight. (Courtesy of the Humboldt County Historical Society.)

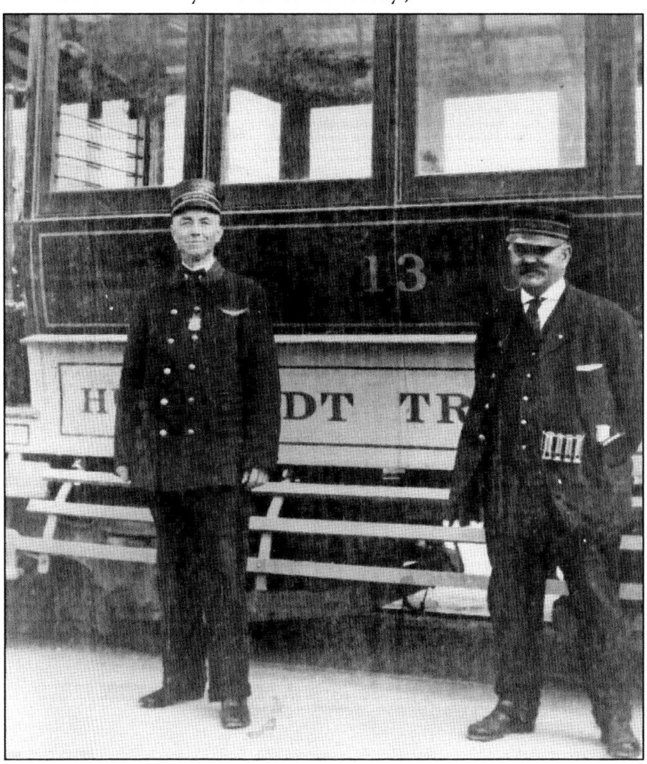

This 1912 photograph shows, from left to right, William Tripp (motorman) and George B. Hinde (conductor). Hugh Jones (not shown), who worked for Humboldt Transit Company as a conductor and motorman, recalls that the years 1909 to 1916 were filled with good days where everyone knew everyone because they all rode the streetcars. (Courtesy of the Clarke Historical Museum.)

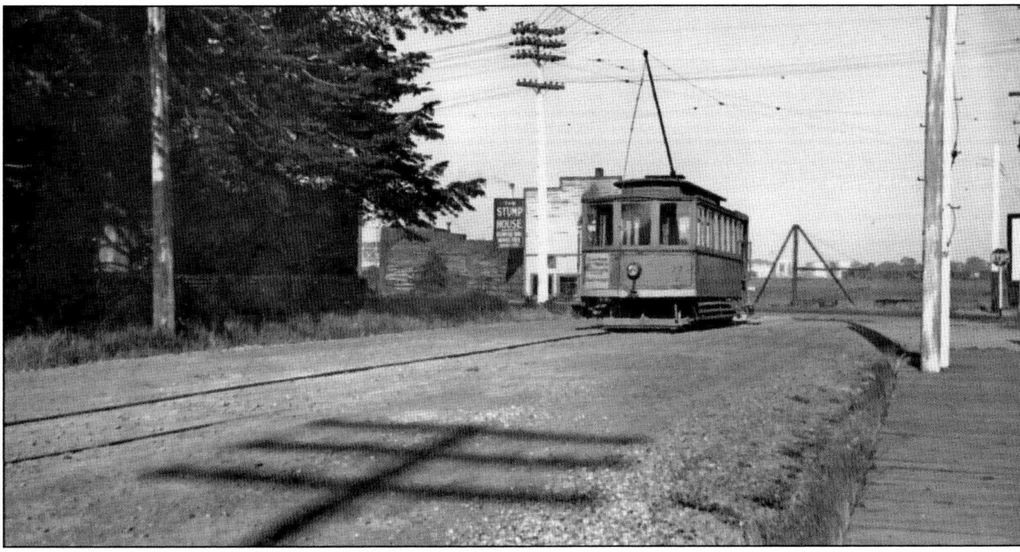

This photograph shows a trolley car at Clark Street and Broadway near the famous Eureka Stump House. The Stump House, established in 1900, was a tourist attraction and souvenir shop made out of a tar-paper-covered wood framework covered with redwood bark and with giant redwood rounds at each end. It closed in the early 1990s. (Courtesy of the Humboldt County Historical Society.)

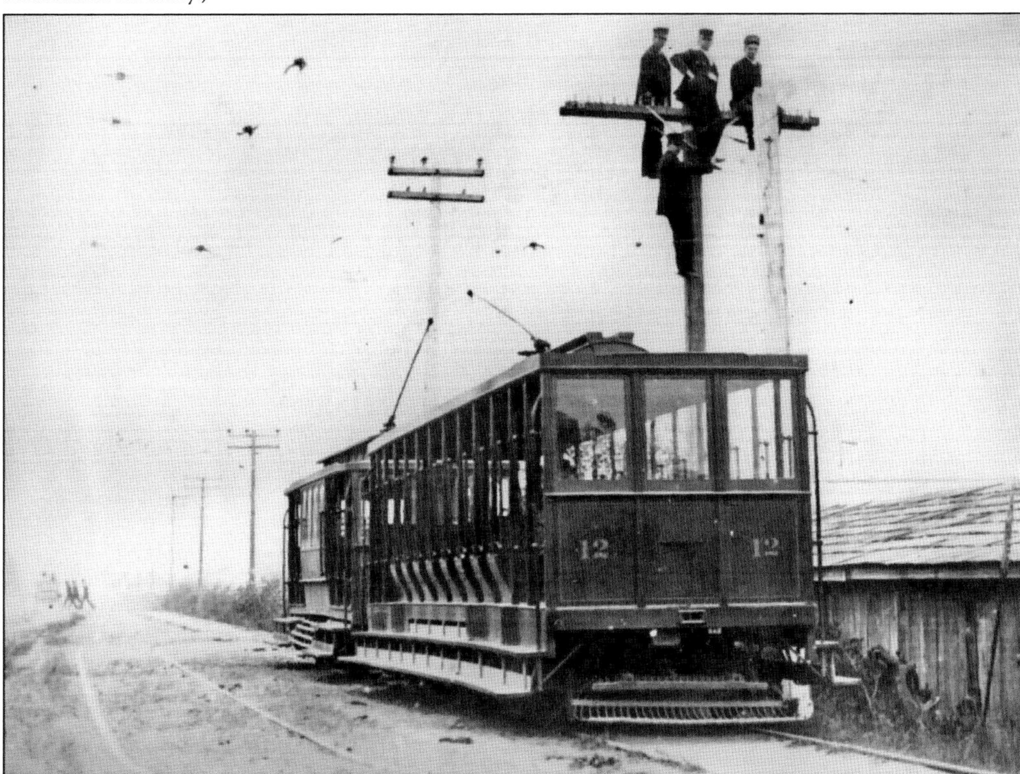

This photograph shows trolley car personnel atop a telephone pole on Broadway near the South Park Race Track. (Courtesy of the Humboldt County Historical Society.)

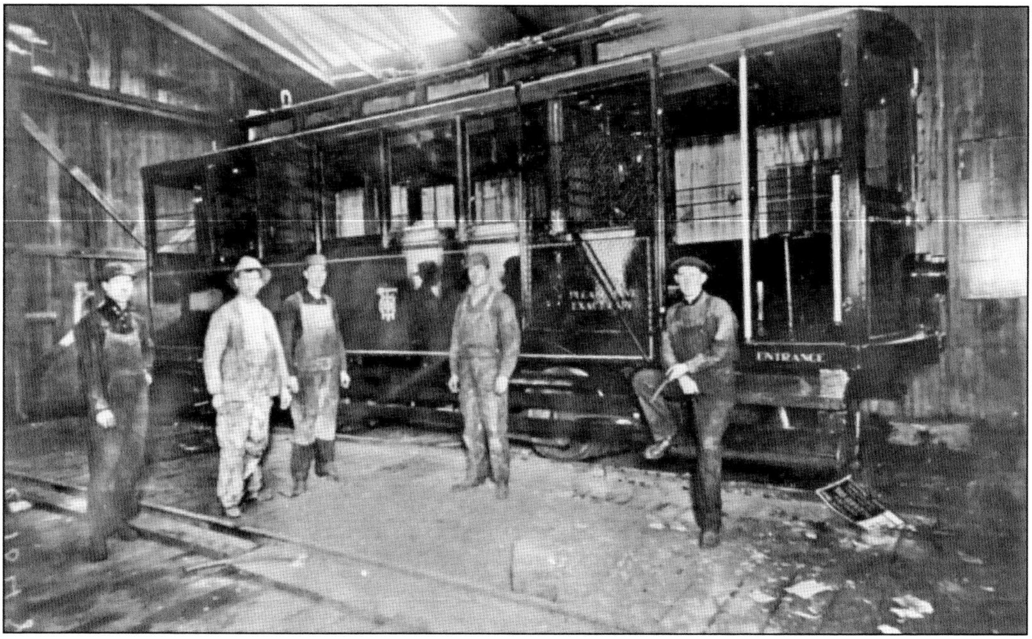

This group photograph shows Humboldt Transit Company personnel in the Eureka carbarn with a trolley car. Carbarns typically are equipped so that the cars can turn around inside the building, entering in one direction and exiting in the other. (Courtesy of the Clarke Historical Museum.)

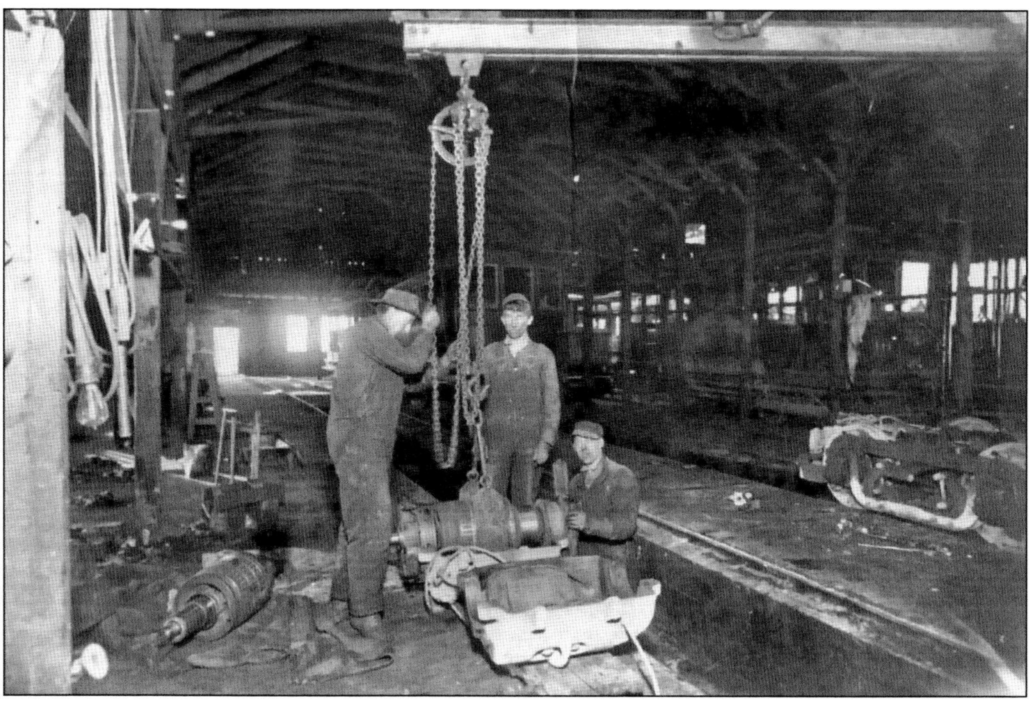

This photograph shows, from left to right, William Ford, an unidentified man, and George Ford in the Eureka carbarn in 1913. A new carbarn at J and Harris Streets was built in 1915. (Courtesy of the Humboldt County Historical Society.)

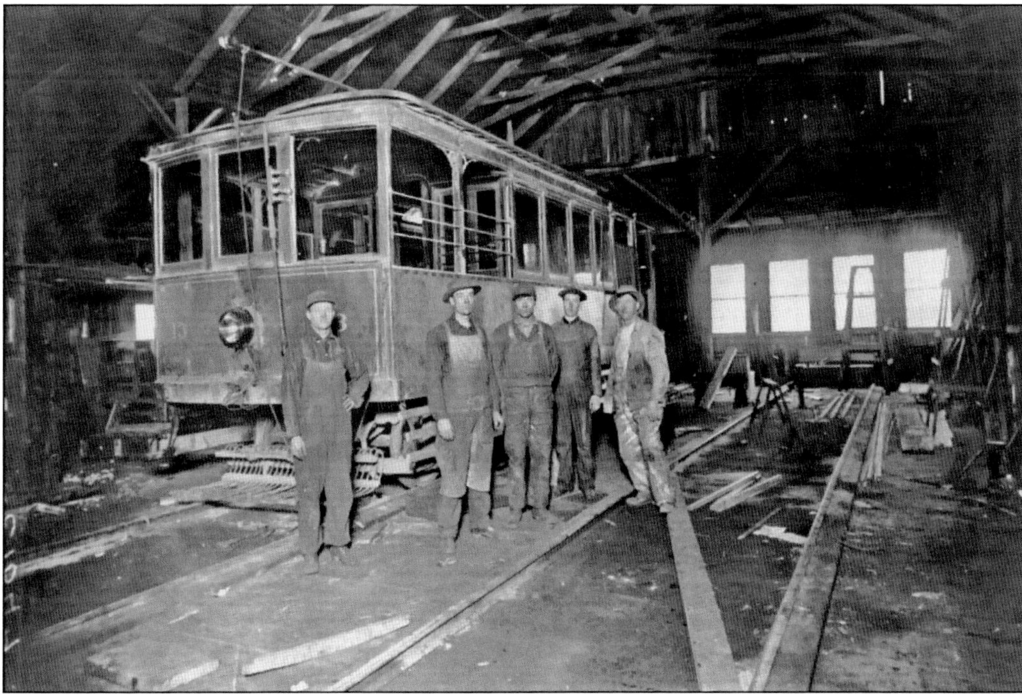

This photograph shows the Humboldt Transit Company shop around 1915 with the first No. 13 streetcar slated for rebuilding and renumbering as second No. 3. The second man from the left is Frank Casedy and the fifth man is Jack Clark. Others are unidentified. (Courtesy of the Humboldt County Historical Society.)

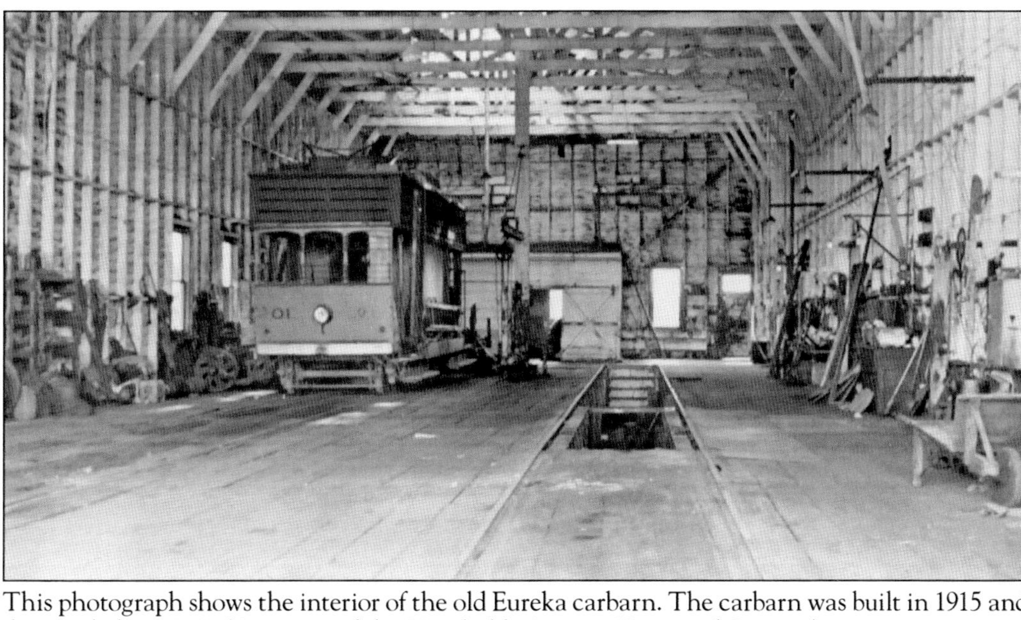

This photograph shows the interior of the old Eureka carbarn. The carbarn was built in 1915 and dismantled in 1940. (Courtesy of the Humboldt County Historical Society.)

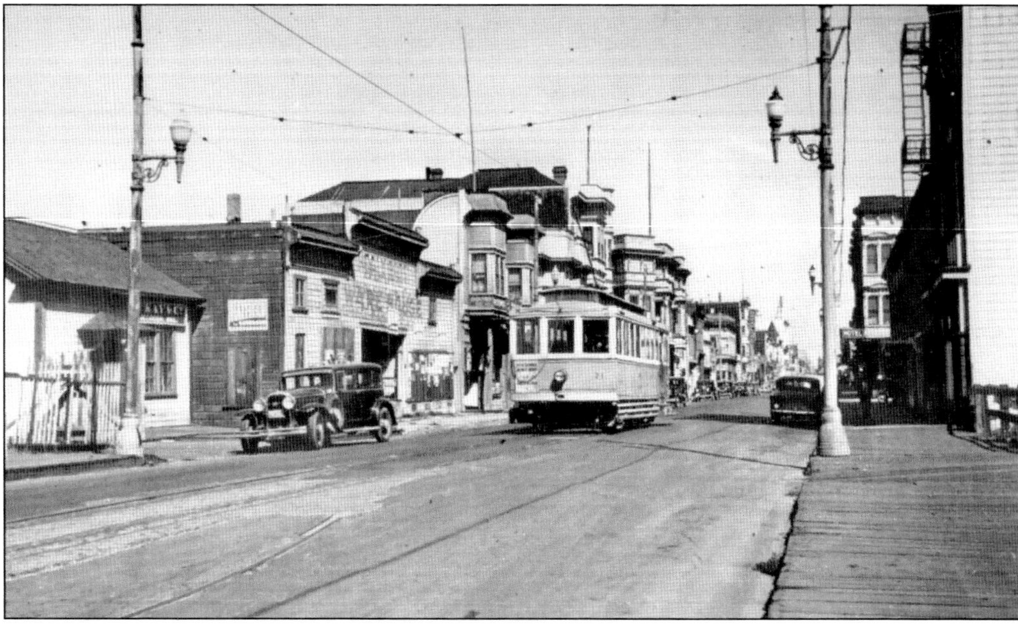

This 1938 photograph shows the trolley car making its way along Second Street near B Street. The redwood plank sidewalk shown was a common sight throughout Eureka until concrete technology improved and timber became less plentiful. (Courtesy of the Clarke Historical Museum.)

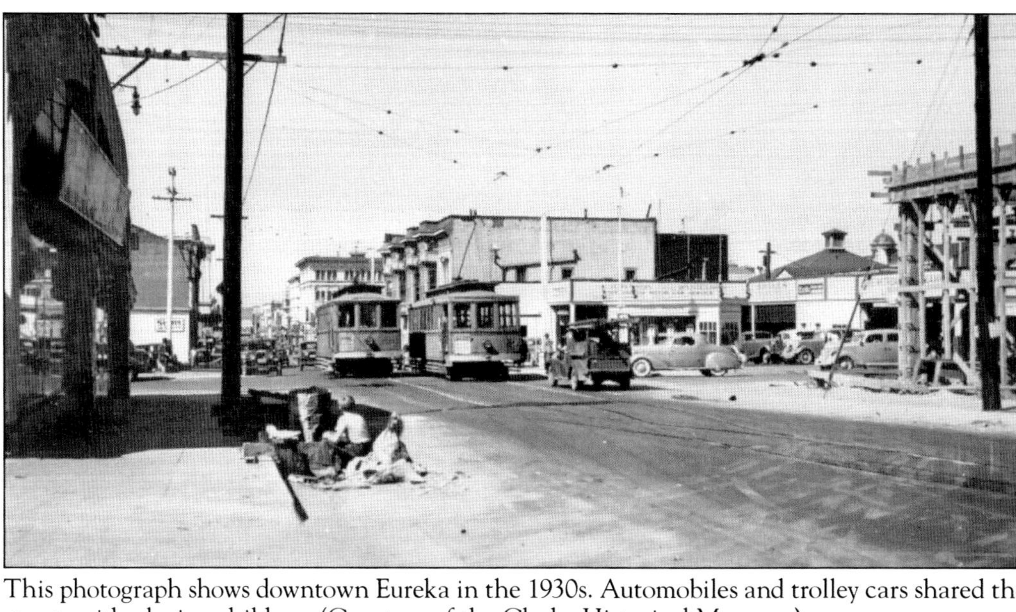

This photograph shows downtown Eureka in the 1930s. Automobiles and trolley cars shared the streets with playing children. (Courtesy of the Clarke Historical Museum.)

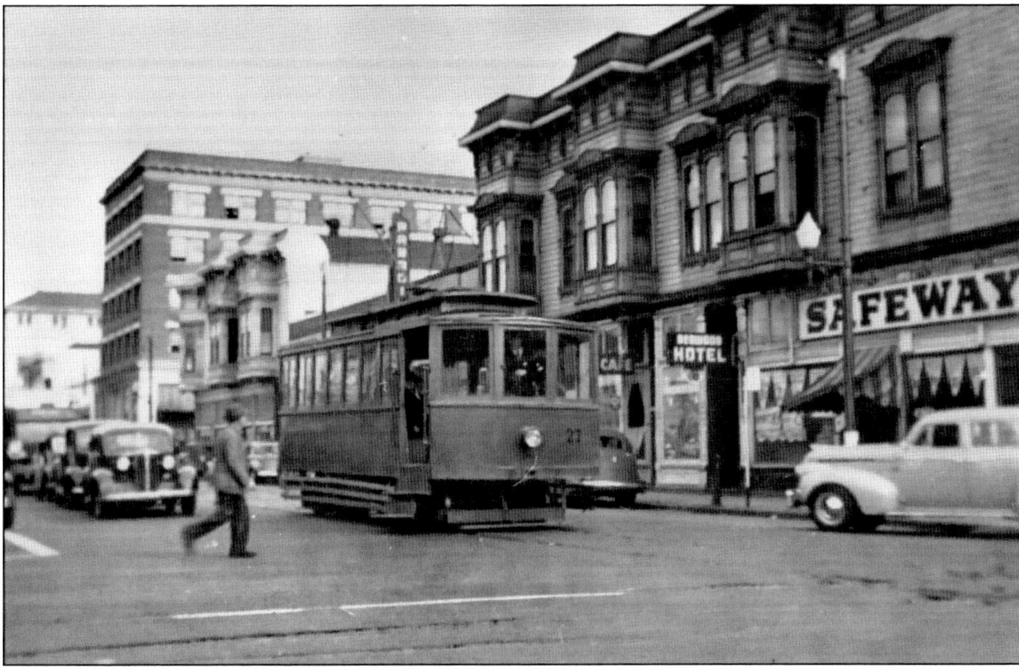

This 1938 photograph shows the old downtown Safeway store in 1938. Safeway stores were incorporated in 1914 to operate a chain of grocery stores in southern California. After merging with Skagg's grocery stores in 1926, Safeway had 332 stores, and Skagg's operated almost as many in northern California, the Rocky Mountain states, and the Pacific Northwest. In 1931, the MacMarr grocery chain was merged into Safeway, and in 1934, MacMarr's president, Lingan A. Warren, became president of Safeway. (Courtesy of the Clarke Historical Museum.)

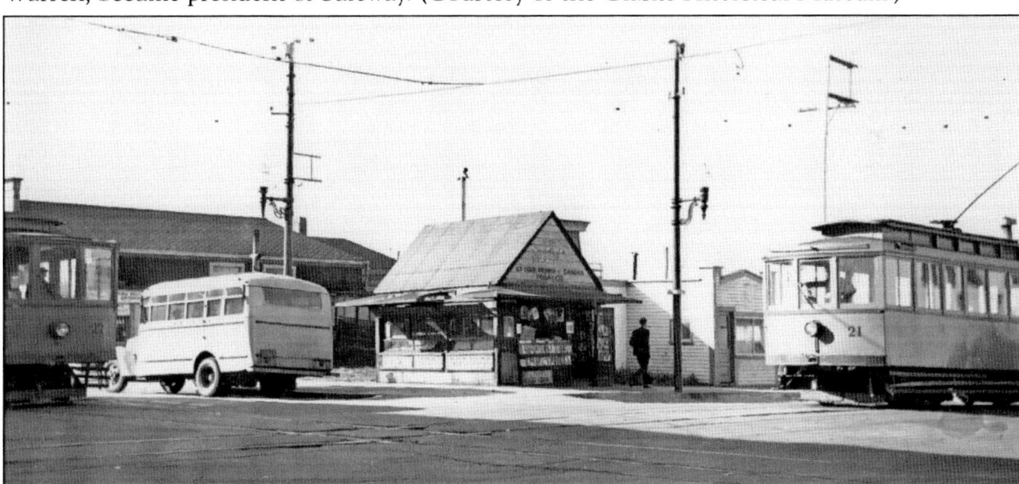

Taken in 1940 at the corner of Fifth and E Streets in Eureka, this photograph showing both a city bus and a trolley hints at the end of the electric trolley system coming soon to Eureka. Because of declining ridership, the city council proposed in September 1939 to junk the railway and replace it with either a city-owned or privately owned bus system. A special election was called on November 7, 1939. The vote to junk the trolley system prevailed 4,933 to 2,597. The proposed expenditure of $50,000 for new buses failed by 87 votes. (Courtesy of the Humboldt County Historical Society.)

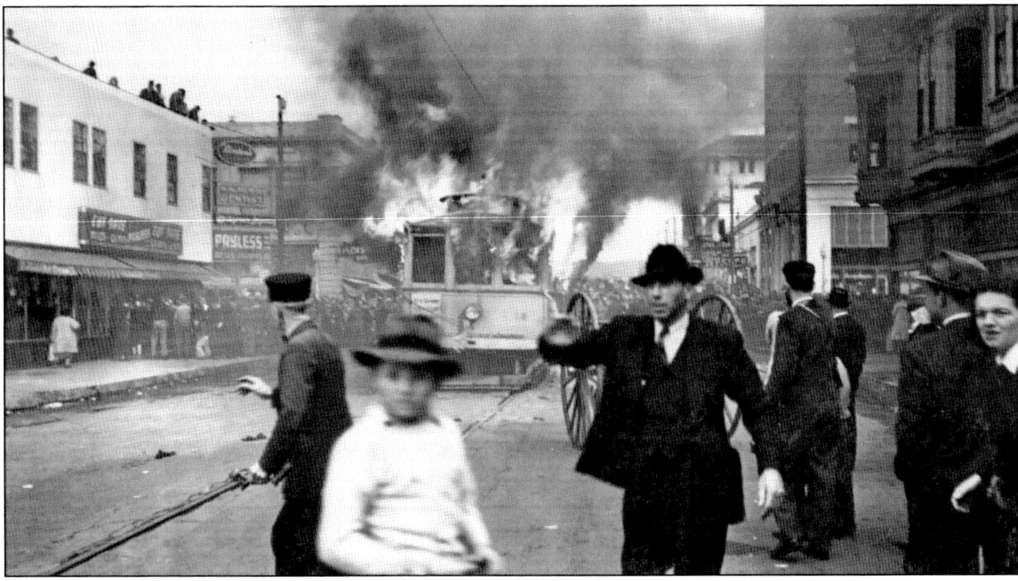

Tuesday, February 20, 1940, was the last day of regular streetcar service. A celebration was planned for the following Saturday. Two of the men identified, Jack Tierney (far left) and Jack Villa (middle foreground), react to the intentional burning of a trolley car on Fifth Street between E and F Streets during the city celebration of what was then seen as a step toward modernization. (Courtesy of the Clarke Historical Museum.)

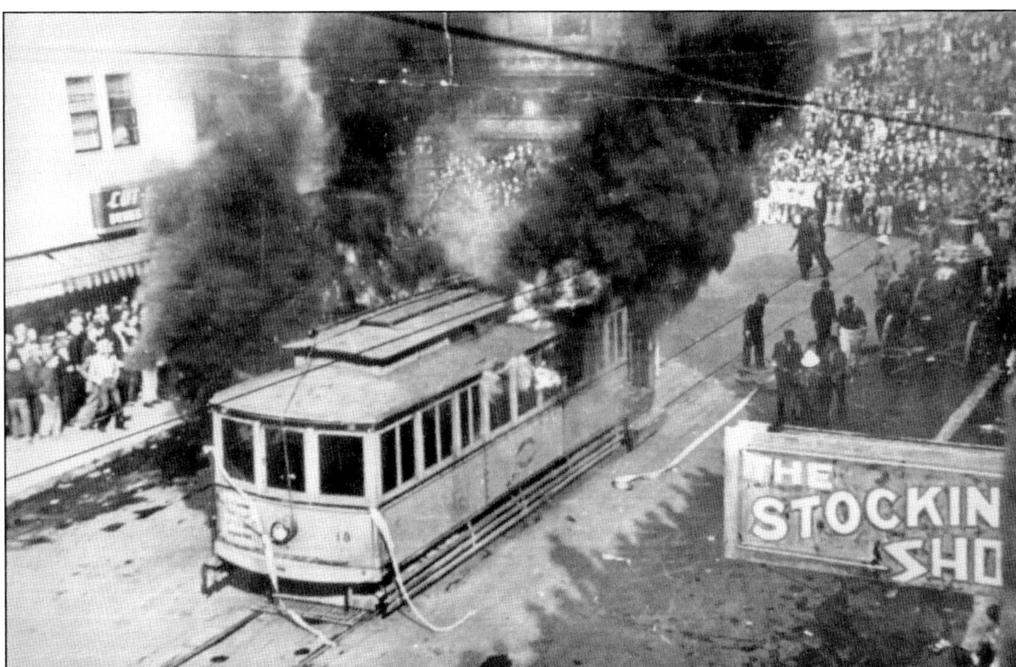

After a large celebration and parade, Mayor H. R. Simmonds addressed the crowd and expressed the belief that Eureka was entering an era of rapid growth and improvement. Car No. 18 was set on fire, and the fire quickly burned out of control. (Courtesy of the Clarke Historical Museum.)

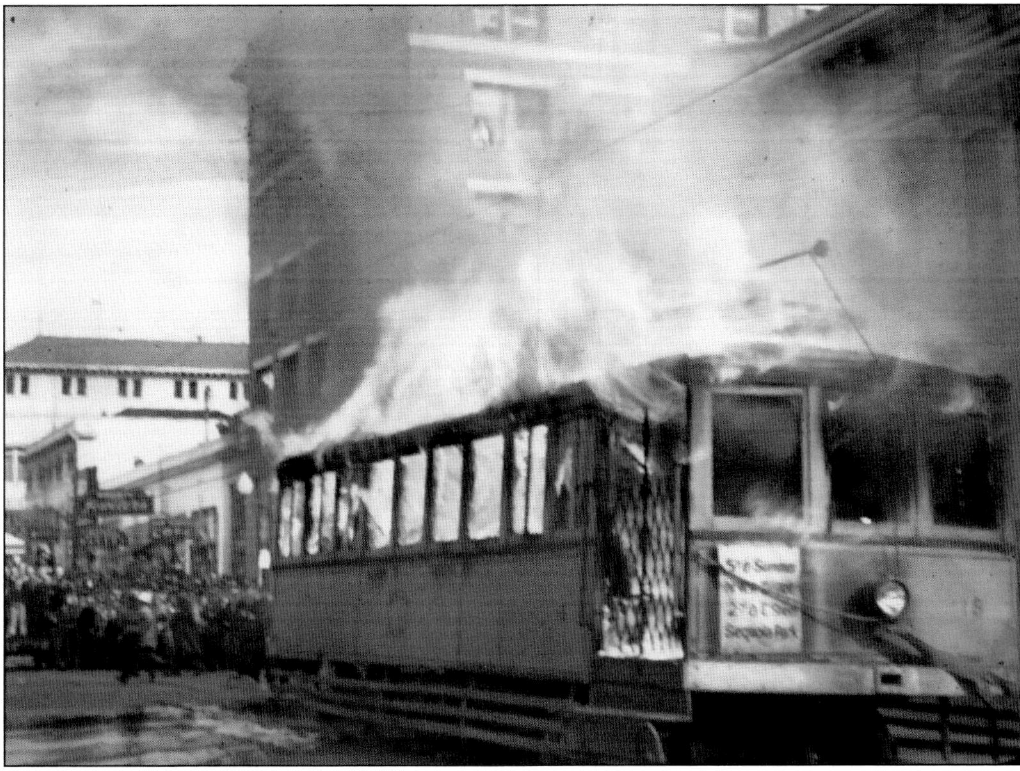

This photograph shows how badly out of control this symbolic fire became. Ironically, the burning trolley car was one of the Sequoia Park cars. The era of Eureka families riding the trolley cars out to Sequoia Park was over. (Courtesy of the Humboldt County Historical Society.)

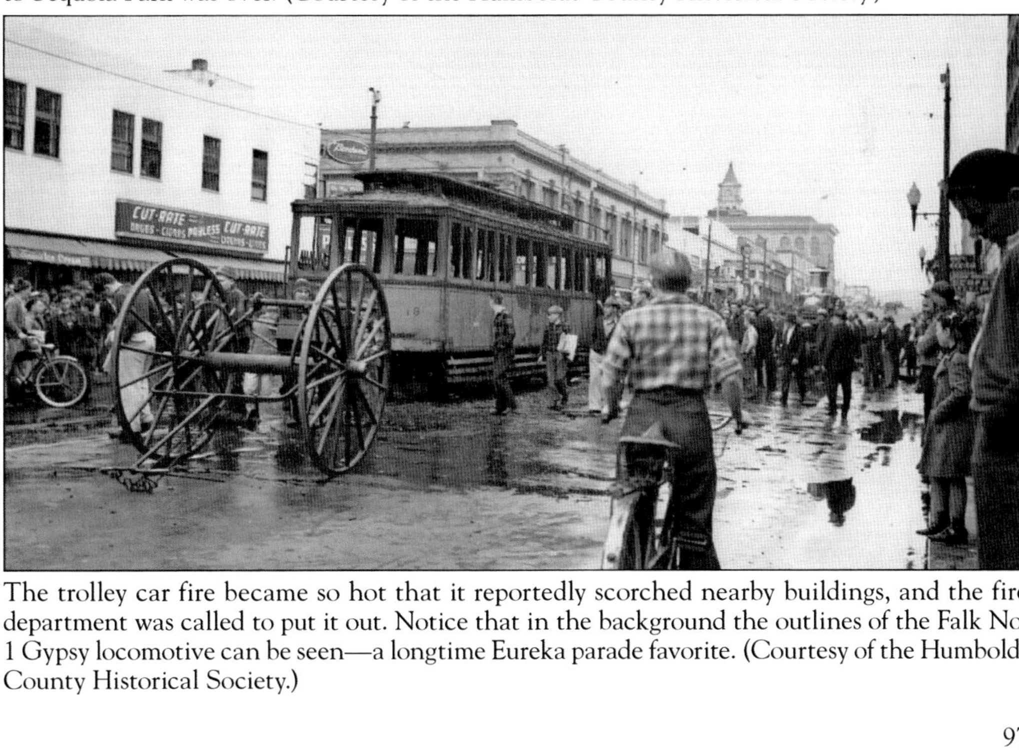

The trolley car fire became so hot that it reportedly scorched nearby buildings, and the fire department was called to put it out. Notice that in the background the outlines of the Falk No. 1 Gypsy locomotive can be seen—a longtime Eureka parade favorite. (Courtesy of the Humboldt County Historical Society.)

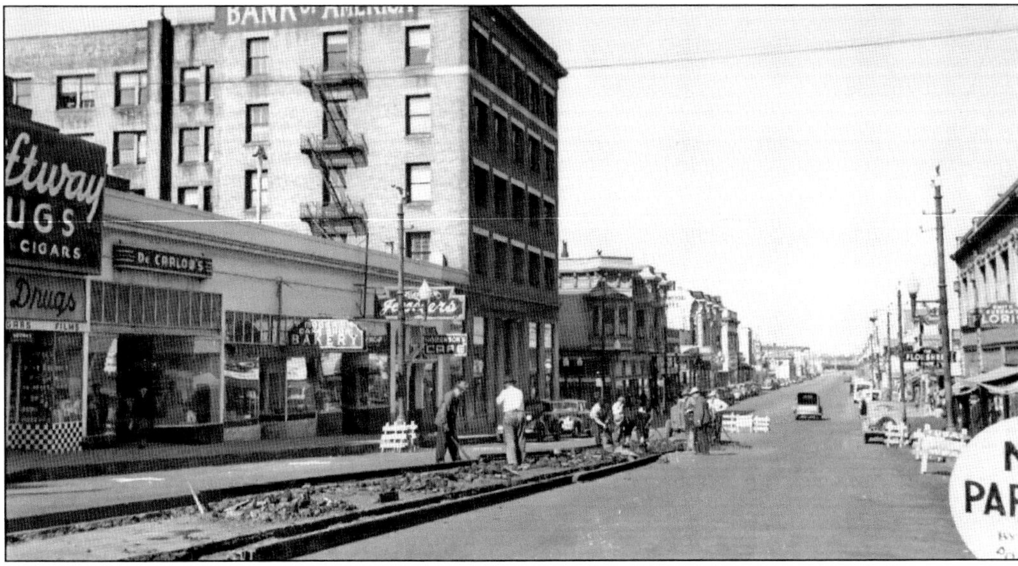

The laborious process of pulling up the existing trolley tracks and pouring asphalt to produce a smooth, car- and truck-friendly surface was slow going. This photograph, taken in May 1942, shows the removal of tracks on Fifth Street. (Courtesy of the Clarke Historical Museum.)

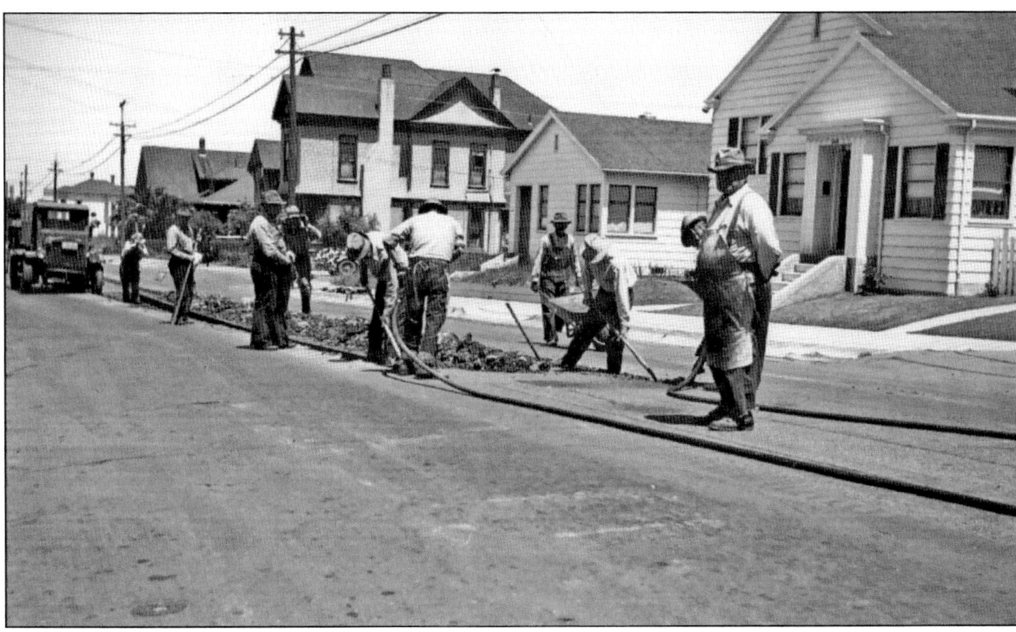

This photograph shows the work of trolley-track removal progressing up E Street on July 6, 1942. The resulting ease of car and truck traffic flow once the trolley tracks were removed was important as the logging boom of the late 1940s would send hundreds of trucks through Eureka on the way to and from logging sites. (Courtesy of the Humboldt County Historical Society.)

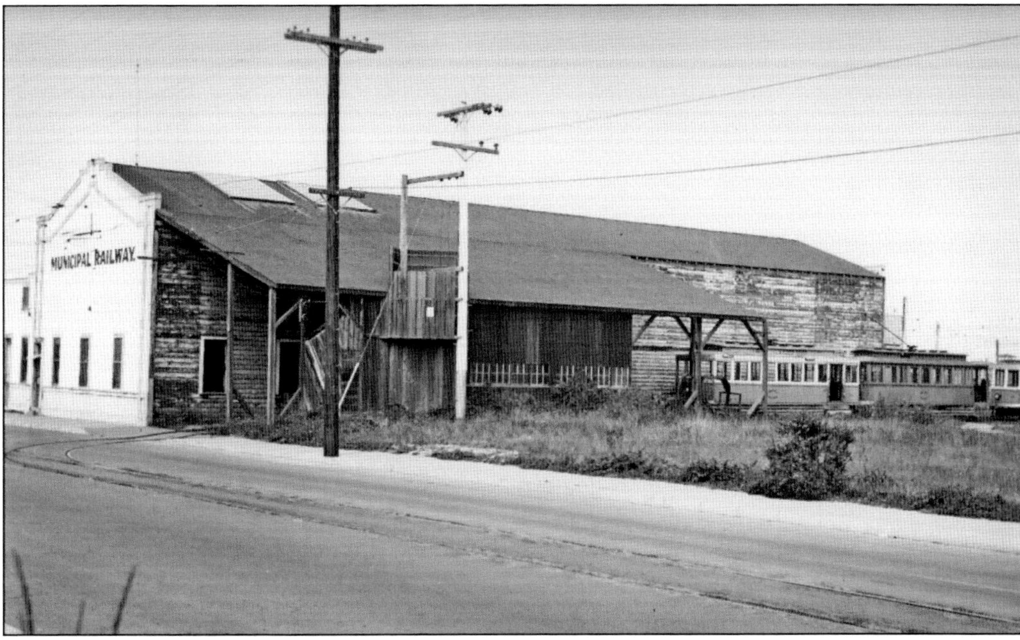

This 1938 photograph shows the old municipal railway carbarn at Harris and J Streets shortly before it was torn down. The land on which it was built was purchased by the Humboldt Transit Company in 1915 for $4,000. Between August and November 1915, the carbarn, which measured 240 feet by 240 feet and included a generous shop, was constructed. In 1940, not long after the trolley cars stopped operation, the carbarn was torn down, and all the trolley cars were junked. (Courtesy of the Clarke Historical Museum.)

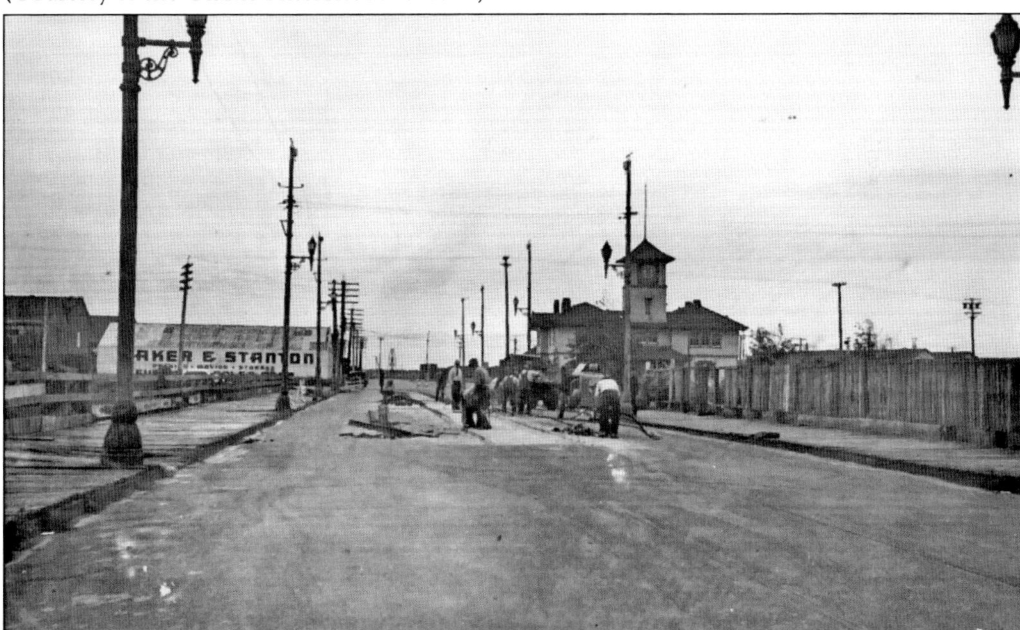

This photograph, looking west on Second Street, shows men removing trolley tracks on May 30, 1942. Notice the old-style streetlamps and the redwood plank sidewalks. (Courtesy of the Humboldt County Historical Society.)

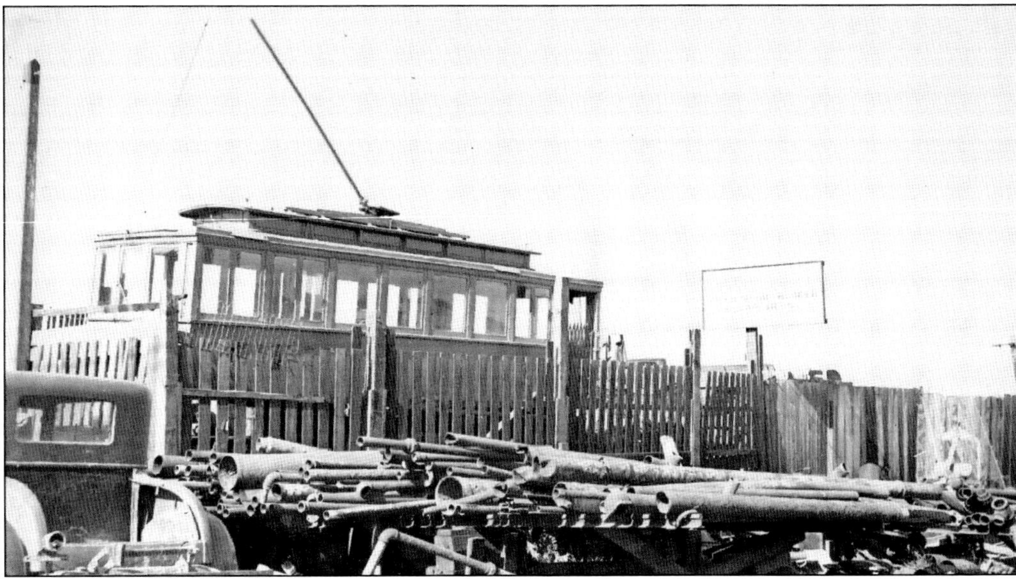

The abandoned No. 17 trolley car sits in Breeden's Junk Yard at 530 First Street in Eureka. (Courtesy of the Humboldt County Historical Society.)

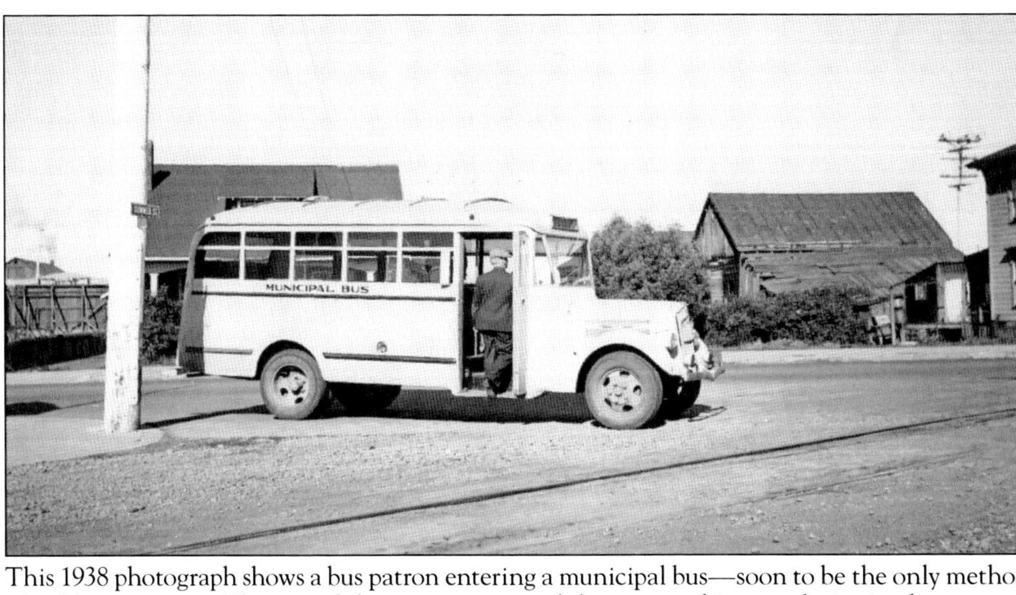

This 1938 photograph shows a bus patron entering a municipal bus—soon to be the only method of public transport. The use of the private automobile increased in popularity in the years to follow. (Courtesy of the Humboldt County Historical Society.)

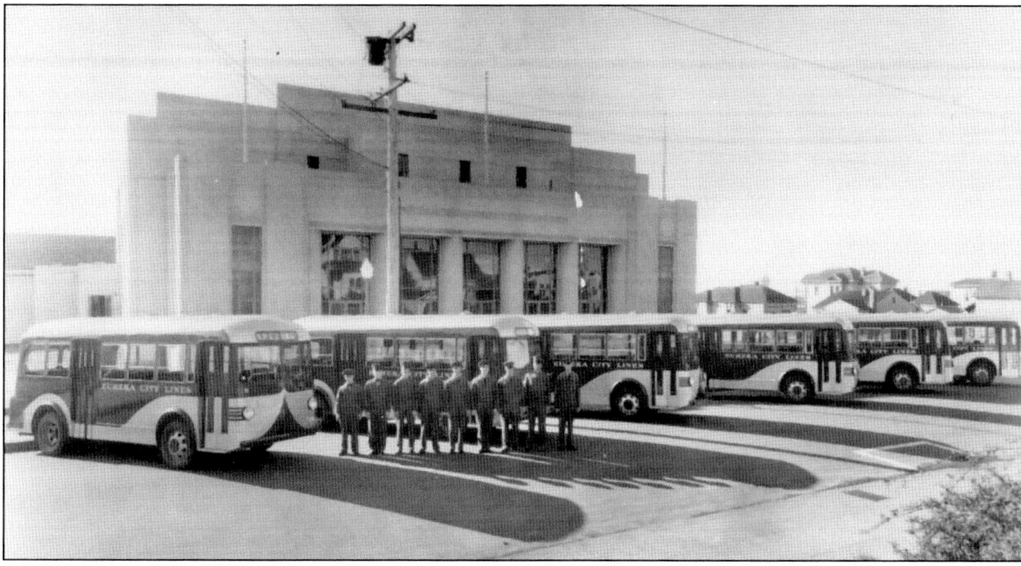

This photograph shows the Eureka City Lines bus fleet in front of the Eureka Municipal Auditorium on F Street. The Eureka Municipal Auditorium building was a Works Progress Administration (WPA) project and is an example of the art deco style. (Courtesy of the Humboldt County Historical Society.)

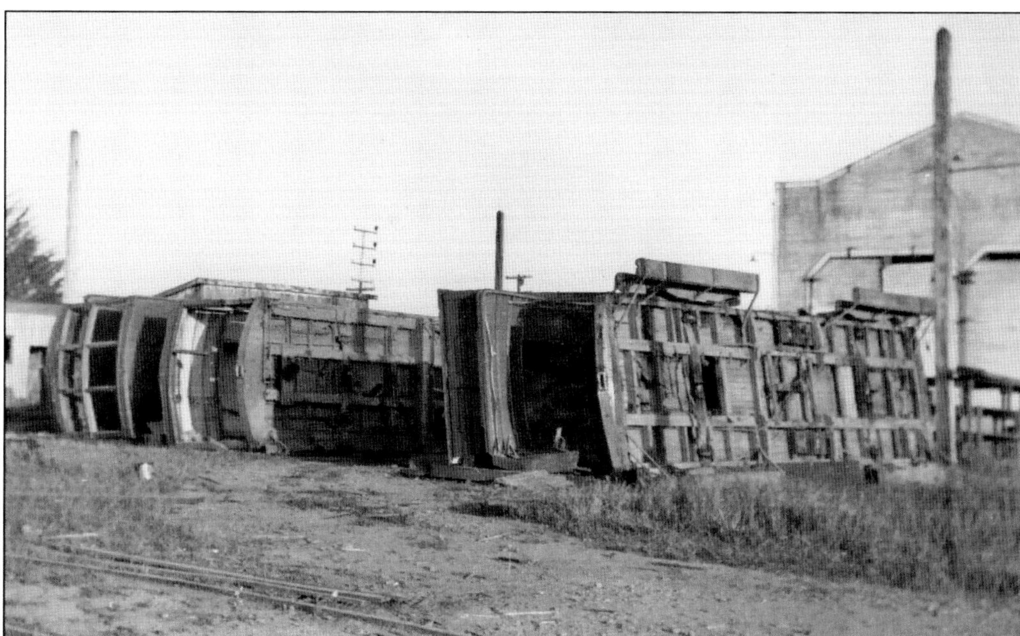

This photograph shows the junked trolleys next to the old Municipal Railway building near the Eureka waterfront. (Courtesy of the Humboldt County Historical Society.)

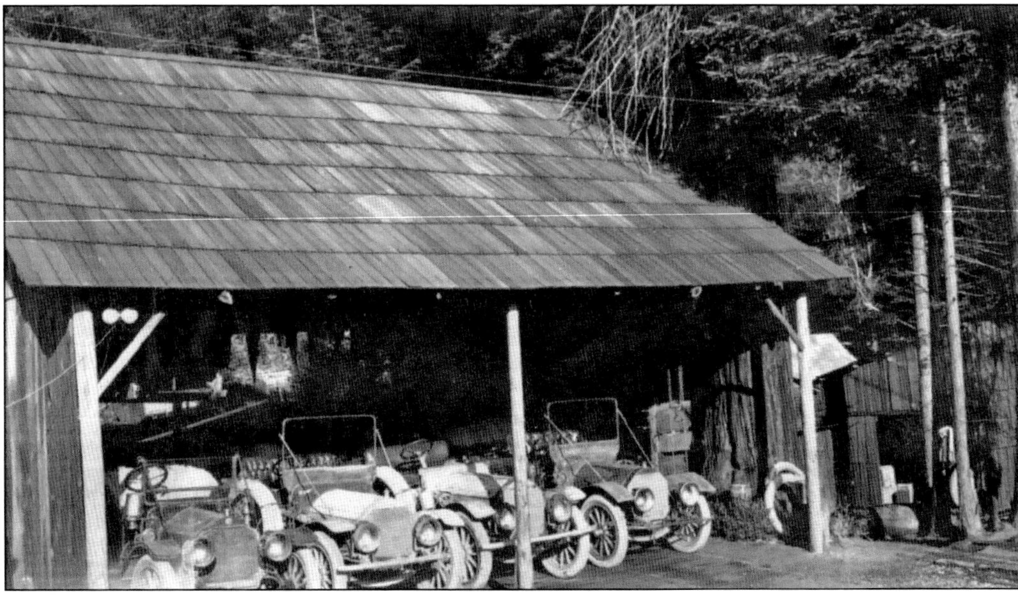

This photograph, taken of an automobile shed near Sequoia Park, shows the open car models common during the early automobile era. Open cars were cheaper to make and were therefore more widely available. By the 1920s and 1930s, thanks to Henry Ford's mass-produced Model T, car ownership became a reality for many families. (Courtesy of the Clarke Historical Museum.)

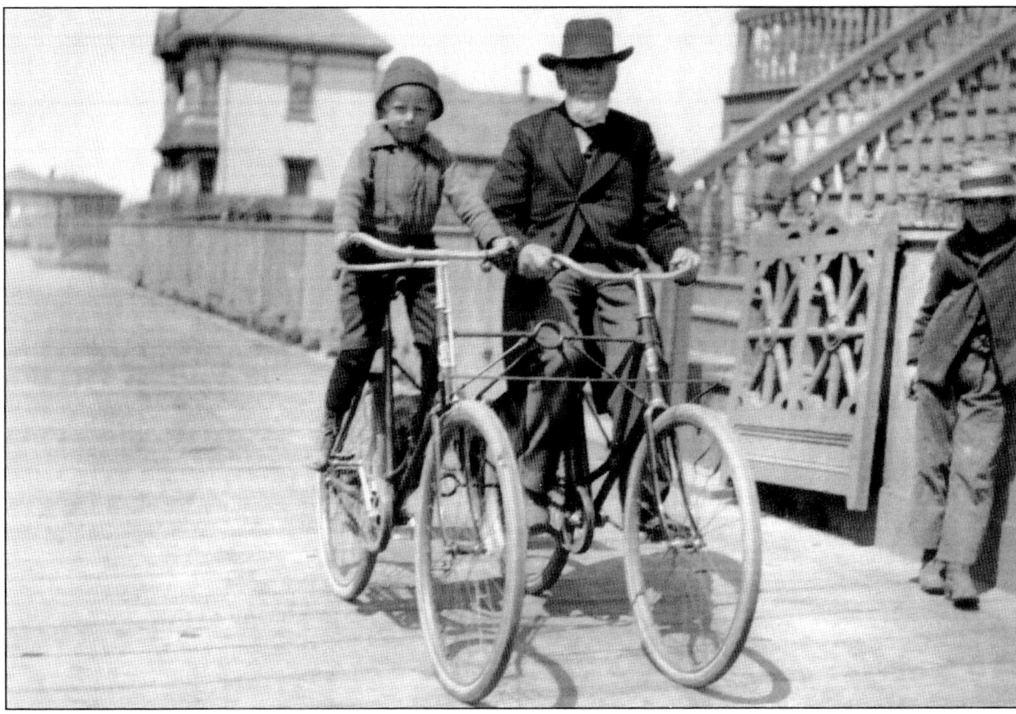

Notice that young and old alike used the same mass-produced bicycle model, in this case welded into a tandem. Redwood plank sidewalks formed the first sidewalks in Eureka. In the downtown area, the sidewalks were 12-feet wide with planks running crosswise. The last remaining plank sidewalk was removed in 1993. (Courtesy of the Clarke Historical Museum.)

Six

Performers in Eureka and Sequoia Park

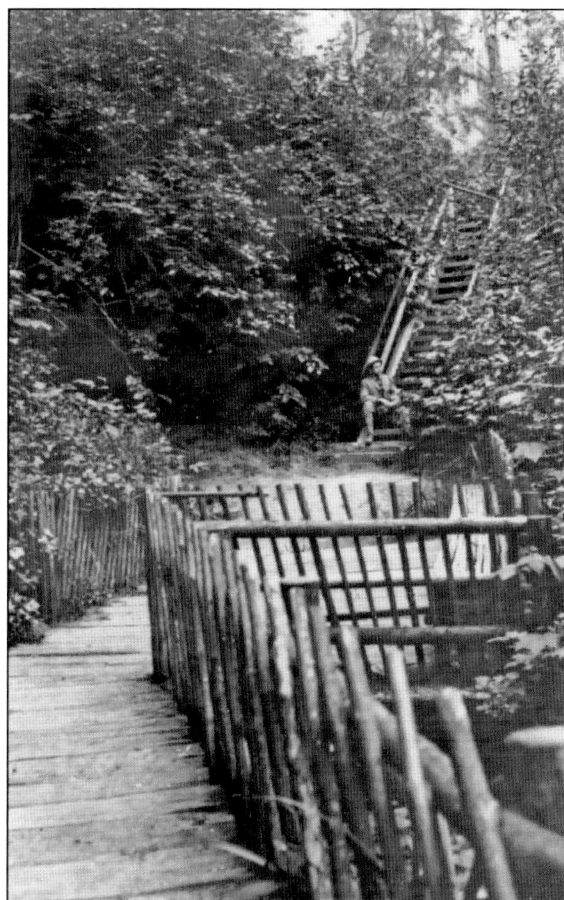

Sequoia Park was not only a draw for local picnickers and community groups, but also for actors and other performers. Where there were crowds, so too were there performers eager to be seen by park visitors. Traveling performers of all kinds were common throughout the late 19th and early 20th centuries. Sequoia Park provided a beautiful backdrop for publicity images. The romantic tale of the park's origins also inspired three versions of the film *The Valley of the Giants*. (Courtesy Humboldt County Historical Society, Phegley Collection.)

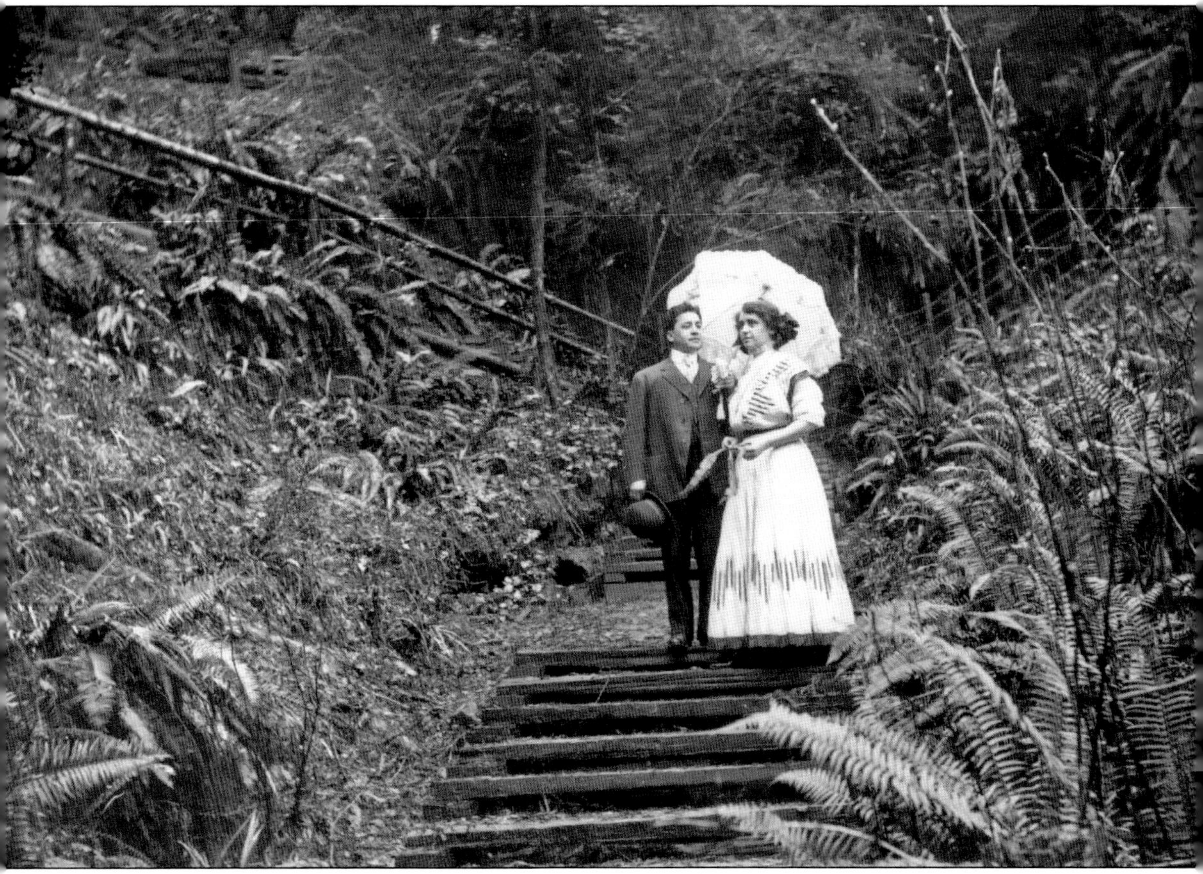

This photograph shows a man and woman, most likely actors, at the top of one of the natural walkways in Sequoia Park. R. J. Baker, a photographer who resided in Eureka from 1904 to 1910 and maintained ties to Humboldt County throughout his life, took this photograph and others around 1907 as part of a series. It is typical of the kind of dramatic still photographs sought by actors at the time. (Courtesy of Humboldt State University.)

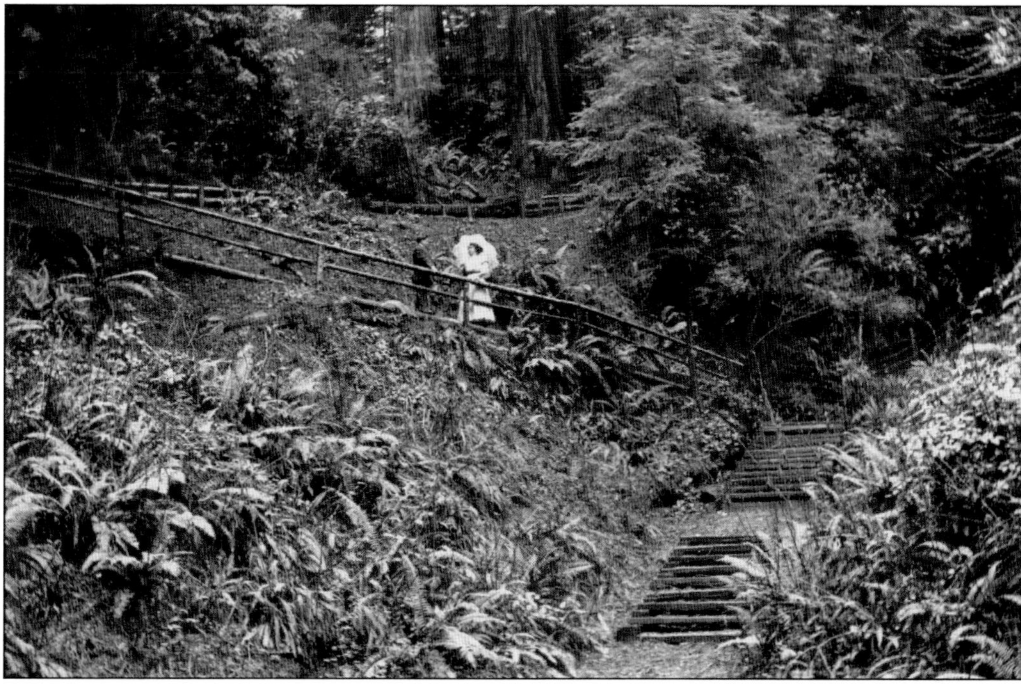

This photograph is one of a series of photographs taken by R. J. Baker of various stock company actors who came to him around 1907 for publicity photographs. (Courtesy of Humboldt State University.)

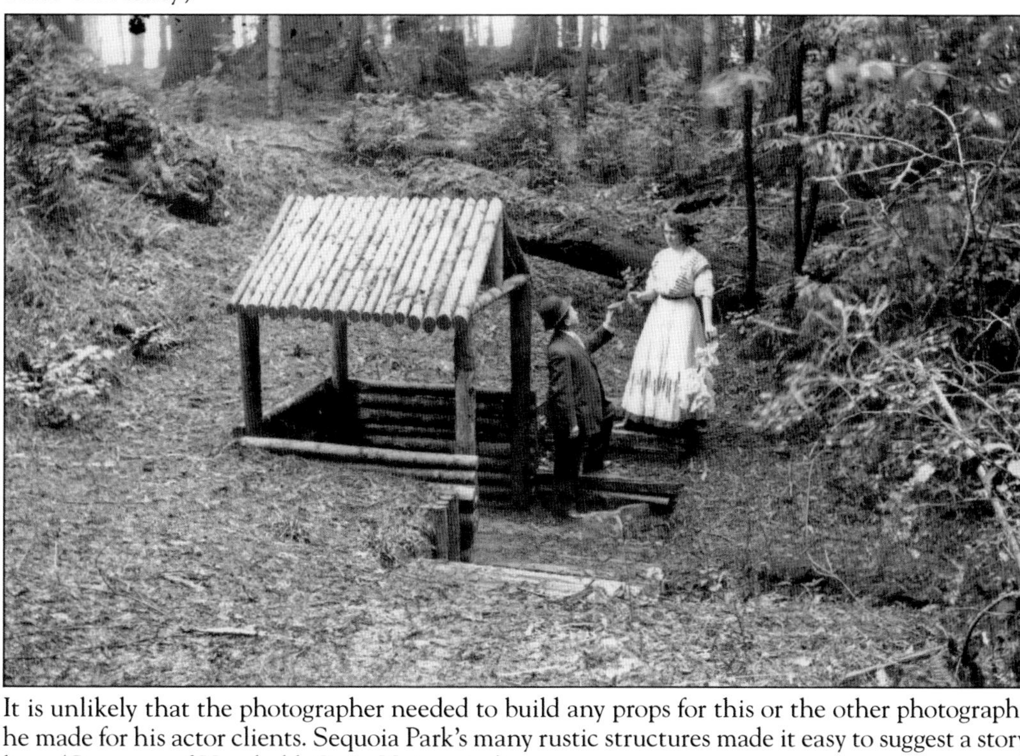

It is unlikely that the photographer needed to build any props for this or the other photographs he made for his actor clients. Sequoia Park's many rustic structures made it easy to suggest a story line. (Courtesy of Humboldt State University.)

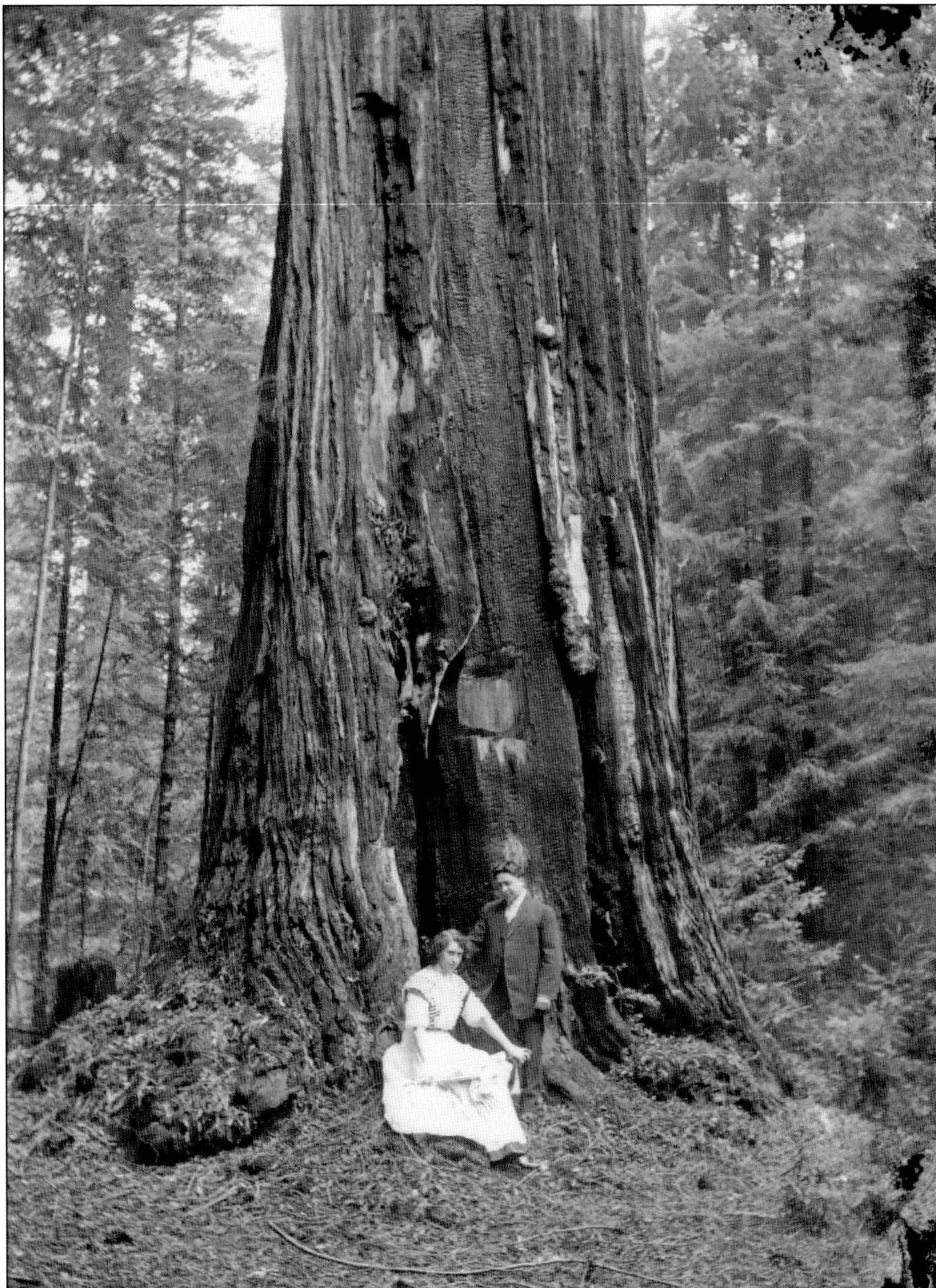

This R. J. Baker photograph, showing the same unidentified man and woman seen in other images from the series, indicates that perhaps this particular tree was a favorite of his for posing his photographic subjects. This giant redwood appears many times throughout his work and is today still standing on the north side of Sequoia Park. (Courtesy of Humboldt State University.)

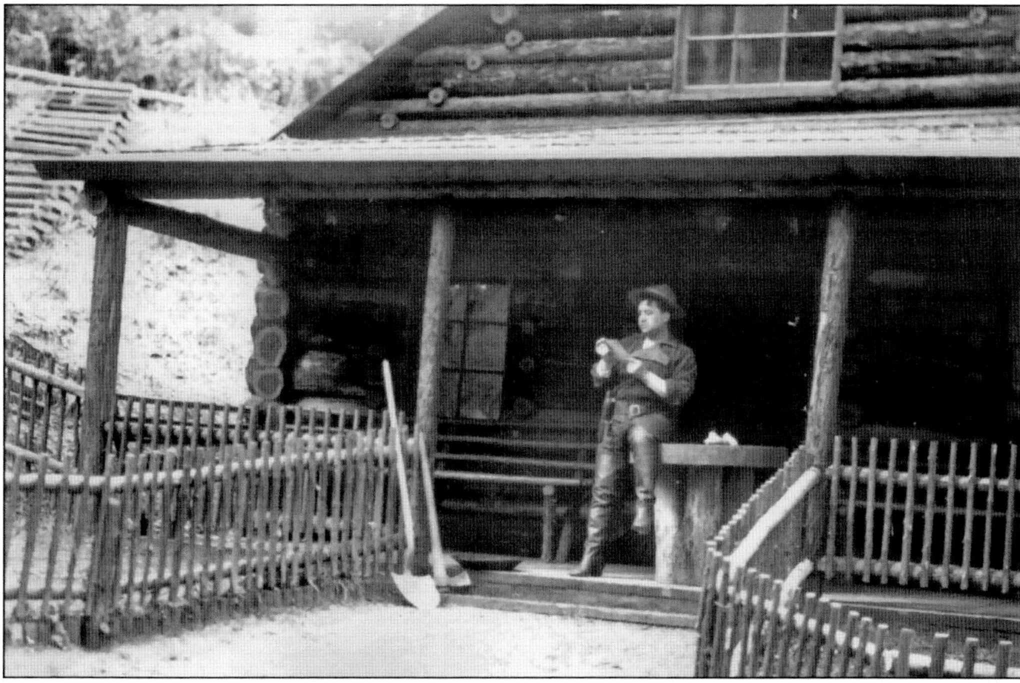

This unidentified actor is shown reading a letter on the porch of the old log cabin at Sequoia Park in 1907. R. J. Baker recorded that this photograph and others in the series were taken for use in a song illustration for George Sousa. (Courtesy of Humboldt State University.)

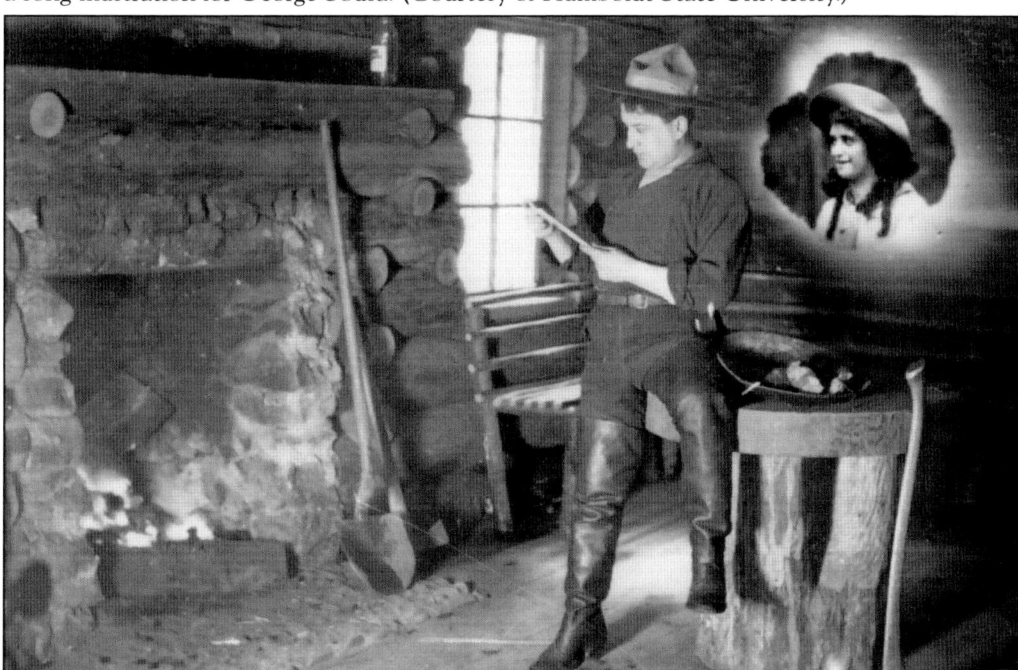

This unusual photograph is from a glass plate negative of another negative with the woman's face incorporated into the image. It shows the actor inside the log cabin at Sequoia Park. Today all that remains of the log cabin is the stone hearth shown. (Courtesy of Humboldt State University.)

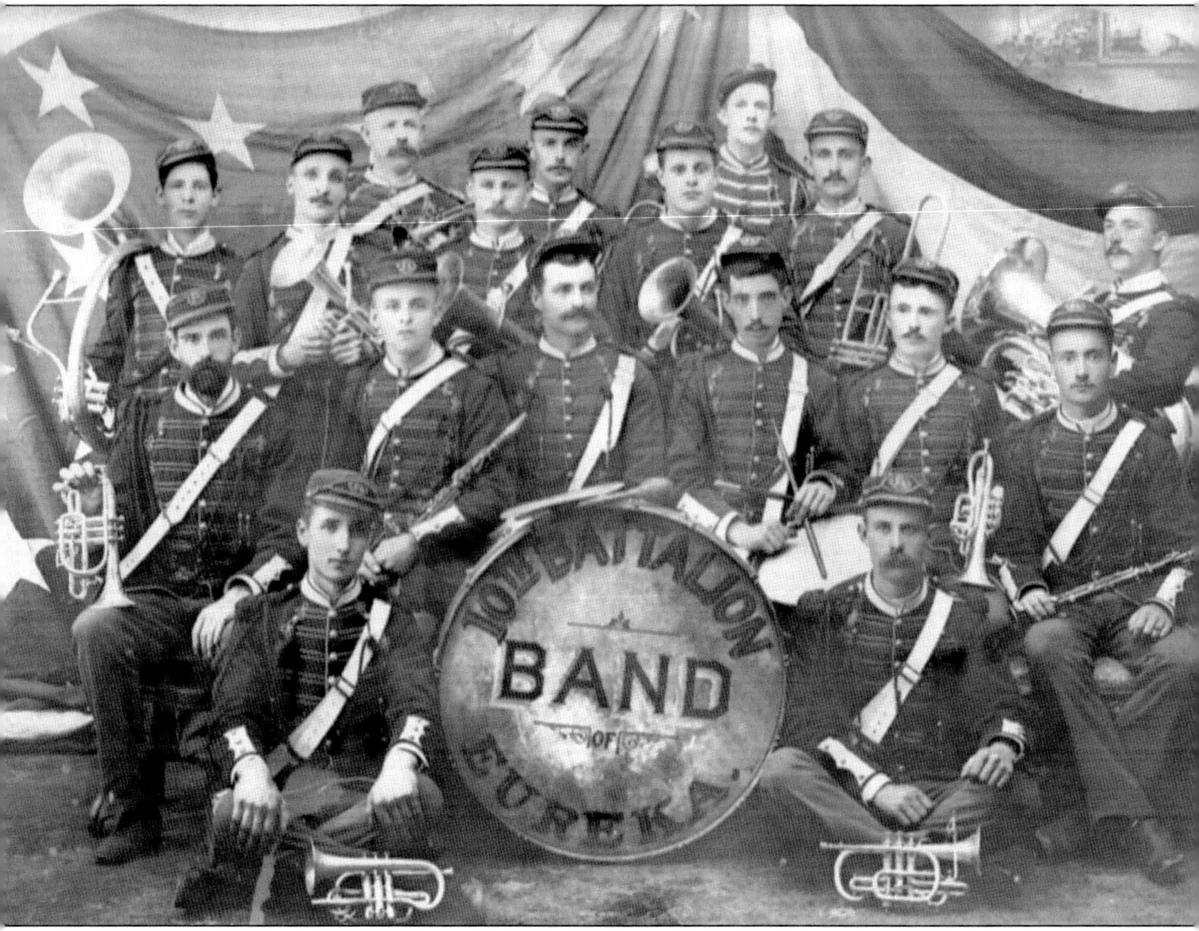

March music enjoyed a lengthy period of popularity in the United States from around 1850 to 1940, when it started to be eclipsed by other musical forms. This photograph shows the 10th Battalion Band of Eureka. The members shown are identified as: (standing) G. L. Willock, A. E. Wunderlich, Prof. McLaren, I. M. Ring, John H. Young, Chas E. Langford, Ambrose Murray, George Wing, and Alfred McGarty; (seated) Harry Wombold, Fred Roberts, Rober Kellen, Jacko Johnson, W. B. Bailey, and A. McDermott; (on floor) Arthur McConnell and John H. Mercer. (Courtesy of the Clarke Historical Museum.)

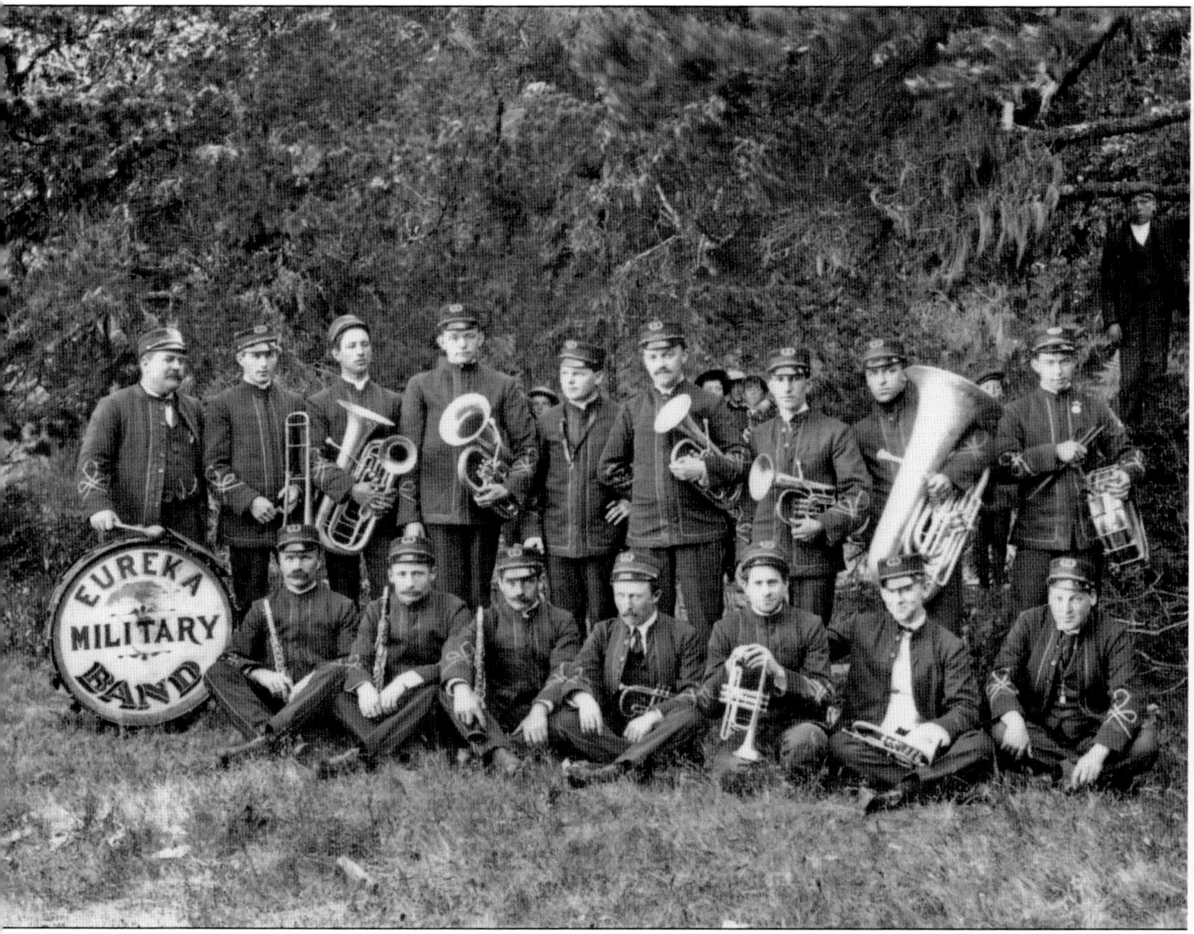

The Eureka Military Band, shown here in 1907, was a favorite at Sequoia Park during the park's early years. They performed in the park nearly every Sunday and at holiday concerts as well. By the early 19th century, published marches for bands such as the Eureka Military Band were plentiful due to prolific composers such as John Philip Sousa and Henry Fillmore. (Courtesy of Humboldt State University.)

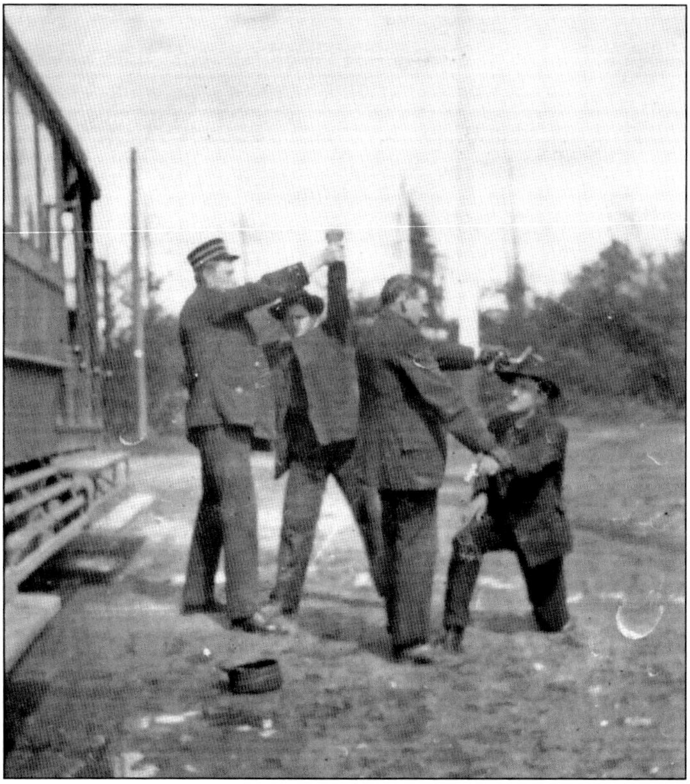

This photograph shows Ed Pike (left) and Gus Hornbrook (right) enacting a mock holdup in front of a trolley car near Sequoia Park. The two men were the conductor and motorman of the trolley shown, which ran on the Sequoia Park line. It is not known whether this was done as a theatrical stunt or as a training exercise. In the two photographs shown it is clear that the trolley conductor and motorman prevail in the scuffle. The two would-be crooks (unidentified) are shown subdued in the second frame. (Both courtesy of the Humboldt County Historical Society.)

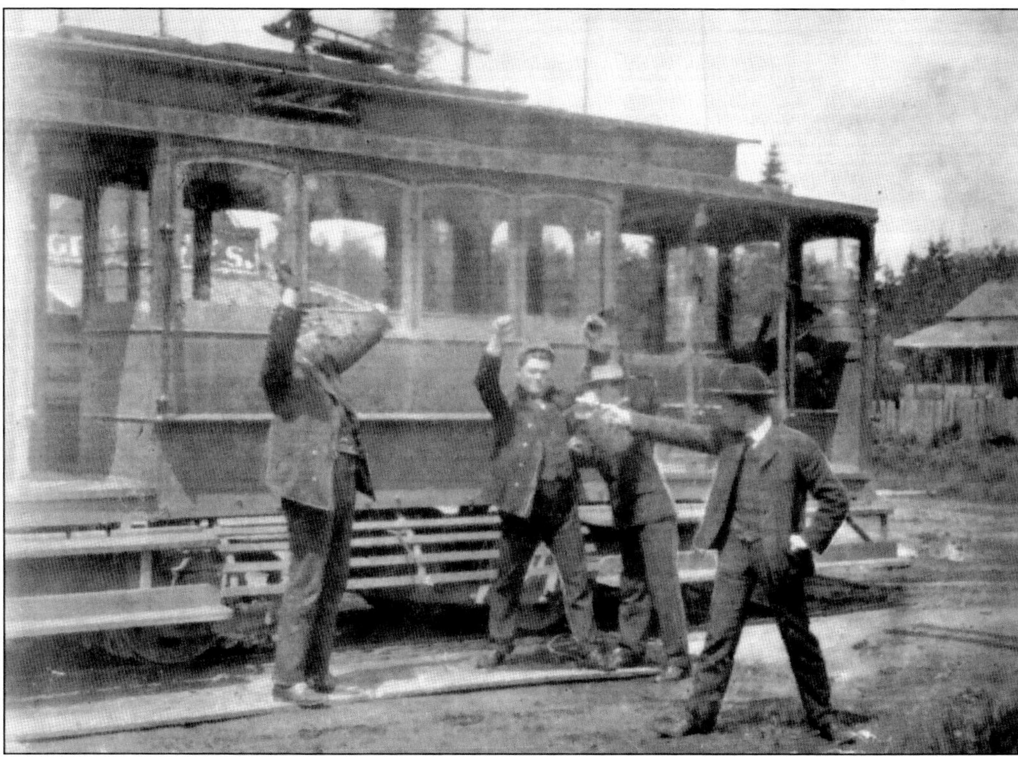

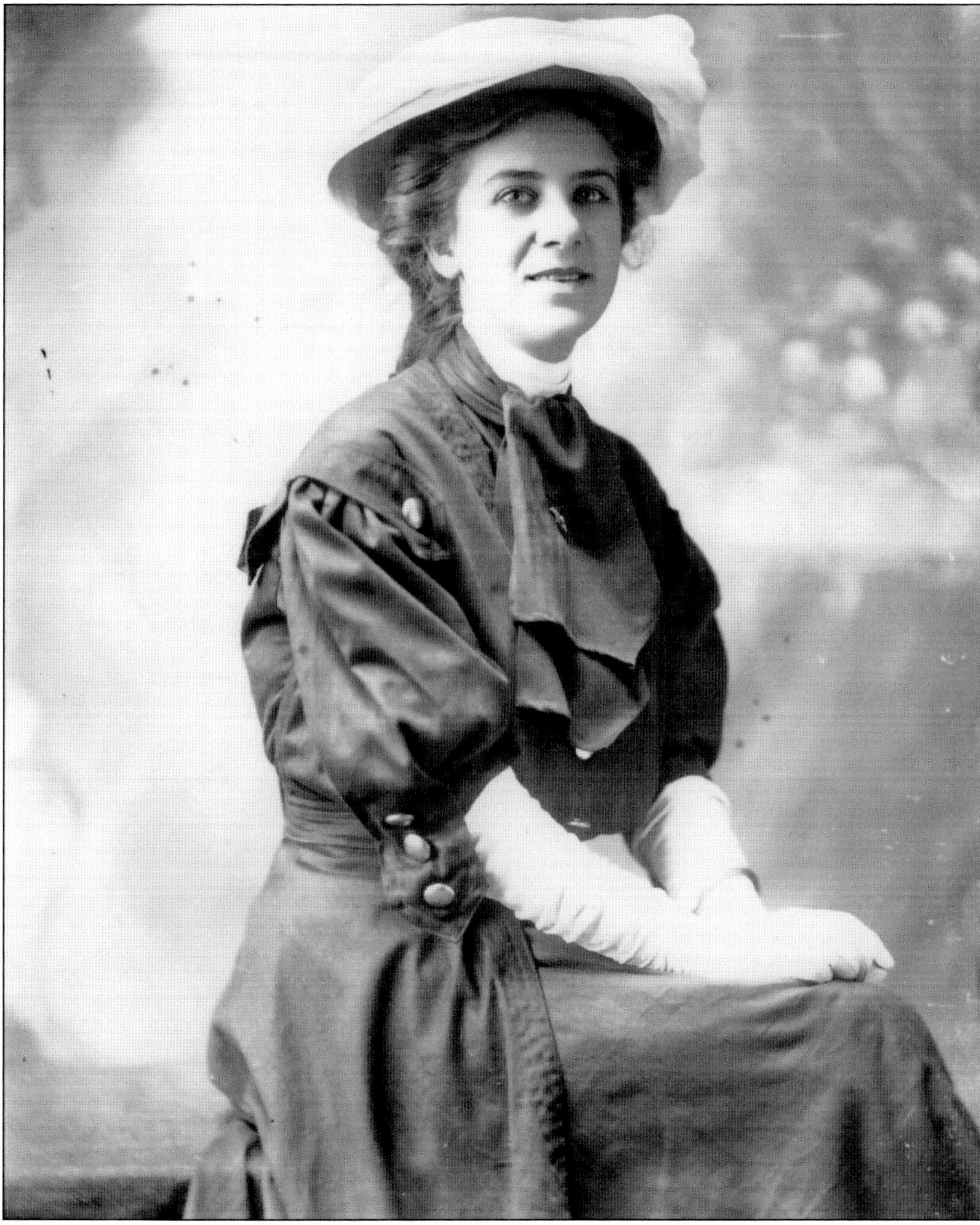

Auda Due, like many actresses of her time, traveled around the country. She visited Sequoia Park around 1909, during which time the photographer R. J. Baker made a series of theatrical stills. Although details could not be found, notes on the series indicate that Baker took the photographs as part of a song illustration for George Sousa. An additional photograph series, part of the J. Willis Sayre Collection at the University of Washington, shows Due in a series of theatrical stills taken in Seattle in 1914. In New York City, she played Nell Thurston in the 1925 Apollo Theatre production of *The Valley of Content*, which was written by Blanche Upright. Her husband, Pietro (Pete) Sosso, became a well-known film actor, appearing in more than 50 films from 1910 to 1948. (Courtesy of Humboldt State University.)

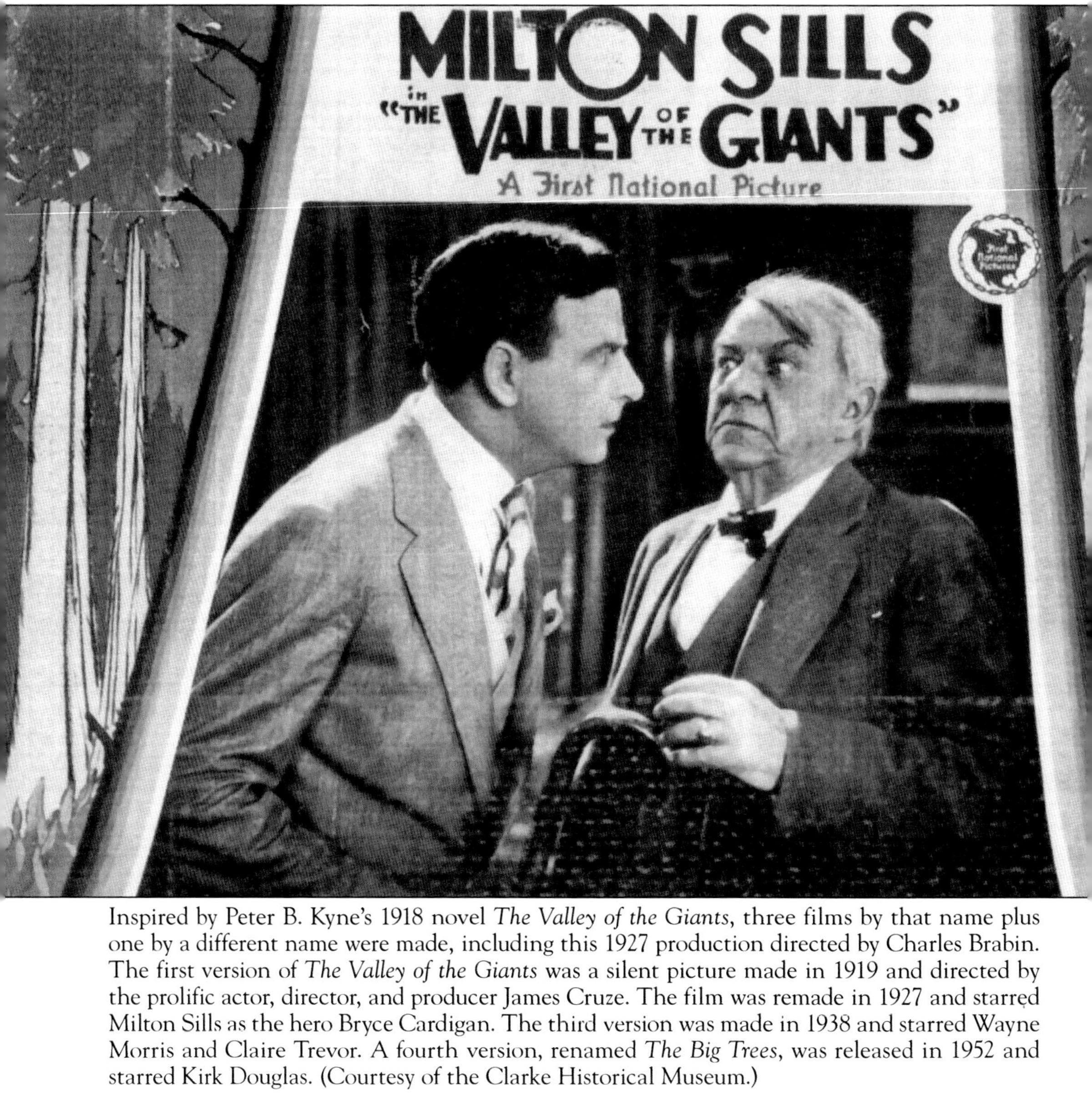

Inspired by Peter B. Kyne's 1918 novel *The Valley of the Giants*, three films by that name plus one by a different name were made, including this 1927 production directed by Charles Brabin. The first version of *The Valley of the Giants* was a silent picture made in 1919 and directed by the prolific actor, director, and producer James Cruze. The film was remade in 1927 and starred Milton Sills as the hero Bryce Cardigan. The third version was made in 1938 and starred Wayne Morris and Claire Trevor. A fourth version, renamed *The Big Trees*, was released in 1952 and starred Kirk Douglas. (Courtesy of the Clarke Historical Museum.)

Doris Kenyon starred in the 1927 production of *The Valley of the Giants*, which was shot on location in Humboldt County in often challenging conditions. Kenyon made her screen debut in 1915 and costarred with many popular silent actors such as Rudolph Valentino and her future husband, Milton Sills. She made the transition from silent films to sound and even to television, where she could still be seen in the 1960s. (Courtesy of the Clarke Historical Museum.)

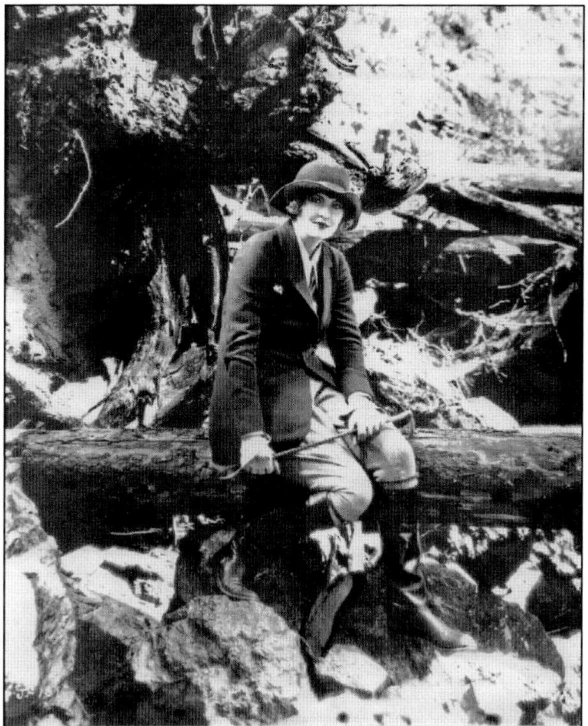

VALLEY OF THE GIANTS, 1927. ***Doris Kenyon on the set in Humboldt County.***

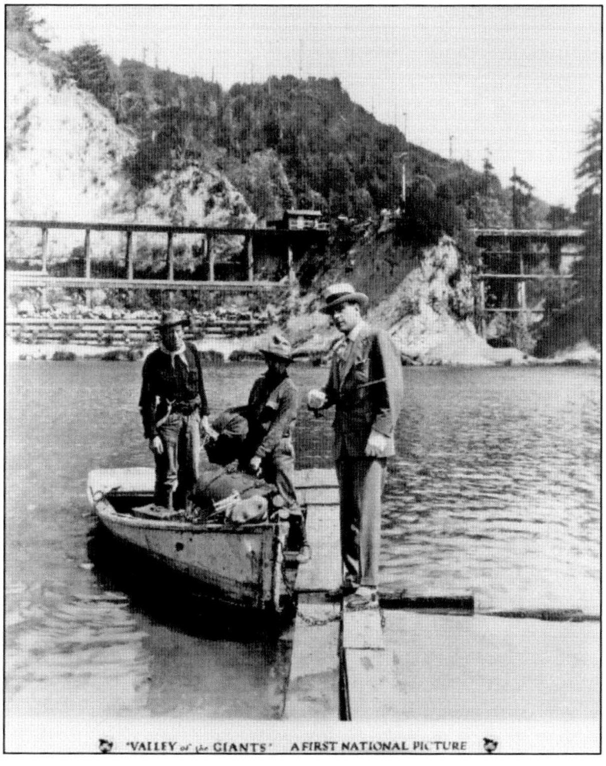

"VALLEY of the GIANTS" A FIRST NATIONAL PICTURE

This film still from the 1927 production of *The Valley of the Giants* shows the wild setting of the film, which was shot on location in Humboldt County. (Courtesy of the Clarke Historical Museum.)

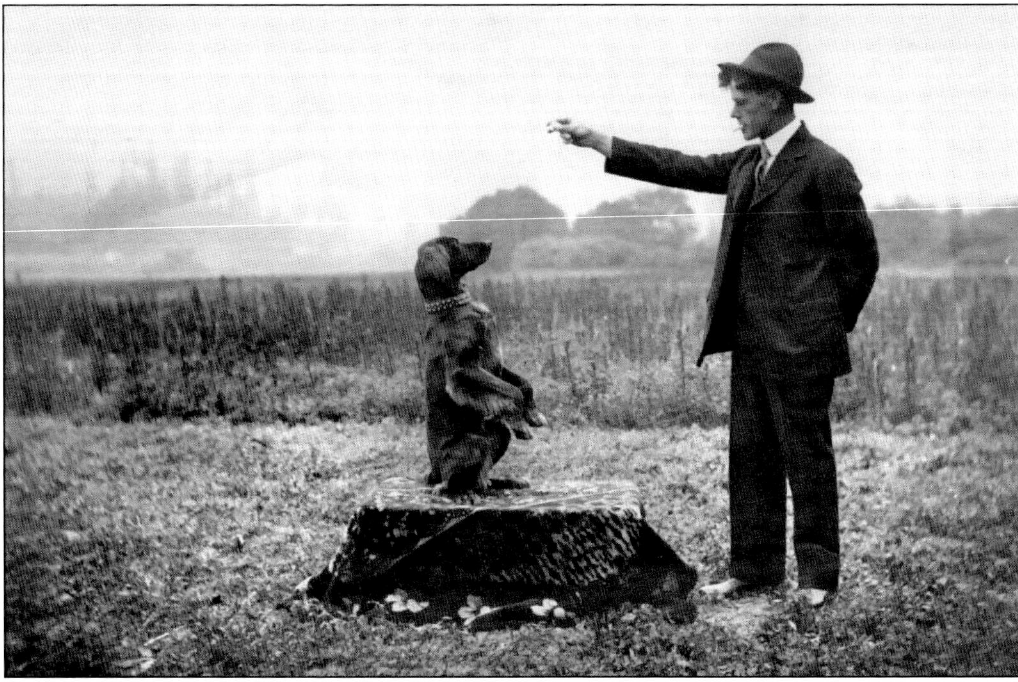

This photograph of a man with a dog performing tricks may have been taken across the street from Sequoia Park, although the exact location is unknown. Traveling performers of all kinds were common throughout the country at the time. (Courtesy of the Clarke Historical Museum.)

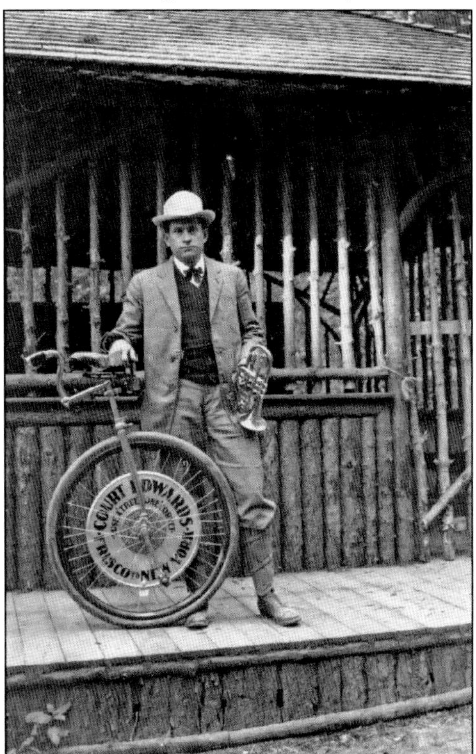

Court Edwards with his cornet traveled from town to town (from "Frisco to New York") on his unicycle. He is shown in front of one the Sequoia Park pavilion buildings. (Courtesy of Humboldt State University.)

Seven

Sequoia Park Today

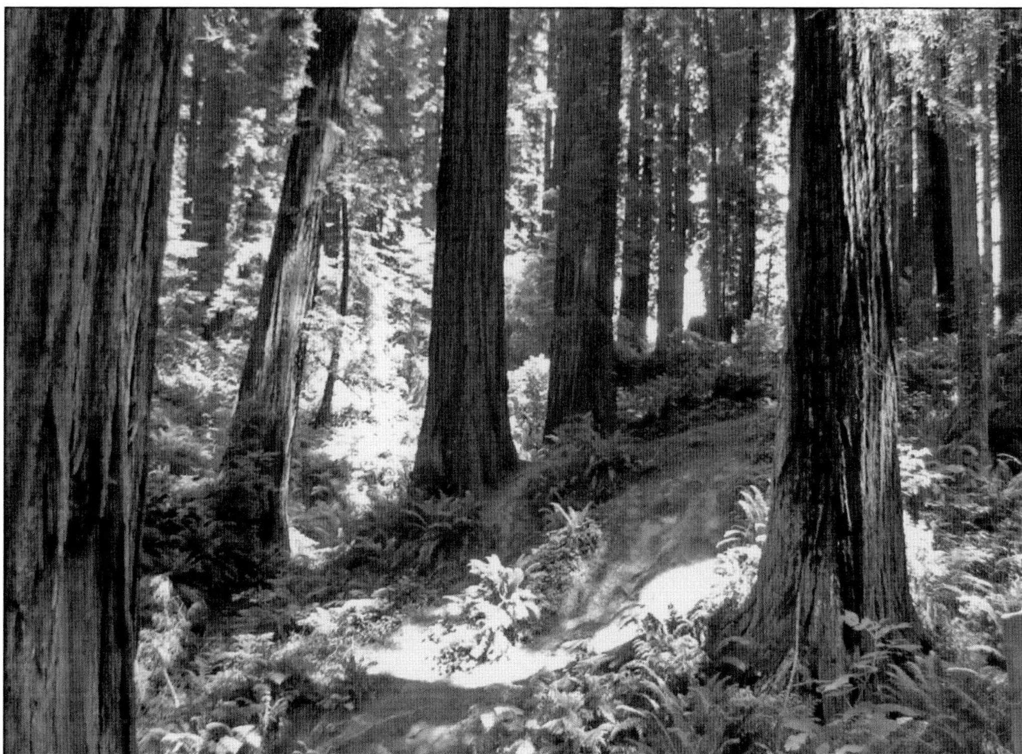

Eureka's Sequoia Park stands today both changed and unchanged. Most of the man-made structures have deteriorated or have been removed. The ancient trees, by contrast, remain, except for those taken out by human intervention. As long as we continue to cherish Sequoia Park, its magnificent forest will be there for the great-grandchildren of our children and beyond. (Courtesy of Dione F. Armand.)

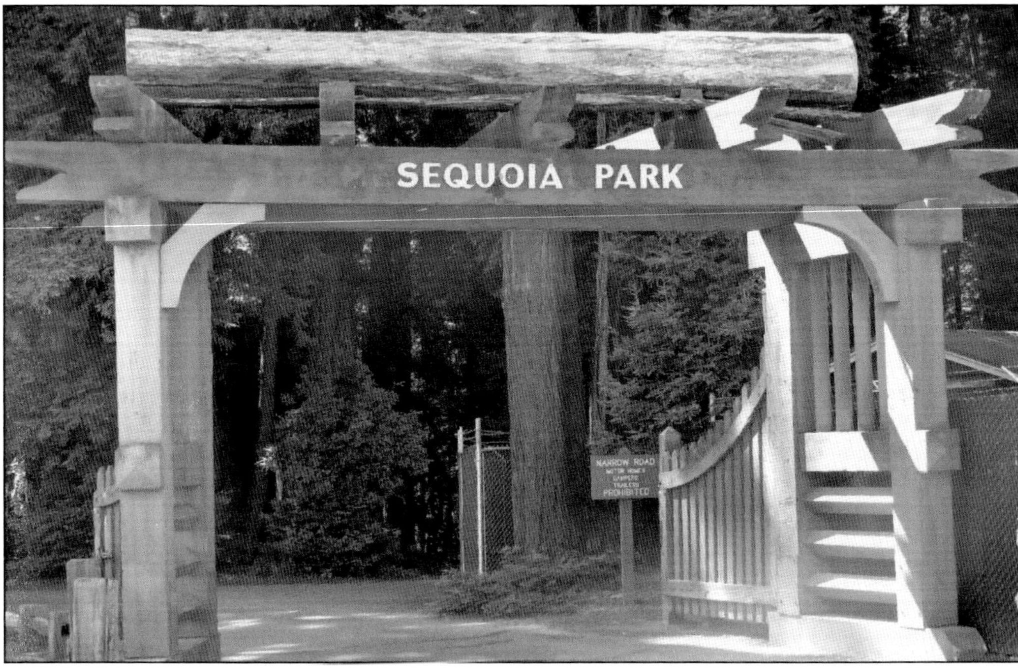

George Cartwright designed this gate for Holmes Eureka Lumber Company in 1938. He used several thousand feet of redwood in its construction and topped it with a life-size logger statue. The gate was moved to Sequoia Park in January 1989 to save it from the wrecking ball when the lumber company site was being converted to the Bayshore Mall. The logger statue was eventually removed. (Courtesy of Christian V. Pennington.)

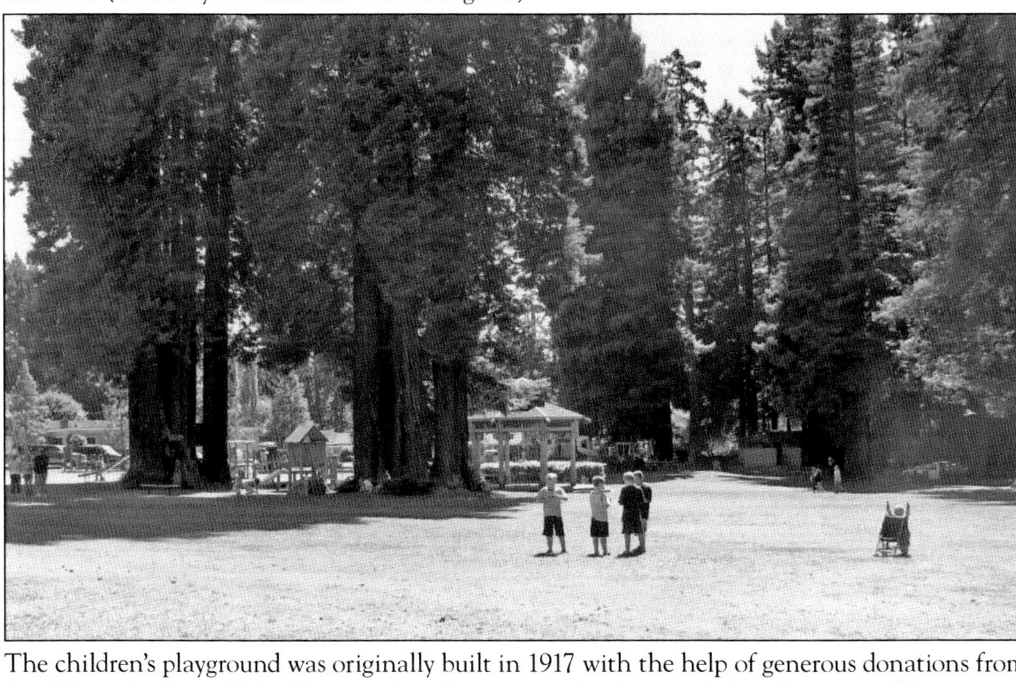

The children's playground was originally built in 1917 with the help of generous donations from the Woman's Civic Club. The meadow shown was also first seeded at that time. (Courtesy of Christian V. Pennington.)

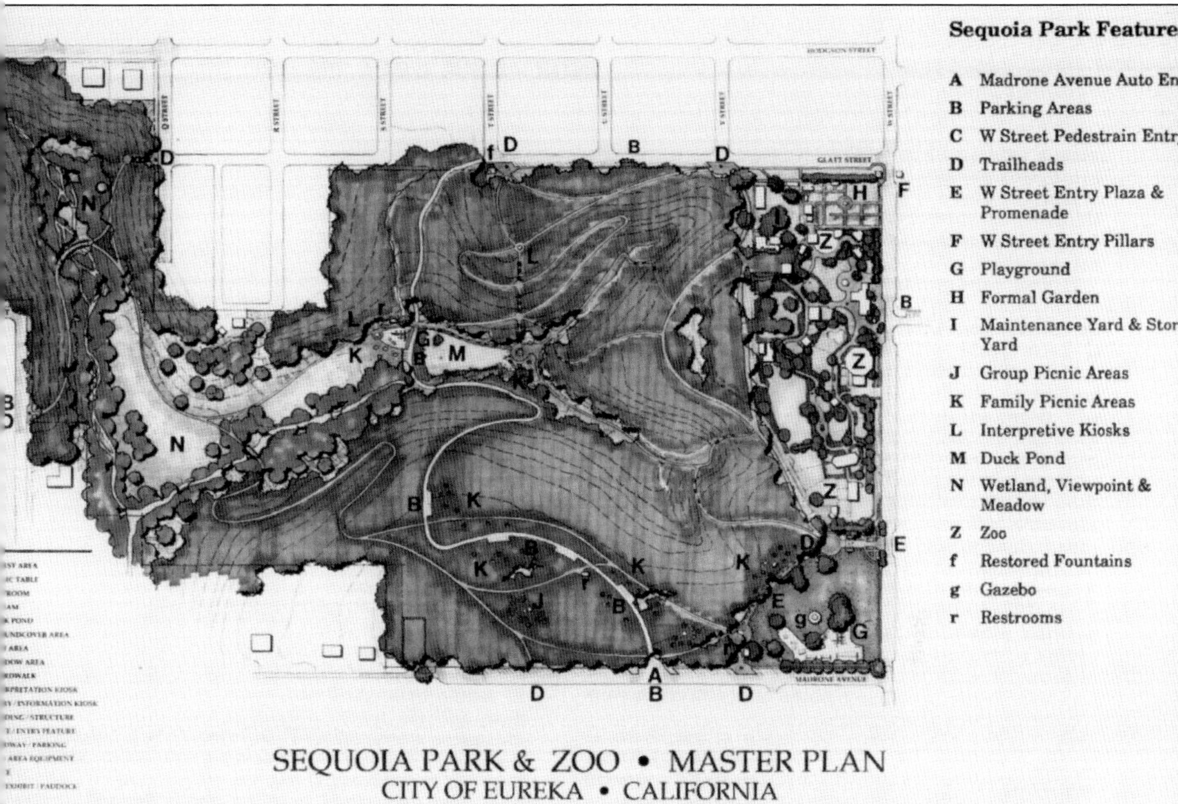

This map of Sequoia Park and the Sequoia Park Zoo shows the master plan adopted in 1993. The Sequoia Zoological Society worked with the City of Eureka for many years to come up with a master plan. The 1993 plan, published by the City of Eureka Parks and Recreation Department, outlines improvements envisioned as taking place during the next 20 years. The estimated cost at the time was $5.5 million. Since then, the 4,000-square-foot barnyard structure was added, as well as a multipurpose entrance pavilion, including a new gift shop, café, interpretive center, and lecture hall. (Courtesy of Humboldt State University.)

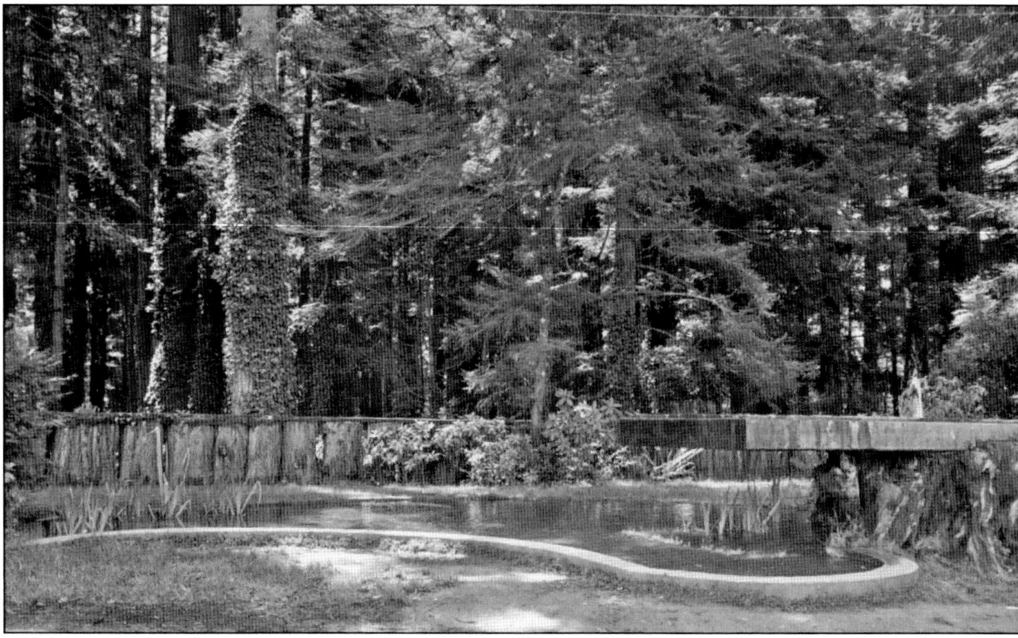

The Glatt Street fountain on the northern edge of Sequoia Park was built in 1952 with funds given to the City of Eureka in memory of L. C. Tuttle. The majority of the donation was used to develop the existing road system through the park. To design the fountain, Eureka mayor Robert Madsen formed a citizens committee to work with designer Bob Usher. The fountain was built with volunteer labor. (Courtesy of the Humboldt County Historical Society.)

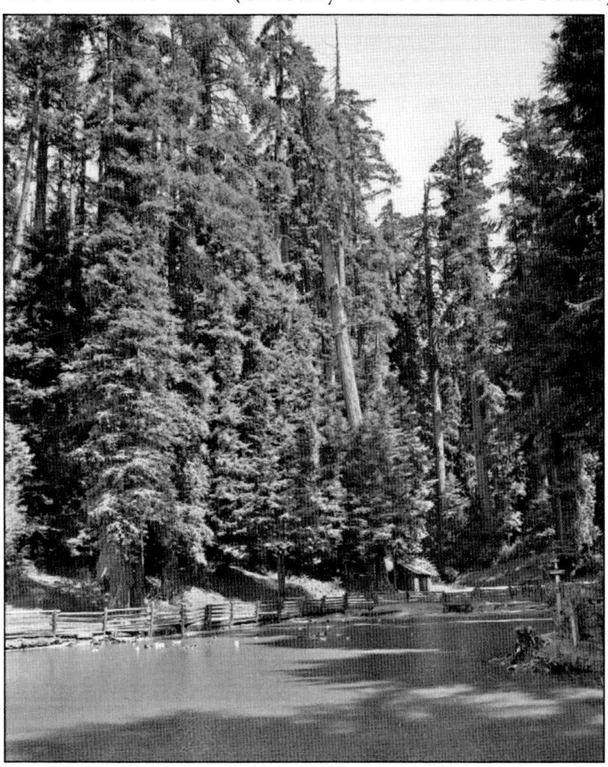

This photograph shows the Sequoia Park duck pond around 1952. The duck pond today is a smaller version of what was once called Mirror Lake. The duck pond was filled with sand in the 1980s to ameliorate safety concerns and a safety berm was added. (Courtesy of the Humboldt County Historical Society.)

The Victorian three-tiered fountain was placed in Sequoia Park some time before 1917, when a newspaper article reported that it had been built thanks to the local lodge of the Native Daughters of the Golden West. This photograph shows the fountain still in operation in the 1950s. (Courtesy of the Humboldt County Historical Society.)

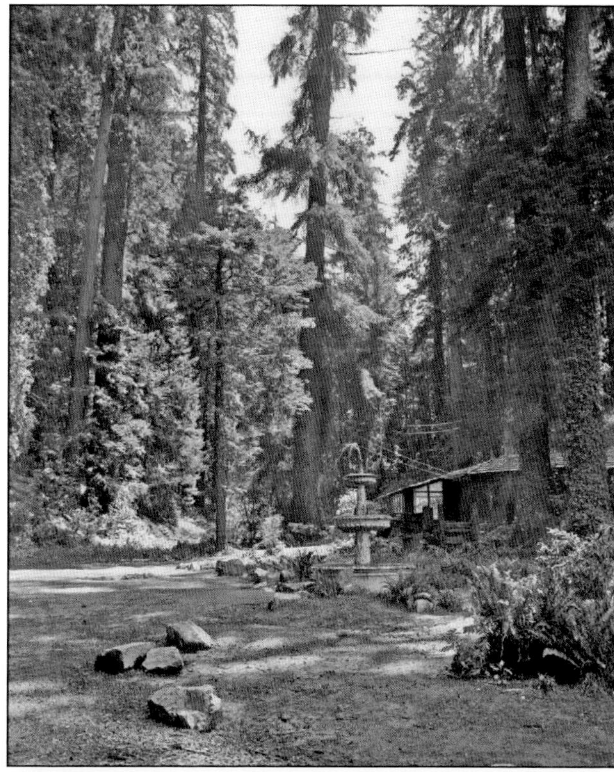

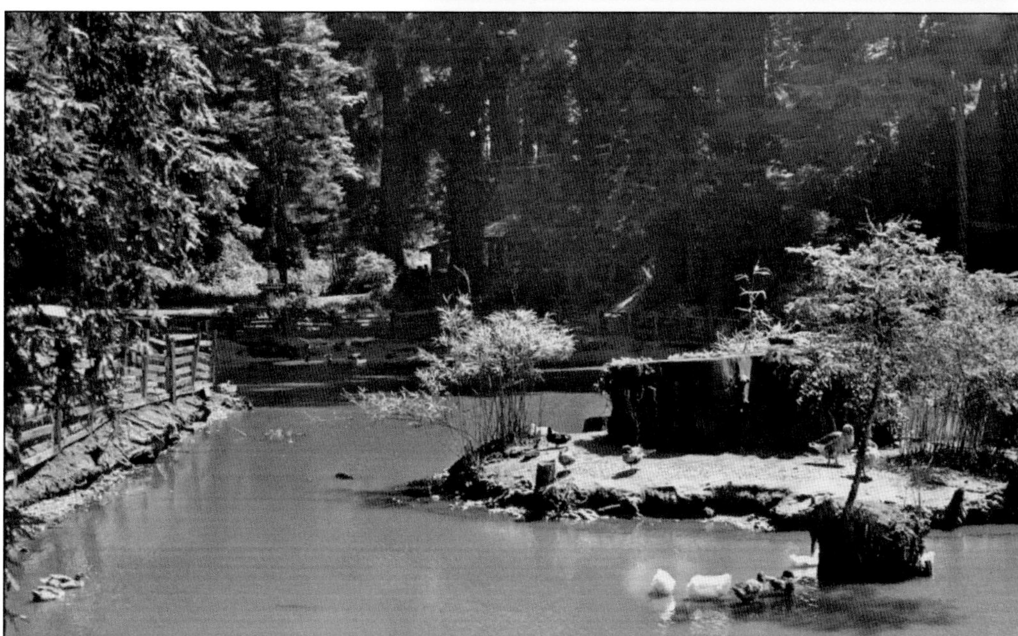

The twin trunks of a giant old-growth redwood tree made Redwood Island a landmark in Sequoia Park for decades. (For comparison, see page 29.) Taken in the early 1950s, this photograph shows that the ancient tree was removed. The raw stump, shown here, has now sprouted a new redwood tree. (Courtesy of the Humboldt County Historical Society.)

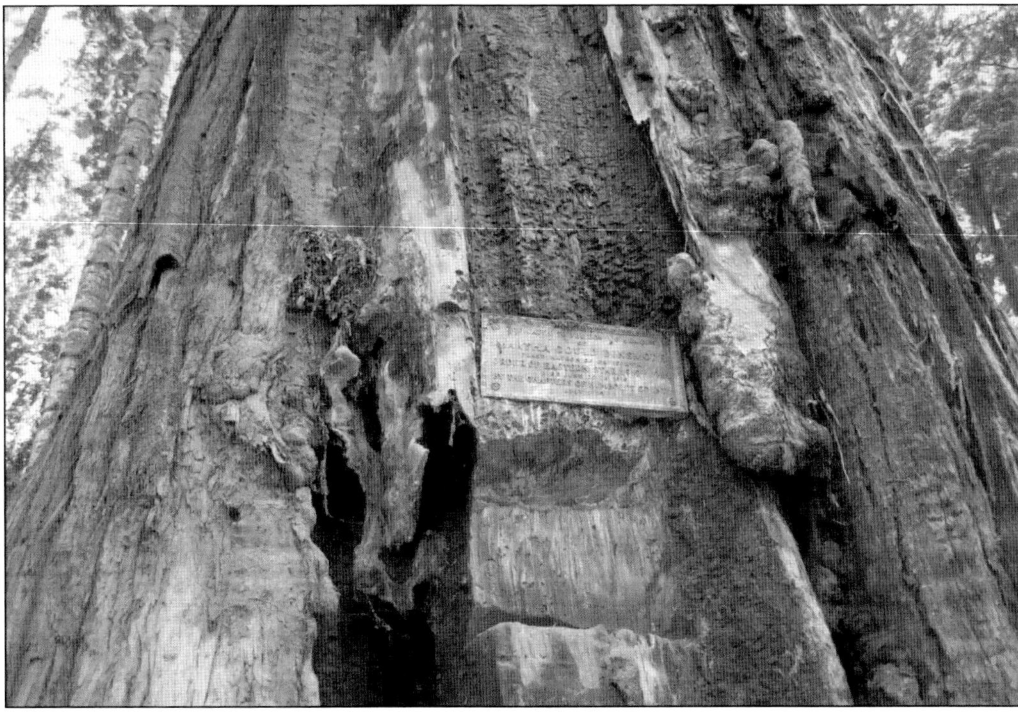

This plaque was placed by the Humboldt County Order of the Eastern Star chapters and dedicated in 1920. It honors Martha Dinsmore Gould, grand matron of California (1912–1918), who died on June 25, 1919. The Order of the Eastern Star is the women's fraternal organization associated with the Freemasons. The tree upon which the plaque is mounted is none other than the grand redwood that figures prominently in early Sequoia Park portraits. (Courtesy of Dione F. Armand.)

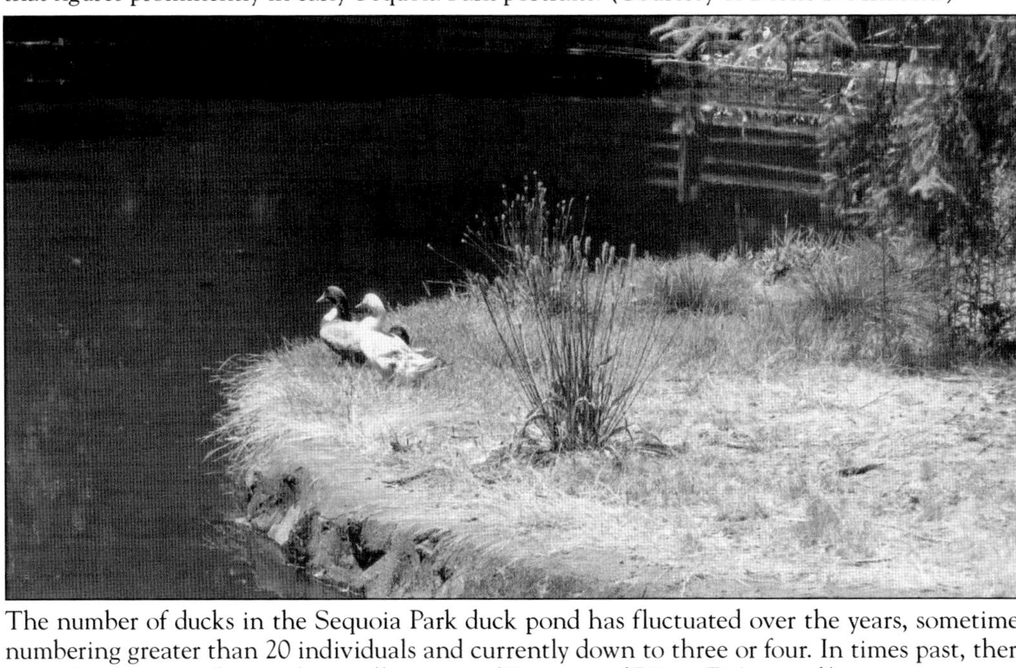

The number of ducks in the Sequoia Park duck pond has fluctuated over the years, sometimes numbering greater than 20 individuals and currently down to three or four. In times past, there were also swans in the pond, as well as geese. (Courtesy of Dione F. Armand.)

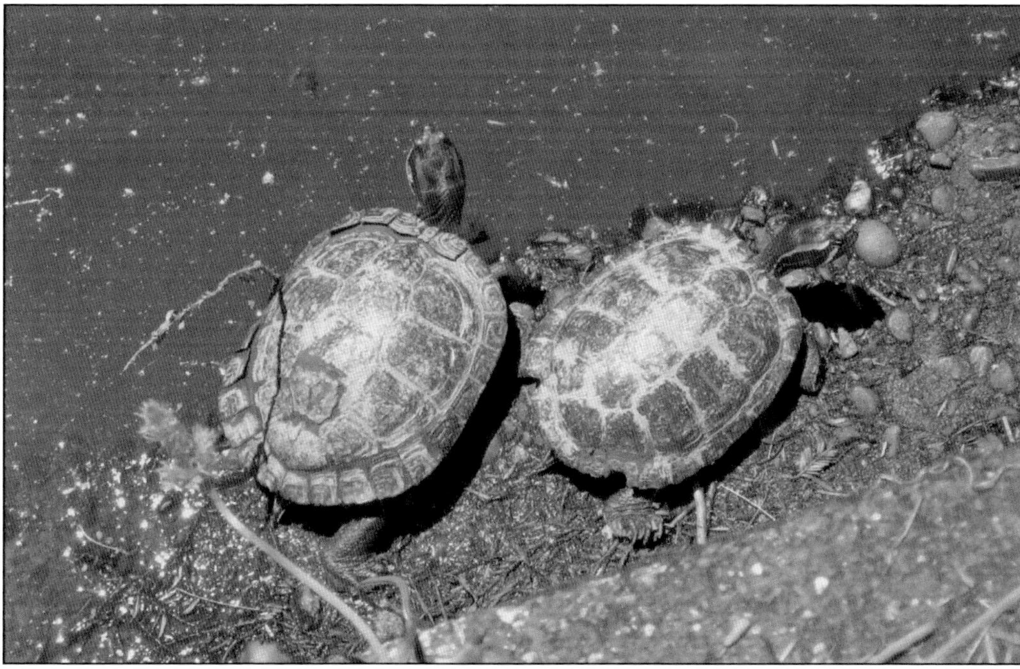

This photograph shows two turtles sunning themselves on the banks of the Sequoia Park duck pond. There are quite a few turtles in the pond, as well as local trout. Fishing is not allowed. (Courtesy of Dione F. Armand.)

This photograph shows some of the hiking trails in present-day Sequoia Park. Because of erosion—both natural and that caused by motorized dirt bikes being illegally ridden in the park—the trails require a lot of work to maintain. (Courtesy of Dione F. Armand.)

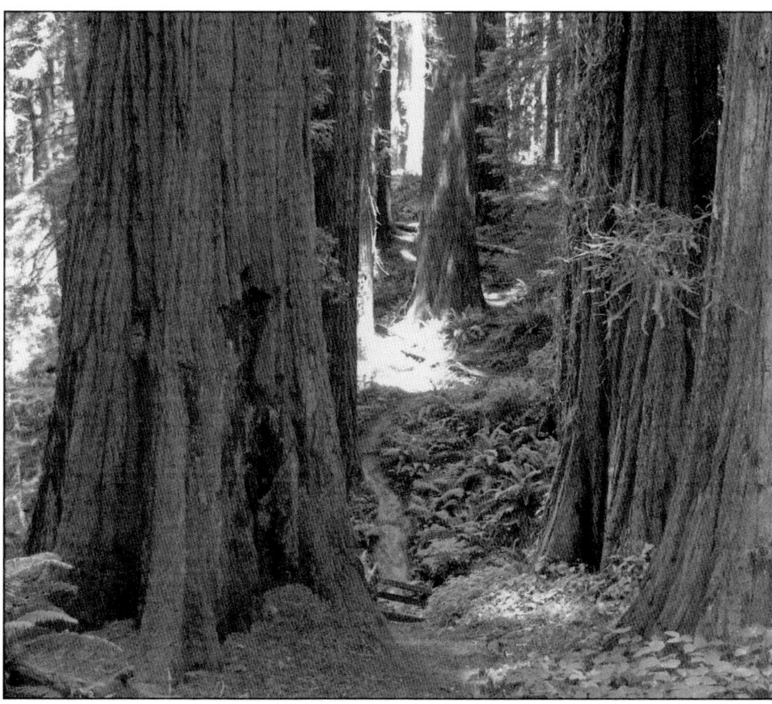

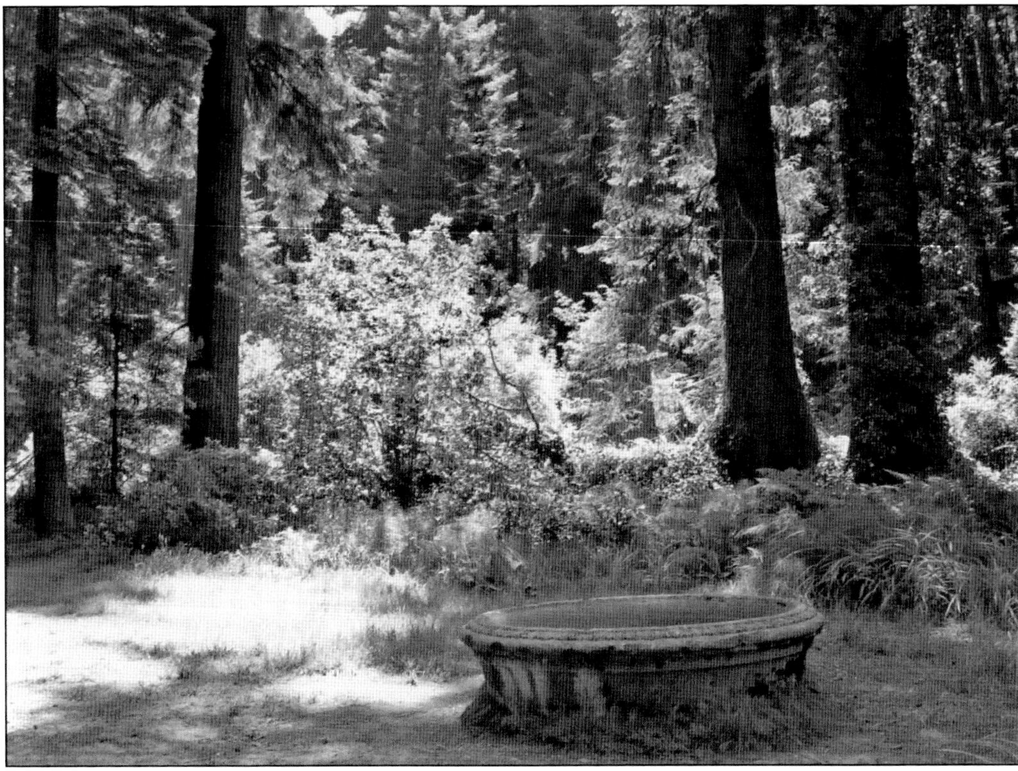

The bottom tier of the once three-tiered Victorian fountain is all that remains today. This old fountain remnant can still be found on the east side of the duck pond. (Courtesy of Dione F. Armand.)

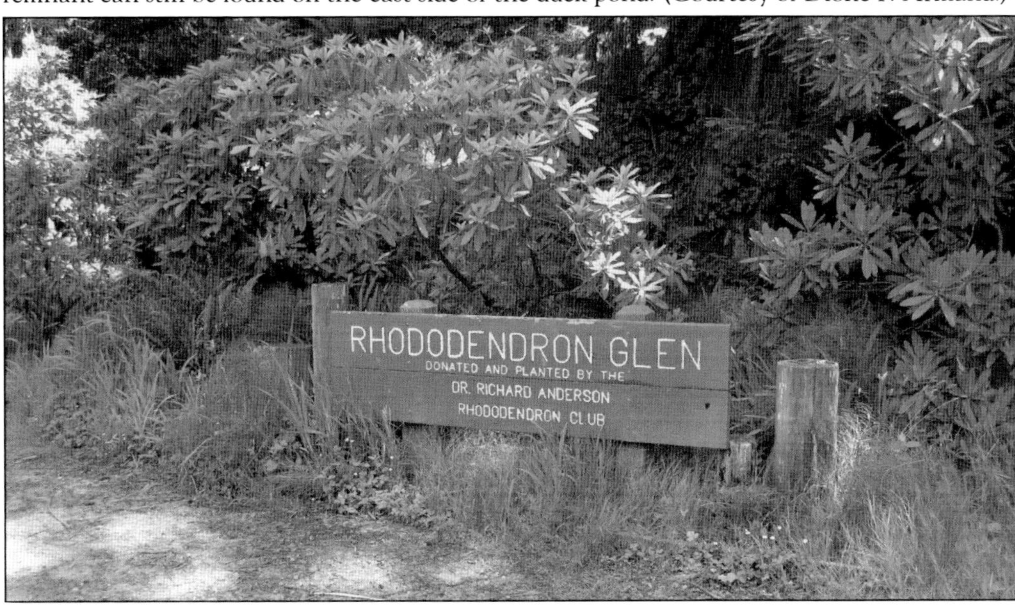

Rhododendron Glen, planted by the Eureka Rhododendron Club, is a marvelous collection of the flowering tree-like shrubs located on the east end of the duck pond along the valley path. It features not only native varieties, but also exotic Himalayan rhododendrons that soar high overhead. (Courtesy of Dione F. Armand.)

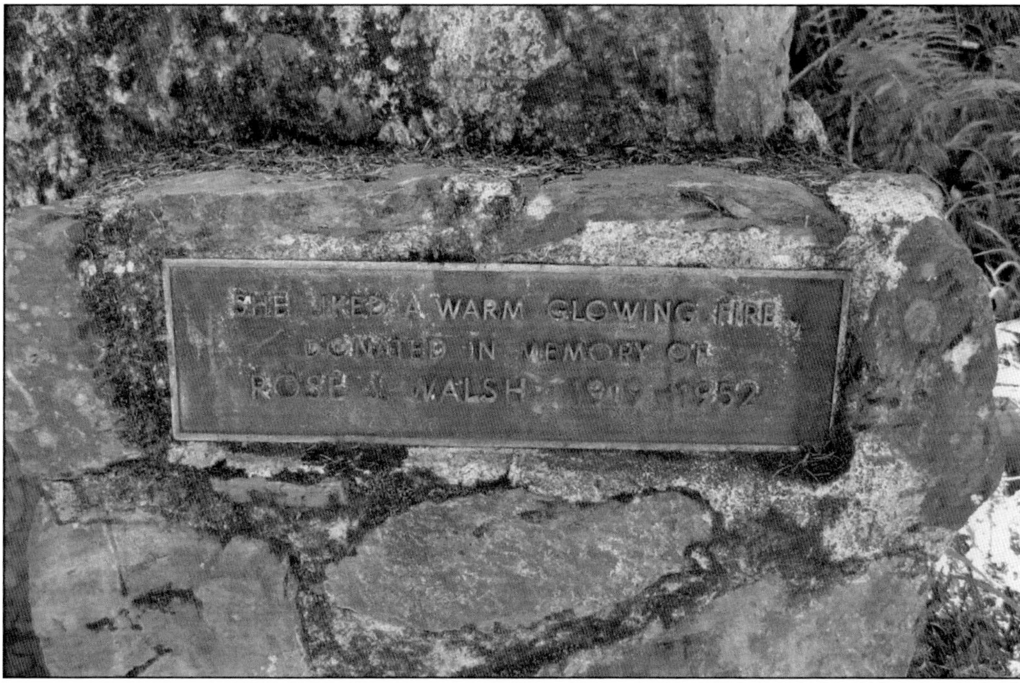

In 1953, the family of Rose Ivancich Walsh dedicated a plaque in her honor. It is placed on the stone hearth to the east of the Sequoia Park duck pond. The plaque reads: "She liked a warm glowing fire. In memory of Rose Ivancich Walsh, 1919–1952." (Courtesy of Dione F. Armand.)

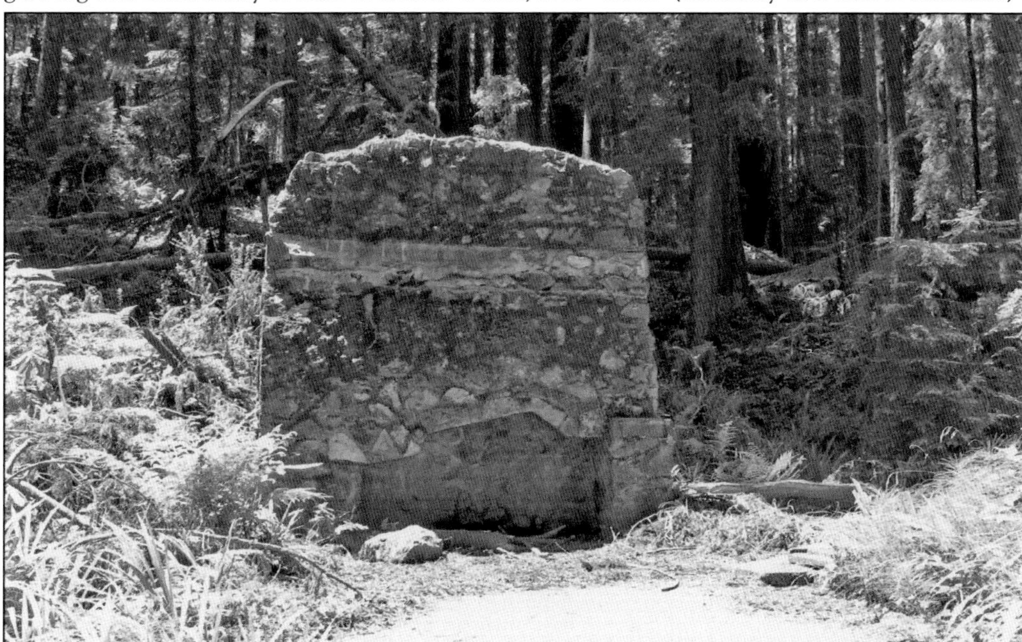

The concrete foundation and stone hearth are all that remain of the log cabin that delighted Sequoia Park visitors for decades. It is located on the east side of the duck pond. The old-style hearth hook, used to hang a cooking pot over the wood fire, is still there but is barely visible in the photograph. (Courtesy of Dione F. Armand.)

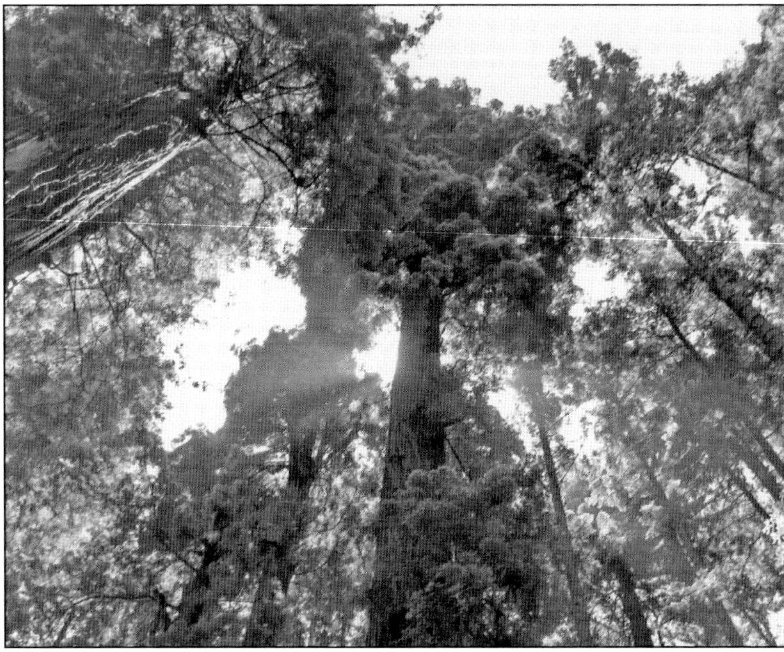

The redwood canopy is a realm all its own and has recently become a hot topic of scientific inquiry. Many animals in the redwood forest spend their lives in the canopy hundreds of feet from the forest floor. In Sequoia Park, raccoons make their homes high in the trees, as do nesting ospreys and woodpeckers. (Courtesy of Dione F. Armand.)

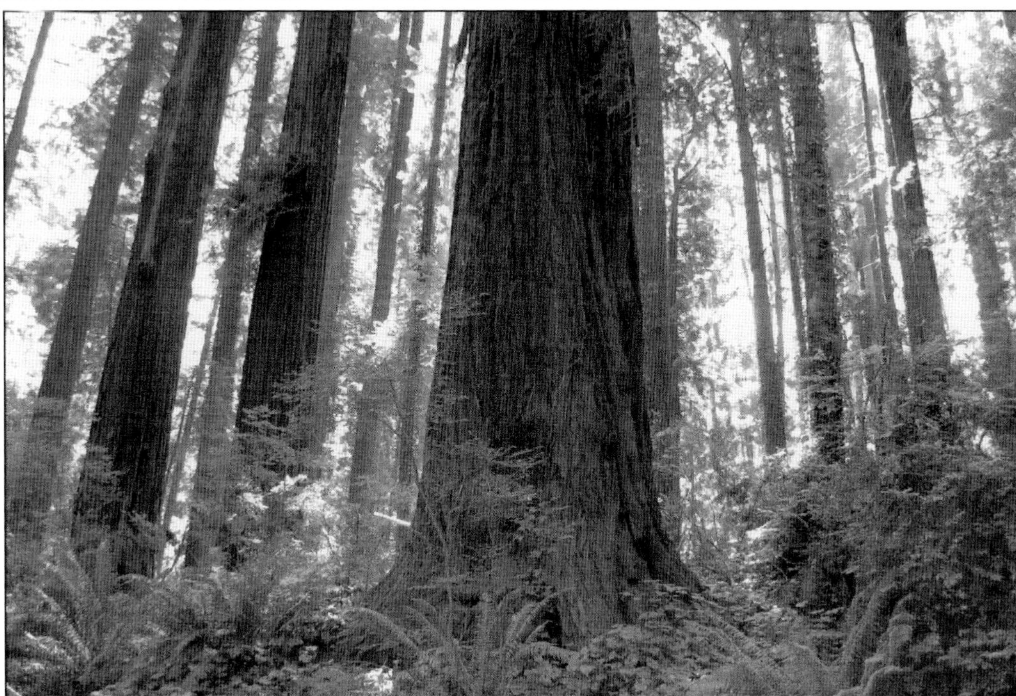

In addition to the simple quiet of walking in woods like those shown in this photograph, Esma Hunt offers this recollection of the park in 1915: "On long summer weekends, we took our supper to Sequoia Park. There were huge iron stoves with wood supplied, and as our parents and friends prepared a hot meal, we children would run to look at the birds and the animals in the zoo. If there was time, we would take bread to feed the ducks down the hill at the pond." (Courtesy of Dione F. Armand.)

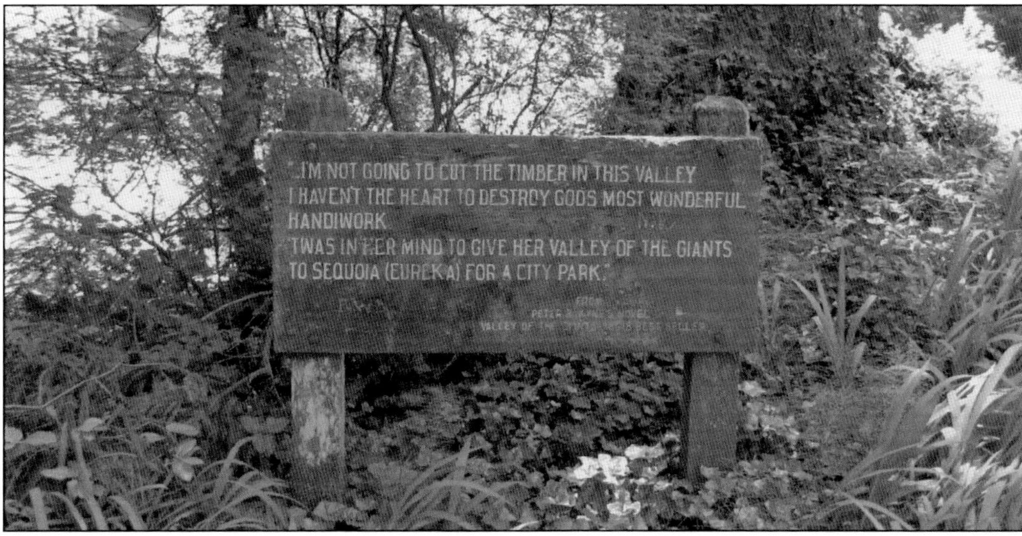

The wooden plaque that commemorates Peter B. Kyne's 1918 novel *The Valley of the Giants* remains in the park, although it does show its age. One thing to note is the absence of the giant redwood that stood behind the plaque on the day of its dedication (see page 62). (Courtesy of Dione F. Armand.)

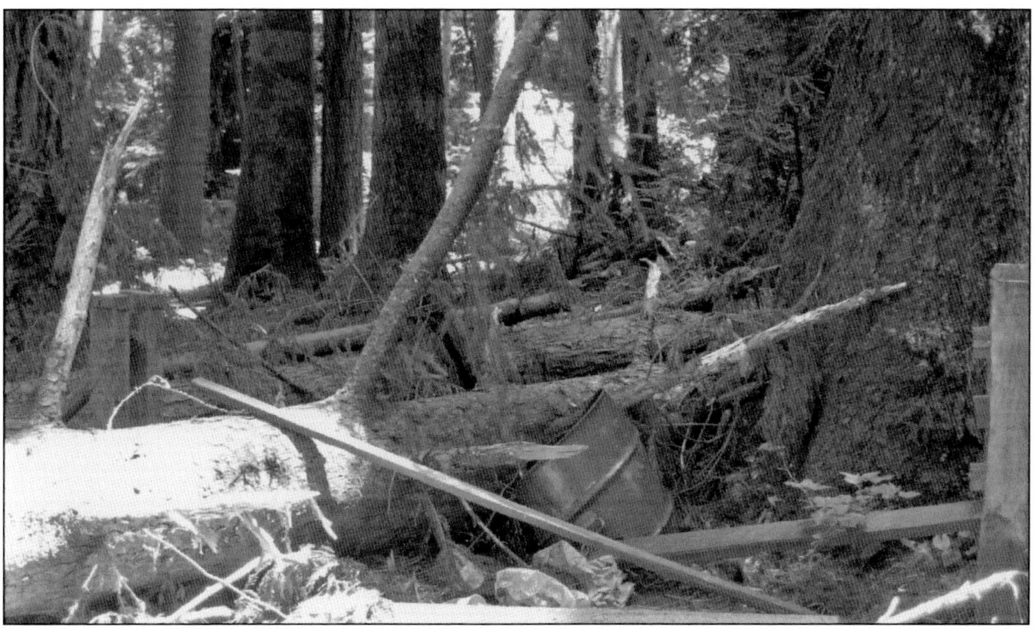

On New Year's Eve 2006, high winds toppled 75 trees in Sequoia Park. Most of the damage occurred between the Sequoia Park Zoo and the duck pond, and along the park road toward Madrone Street. It is estimated that 50 MBF (1 MBF = 1,000 board feet) of second-growth redwood and 90 MBF of grand fir were knocked over by the high winds, which gusted up to 85 miles per hour. Blowdown Meadow will fill in the once-forested area; however, only by replanting trees will the forest truly resume its former grandeur. Planting redwood rather than grand fir, which is shorter-lived than redwood, would reforest the area lost to the storm, and the resulting increase in forest density would help to protect other trees in the park from future storms. (Courtesy of Dione F. Armand.)

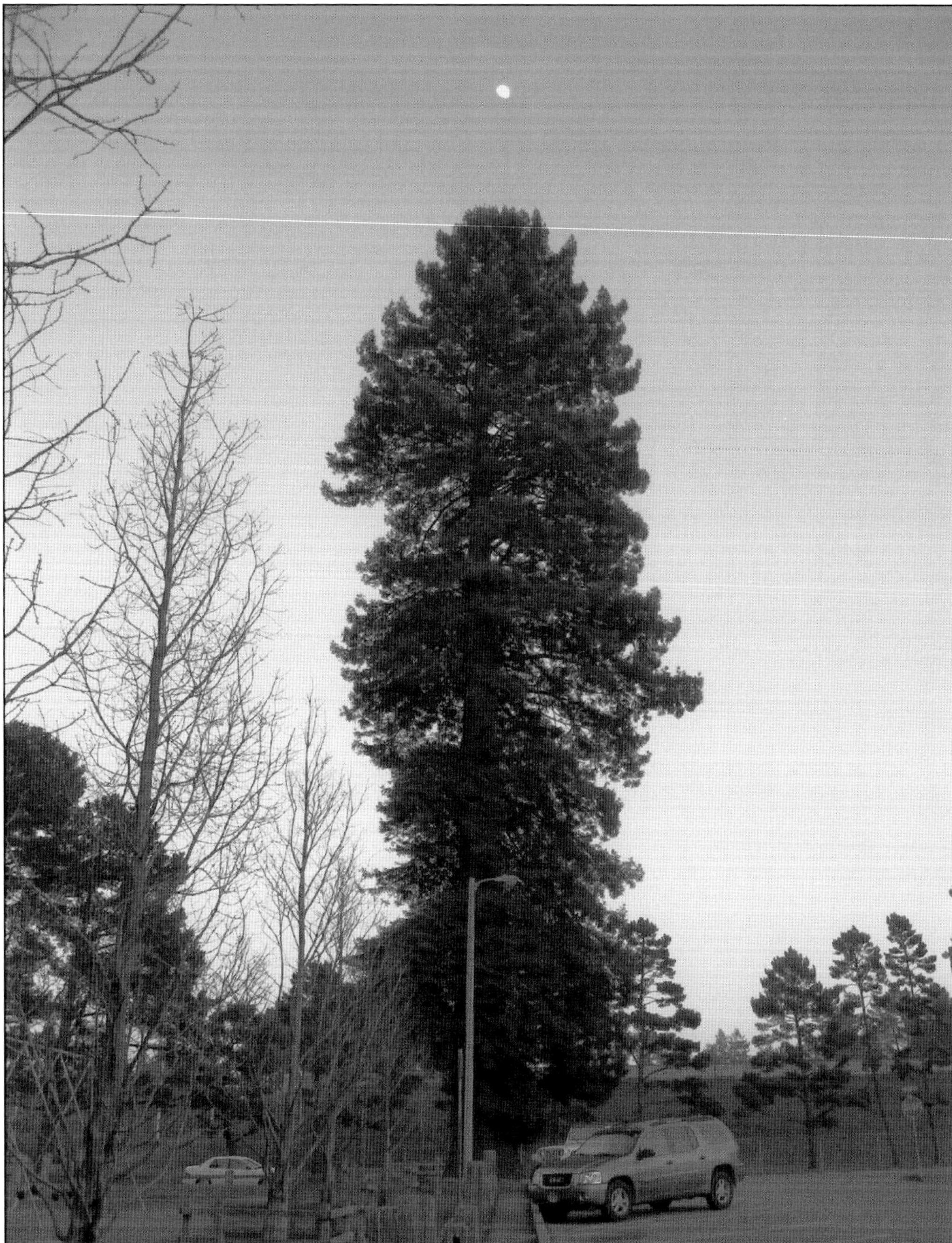

This photograph shows the moon above the giant redwood at the corner of W and Madrone Streets on the south edge of Sequoia Park. The area also contains the children's playground and picnic benches. (Courtesy of Dione F. Armand.)

BIBLIOGRAPHY

Barbour, Michael and Sandy Lydon et al. *Coast Redwood: A Natural and Cultural History*. Los Olivos, CA: Cachuma Press, 2001.

Borden, Stanley T. *Street Railways of Eureka*. 1964.

Carlson, Peter. *Roughneck: The Life and Times of Big Bill Haywood*. New York: W. W. Norton and Company, 1983.

Eifert, Larry. *Field Guide to Old-Growth Forests*. Seattle, WA: Sasquatch Books, 2000.

Guerin, Daniel. 100 *Years of Labor in the USA*. Trans. Alan Adler. London: Ink Links Ltd, 1979.

Johnstone, Peter, Ed. *Giants in the Earth: The California Redwoods*. Berkeley, CA: Heyday Books, 2001.

Kync, Peter B. *The Valley of the Giants*. New York: Doubleday, Page and Company, 1918.

Palmquist, Peter and Jack Irvine, eds. *In the Redwood's Realm*. Eureka, CA: Chamber of Commerce, originally 1893, facsimile edition reprinted by editors, 1987.

Schmidt, Alvin J. *Fraternal Organizations*. Westport, CT: Greenwood Press, 1980.

Thornbury, D. L. *California's Redwood Wonderland: Humboldt County*. San Francisco, CA: Sunset Press, 1923.

Turner, Dennis W. Place *Names of Humboldt County, California*. Eureka, CA: Eureka Printing Company, 1993.